M000276620

WHAT MAKES
a STAR
TEACHER

Foreword

In 1994, the Haberman Educational Foundation was chartered to promote the research and vision of Dr. Martin Haberman: "Selecting the best teachers and principals for children and youth of America." Prior to Haberman's work, the ideology and best practices of effective teaching for diverse children and youth in poverty were a mystery. For more than five decades, he studied both what successful and failing practitioners believed and how that belief triggered certain behaviors. Haberman wrote the following about what Star Teachers do:

- Make school a positive place and make learning as enjoyable and successful as possible
- Connect learning to students' interests
- Model and teach appreciation of learning for its own sake rather than for rewards
- Convince students they are welcome in the school and in their classroom
- Are gentle while consistently firm; a great manager with much flexibility
- Seek to understand without judging
- Own up to their own mistakes and try to fix them
- Carefully choose homework and assign sparingly
- Base student evaluation at least partly on student effort and progress
- Never "blame the victim"; do whatever is possible in school regardless of the realities of the home, family, and neighborhood

- Find a way to teach in the style they know is best for their students
- Maintain positive ongoing contact with all parents and guardians
- Use behavior management techniques that teach children to take responsibility for their own behavior; avoid arbitrary discipline or punishment measures

After interviewing more than 5,000 teachers, he concluded that the great teachers, Star Teachers, all appeared to have the same undergirding ideology and belief system for teaching and learning and consistently demonstrated the fine art of these teaching behaviors.

Star Teachers are effective with all students, particularly with students of color and students who live in poverty (individuals and groups of students historically underserved by public schools). Haberman often said, "Star Teachers understand students who have these challenges and embrace them as an important part of the classroom learning community." Star Teachers understand students who have many challenges and know how to bring them into the learning. They do not look for ways to remove them, but work tirelessly to find teaching strategies that help them learn at a high level.

Haberman developed interviewing techniques to identify teachers and administrators who would be successful in working with poor children. Distinguished Professor Emeritus of Curriculum and Instruction at University of Wisconsin–Milwaukee School of Education and founder of the Haberman Educational Foundation, he developed an emphasis on teaching in high-poverty schools. Haberman's philosophy of teacher preparation: "For children in poverty, success in school is a matter of life and death, and they need mature people who have a great deal of knowledge about their subject matter, but who can also relate to them. It is also necessary to recognize that most of what effective teachers learn they learn on the job from mentors, colleagues, and self-reflection."

This book is a further effort to share what Star Teachers do to rescue children who are in the process of having their lives destroyed through poor practices in education. Though the content in this book does not reveal the essence or protocol of the interview developed by the Foundation, educators will be able to discover the behaviors of Star Teachers who are at their best when working with children of poverty. Readers will be inspired by this work to become better teachers. For additional resources, you may visit www.habermanfoundation.org.

Alan Hooker
Haberman Educational Foundation

Introduction

Star Teachers can be found in every school, regardless of bureaucratic teaching environments or the negative social forces set in motion against learners. Many of us, whether as students or colleagues, have been fortunate enough to see how these effective teachers behave. These are teachers who do "the small things" with great effect, such as finding innovative ways to encourage students on a spelling test, sharing their passion for the great mathematicians of the Enlightenment period, or inspiring even the most underperforming students to reach their personal best. This book describes the seven dispositions (i.e., beliefs and behaviors) of Star Teachers along with examples and strategies for acquiring stardom in teaching.

We believe that these dispositions are the reasons that some teachers are successful and others are not. These are seven things that Star Teachers believe in and carry out in their classrooms, every day. Consider the following scenario at a failing middle school. It is first period and a class of 7th graders is falling apart. One student tears a blank sheet of paper from his notebook and crumples it up just so he has an excuse to walk to the trashcan. Another student gets up to retrieve a book from the bookshelf that she doesn't need. Several students are busy texting—part of an unspoken deal with the teacher, where they don't make trouble and she does not make them do work. This respected fourth-year teacher graduated at the top of her teacher preparation class and her diploma is prominently framed on the wall, but there is no joy in her class and students are not learning.

After first period, these same students go to a science class where their behavior is completely different. Though it is not a quiet class, the students are working independently except for a group collaborating on a team project. After a few minutes, the serious but approachable fourth-year teacher makes his way to the front of the class, and the students know, almost instinctively, to bring their work to a close to join a class discussion. In this class, there is a beautiful chaotic order and a sense that curiosity is nurtured. In the far corner near the door is a framed letter from the teacher to his students, congratulating his co-learners for their recent honor of being selected to participate in the county science fair. Although student scores in this class exceed those of other science classes in the district year after year, metrics of Adequate Yearly Progress are the furthest concerns from the teacher's mind.

What explains the observable differences in these two teachers? Martin Haberman's writings offer a nuanced way to interpret them. His Star Teacher framework was derived from five decades of research, including countless hours spent observing what teachers do and what motivates them to do it.

Haberman believes that mindset (ideology or beliefs) shapes behavior (practice).[1] The first educator described above is a pre-Star Teacher: she has not developed the personal traits that may contribute to being effective with learners. The second educator is a Star Teacher who has acquired the expertise and the dispositions to be successful. Although the pre-Star and the Star both teach in a failing school with harsh bureaucratic school and district policies, only the Star successfully meets the needs of *all* his students. The good news is that anyone who truly desires to be a Star Teacher can become one.

Haberman defines the merger of mindset and behavior for Star Teachers as midrange functions or dispositions ("midrange" because they represent chunks of teaching behavior that embody interconnected actions that constitute the beliefs that predispose the teachers to act).[2] He notes that Star Teachers can readily be identified by

> their persistence, their physical and emotional stamina, their caring
> relationships with students, their commitment to acknowledging and

appreciating student effort, their willingness to admit mistakes, their focus on deep learning, their commitment to inclusion, and their organization skills. They also protect student learning, translate theory and research into practice, cope with the bureaucracy, create student ownership, engage parents and caregivers as partners in student learning, and support accountability for at-risk students.[3]

Teacher Dispositions

Early research on teacher dispositions focused on teachers' character, honesty, and habits. At the start of the 20th century, education icon John Dewey discussed the idea of teacher conduct as manifestations of their routine thinking, which he famously referred to as "habits of the mind."[4] Dewey made the argument that not all teacher conduct is well informed, but that poor teacher habits can be disrupted when educators deliberately and critically reflect on their practice. Behavior informed by examination and open-mindedness can displace deep-rooted habits that are faulty. In *Disposition as Habits of Mind: Making Professional Conduct More Intelligent,* Erskine Dottin defines dispositions as "a tendency toward a general type of action in pedagogical situations," with "the teacher and learner tending to approach situations in a certain way and displaying a general set of actions associated with the disposition. Pedagogical dispositions should lead to better and more powerful pedagogy."[5]

There are too many definitions of the term *dispositions* to count, but they usually involve one or more of the following:

- Teacher characteristics: Attributes or tendencies that are persistently demonstrated, such as tolerance of differences, open-mindedness, patience, enthusiasm, critical thinking, and so on.
- Teacher behaviors: Observable actions during class, such as speaking Standard English, being punctual, smiling, presenting a neat and orderly appearance, and so on.
- Teacher perceptions: The attitudes, values, and belief systems that undergird characteristics and behaviors.[6]

To Haberman, all three of the above elements work to form dispositions. The characteristics and beliefs (mindset) of Stars cannot be detached from their behavior (classroom practices)—"they are of a piece."[7]

The Seven Dispositions of Star Teachers

The seven dispositions that Haberman outlines and that are the focus of this book are as follows: (1) persistence, (2) positive values about student learning, (3) the ability to adapt general theories into pedagogical practices, (4) an encouraging approach to at-risk students, (5) a professional versus a personal orientation, (6) the ability to avoid burnout, and (7) the tendency to be vulnerable and to admit one's shortcomings.[8] These dispositions are highly symbiotic: like links in a chain, each acts upon and is affected by the other. A Star Teacher is likely to embody most or all of Haberman's seven dispositions to varying degrees and at different points in his or her career.

If you closely examine the individual dispositions (see Figure 1), you will discover that each has two components: (1) a belief or mindset and (2) a set of behaviors. Haberman's seven dispositions help us understand how teachers' ways of thinking connect to their performance in the classroom. As Haberman writes, "teachers' behaviors and the mindset that undergirds their behaviors cannot be unwrapped."[9] Put simply: as a teacher thinks, so she or he does.

Figure 1   **Understanding the Source of Teachers' Dispositions**

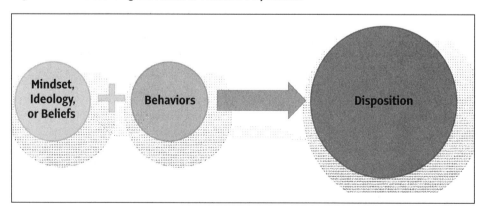

Source: From *Better Teachers, Better Schools: What Star Teachers Know, Believe, and Do* (p. xvii), by V. Hill-Jackson & D. Stafford, Charlotte, NC: Information Age Publishing. Copyright 2017. Used with permission.

Developing Effective Teacher Practice: Knowledge, Skills, and Dispositions

In the field of teacher education, effective teacher practice is determined by the professional triad of knowledge, skills, and dispositions (see Figure 2). Although the domains of teacher knowledge and skills are generally understood, the domain of dispositions is undervalued, underresearched, and fails to attract the same attention when it comes to identifying and selecting teacher candidates or training inservice teachers.

Figure 2   **The Professional Triad of Teacher Education**

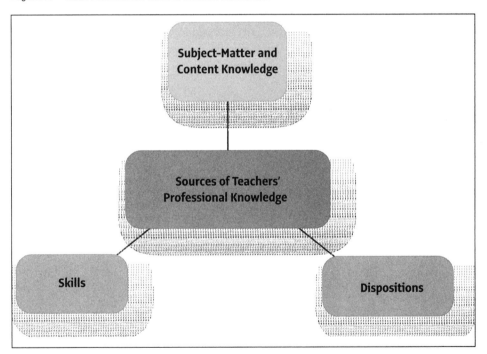

Dispositions are integral elements of teacher preparation programs, professional teaching standards, and teacher evaluation in K–12 schools. The Interstate New Teacher Assessment and Support Consortium (InTASC) outlines 10 standards for effective teaching aligned to the essential knowledge, skills, and dispositions of effective teachers, noting that "habits of professional action and moral commitments that underlie the performances play a key role in how teachers do, in fact, act in practice."[10] The Council for Accreditation of Educator Preparation notes that

> candidates preparing to work in schools as teachers or other school professionals know and demonstrate the content knowledge, pedagogical content knowledge and skills, pedagogical and professional knowledge and skills, and professional dispositions necessary to help all students learn. Assessments indicate that candidates meet professional, state, and institutional standards.[11]

Similarly, the National Board for Professional Teaching Standards outlines five propositions based on dispositions for developing and expert teachers. Professional organizations such as the National Association for the Education of Young Children and the Association for Childhood Education International also emphasize professional dispositions as being equally important to effective teaching as knowledge and skills.

Despite being such important characteristics of educators, dispositions are very difficult to assess.[12] Often they are reduced to such matters as enthusiasm, punctuality and good attendance, professional attire, initiative, strong oral and written communication, and collegiality. Teacher evaluation systems rely heavily on these visibly technical dispositions. For its part, the teacher accountability movement tends to focus more on observable or cognitive aspects of quality teaching such as licensing, subject-matter knowledge, and grade-point averages than on the types of dispositions Haberman espouses. In "Examining the Relationship Between Student Achievement and Observable Teacher Characteristics," Anna Jacob surmises that "educational outcomes depend more on the quality of the teacher a student is assigned to than on any other factor outside of the home, yet only a small proportion of the variation in teacher effectiveness is explained by the types of observable characteristics that are most commonly found in administrative data sets."[13]

One of the biggest challenges facing the educational community is how to measure the impact of teacher dispositions on learners and whether it is possible to factor them into hiring considerations. State and federal initiatives like the Every Student Succeeds Act, Common Core State Standards, and Race to the

Top have forced teacher preparation programs and school districts to primarily focus upon teachers' subject-matter knowledge and pedagogical skills, both of which can be easily measured. Indeed, teacher education has traditionally paid little attention to nonobservable characteristics. Given the need to retain effective teachers, however, educators should consider the value of taking nonobservable traits into consideration. What is missing most from the discussion of dispositions in teacher education is a focus on the *core* of the teacher—that which is invisible, intangible, and speaks to the personal or moral dimensions of the educator's character.

Teaching as a Moral Craft

Teaching is dynamic, deliberative, value-laden work. By virtue of their leadership role in the classroom, teachers are traditionally held to an elevated moral standard. As a human enterprise and as a profession, teaching is inherently moral. Because there are many perspectives on what constitutes morality, teacher education programs have stayed away from engaging in these discussions and, instead, have focused on the technical (i.e., nonpersonal) dimensions of teacher dispositions.

Richard D. Osguthorpe argues that teacher education should promote teachers with moral dispositions. This type of educator, he writes, teaches with fairness, respect, magnificence, honesty, compassion and "addresses multiple learning styles, gives appropriate and relevant homework, and does not favor one student or group over another." He continues:

> Teaching respectfully requires a teacher to give due attention to individual students, show consideration for different viewpoints and opinions, and refrain from embarrassing or humiliating students. A teacher who teaches magnificently exceeds students' highest expectations and impresses colleagues, administrators, and parents with the greatness of her practice. Honest teaching demands that a teacher present controversial issues in an impartial way, be truthful in giving feedback to students, and refrain from cheating students out of worthwhile learning experiences. Finally, a teacher who teaches compassionately shows sympathy for students' inability to comprehend difficult problems, exhibits concern for students who fall behind in their work, and spends time after school helping students.[14]

Similarly, Peter C. Murrell Jr., Mary E. Diez, Sharon Feiman-Nemser, and Deborah L. Schussler argue that teaching involves ethical decisions and that disposition standards should focus on moral or relational attributes of teachers.[15]

Star Teachers embody the essential technical dispositions of effective teachers while also emphasizing teaching as a moral enterprise. Haberman writes that Star Teachers are moral and decent without being moralistic or judgmental,[16] and proposes the seven dispositions of Star Teachers as reflecting teachers' moral center. Pre-Stars and Star Teachers respond differently in the classroom because they have fundamentally different belief systems. Stars also express their dispositions more sharply than Pre-Stars in the classroom as deep-rooted beliefs put into action.

Relational Dispositions: Humanity, Respect, and Care

The dispositions of Star Teachers are best defined as *relational*—that is, speaking to the personal or human aspects of teaching and learning. Although each relational disposition has a unique mindset associated with it, the unifying ideology is a "humane, respectful, caring, and nonviolent form of gentle teaching."[17] Humanity, respect, and care can thus be said to distinguish the beliefs and behaviors of Star Teachers from those of Pre-Stars (see Figures 3 and 4):

- **Humanity:** The *human* dimension of teaching is related to the teacher's heart and philosophy of teaching, which should position the students' needs above all else. Star Teachers see children's success "in school as a matter of life and death for the students and a matter of survival of society."[18]

- **Care:** Teaching is the *caring* profession. Scholars advocate the importance of developing caring relationships in the classroom because it supports students' social, emotional, and academic learning. Behavioral scientists maintain that teaching should be compassionate and honor the social interactions and relationships of the classroom. The work of Haberman and Valerie Hill-Jackson confirms that Star Teachers are adept at various forms of gentle teaching.[19]

Figure 3   **Respect, Humanity, and Care: The Unifying Themes of Haberman's Dimensions**

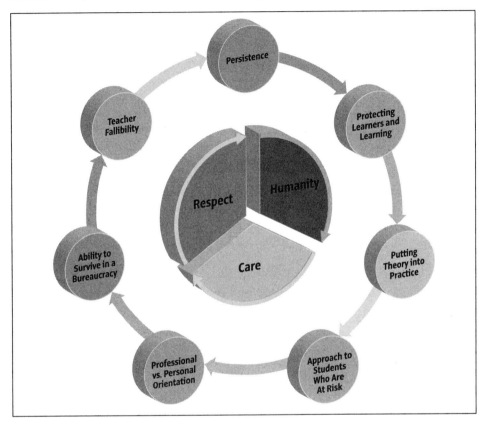

- **Respect:** The level of *respect* for the teacher and students increases when a supportive community is developed in the classroom. Haberman argues that respect in the Star Teacher's classroom goes both ways; the student gives respect to the teacher and the teacher gives respect to the student. Star Teachers do not wait until the Christmas holiday to smile at students or for students to earn their respect, they empower students and give them respect beginning on day one.[20]

Figure 4   **Star Teachers' Beliefs and Behaviors Using Haberman's Disposition Framework**

Pre-Star Teachers	Dispositions: Beliefs and Behaviors	Star Teachers
Have a one-size-fits-all approach to passive learners. If students fail to get the content the first time, then they quickly fall behind or fail.	Persistence	Possess the propensity to work with children who present learning and behavioral problems without giving up on them for the entire 180-day work year.
See protecting their career or just getting through the material as their highest priorities.	Protects and Values Student Learning	Believe that student learning is the teacher's highest priority.
Understand educational theories but fall short of adapting them into practical lessons for their classrooms.	Theory into Practice	See the implications of generalizing theory and the wherewithal to bring theory into practical applications in the classroom.
Cannot relate to, or teach, learners from diverse backgrounds.	Approach to Children in Poverty or Students at Risk	Connect with and teach students of all backgrounds and levels.
Wear their hearts on their sleeves and are easily bruised by the normal behavioral problems or classroom challenges that will arise in underserved classrooms. Their responses are often unprofessional and inappropriate for learners.	Professional vs. Personal Orientation to Students	Expect students to misbehave and attempt to relate to students as an experienced and consummate professional: resist the urge to "take it personally" in difficult classroom interactions.
Are unable to function or thrive in a large depersonalized organization; these teachers often leave the profession by year five or relegate students to impoverished learning experiences.	Survival in a Bureaucracy	Function or thrive in a large depersonalized organization.
Never acknowledge when they're wrong because they see mistakes as a form of weakness.	Fallibility	Readily admit mistakes and create 'teachable moments' from their mistakes for students' benefit.

Source: From *Better Teachers, Better Schools: What Star Teachers Know, Believe, and Do* (p. xix), by V. Hill-Jackson & D. Stafford, Charlotte, NC: Information Age Publishing. Copyright 2017. Adapted and used with permission.

In an essay titled "The Lifeguard: Confessions of a Novice Star Teacher of Children in Poverty," Lauren Williams shares how she applied Haberman's seven dispositions to her teaching. She worked hard to "put the strong focus of content on the backburner," writing that "building relationships with my students was the first and most important part of becoming an effective educator."[21] This investment in the learners on a personal level was returned with academic gains on state tests.

Williams's experience affirms the research on the effects of teacher-student relationships on students' social functioning,[22] engagement in learning,[23] and academic achievement.[24] They are also in line with the findings of Jeffrey Cornelius-White, whose in-depth meta-analysis points to a credible link between person-centered teaching (i.e., empathy and warmth) and student outcomes.[25]

Haberman's Star Teacher framework demonstrates that the personal dimensions of teacher dispositions, once thought of as ethereal and difficult to discern, can be assessed and quantified. Star Teachers are not smarter, more educated, or more caring than pre-Star Teachers; they are merely more conscious of how their belief systems are inextricably connected to what they do and clear-eyed about the ways in which their practice affects students' academic and emotional development.

Characteristics of Effective Teachers

Teaching effectiveness is often associated with experience, teacher training, ongoing professional development, cumulative grade point averages, teacher examination scores, Scholastic Aptitude Test (SAT) scores, and high school rankings, but there is no single attribute that defines an effective teacher. In their book *The Teacher Quality Index: A Protocol for Teacher Selection,* James H. Stronge and Jennifer L. Hindman suggest that effective teaching is composed of the following six areas:

1. Impressive oral and written communication skills, prior teaching experience, and a high command of the content area;
2. Caring teacher-student relationships with high expectations for learners and themselves;
3. Engaging learning environment;
4. Remarkable organization and planning astuteness;

5. Exciting learning experiences for learners that provide a medium for critical thinking, problem solving, and high-level questions;

6. Formative and summative assessment that adjusts to meet the needs of all learners.[26]

Other scholars define effective teachers as those who can increase student performance,[27] teach a variety of learning styles,[28] and assess and adjust instruction.[29] Many advocate knowledge of subject matter as the best criteria for predicting teacher effectiveness.[30] But if command over content and pedagogy were enough, then university math professors and school of education faculty would be able to teach successfully for sustained periods of time in urban middle schools. We recognize that such an idea is preposterous because more than knowledge of content and pedagogy is required.

In an article titled "Teachers Need Affective Competencies," Carl Olson and Jerry Wyett propose that teachers should be equally as capable in relational matters as they are in matters related to content.[31] An impressive volume of studies proposes that teachers' beliefs about teaching and learning affect their teaching practices.[32] If a teacher believes that all students can learn, she or he will move heaven and earth to ensure that the learners on his or her watch will experience academic success. However, if a teacher feels in his or her heart that there is no hope for learners, then he or she is unlikely to implement practices that support student learning to the detriment of their performance, aspirations, and self-concepts.

Development of the Star Teacher Framework

Since 1959, Haberman has completed hundreds of research trials to confirm the dispositions of pre-Stars and Stars, including thousands of hours of classroom observations. After five decades of research, the Star Teacher dispositions are now highly developed and extremely predictive of highly effective teachers.[33] Haberman's contributions to understanding teacher dispositions become meaningful when results are measurable student achievement.

In a book chapter titled "Victory at Buffalo Creek: What Makes a School Serving Low-Income Hispanic Children Successful?" Haberman discusses 29 teachers and a principal who were all selected by using the Star Teacher framework. Several years later, most of the staff was still employed at Buffalo Creek Elementary

School (BCES) and the students continued to receive state recognition on mandated tests:

> What these teachers (and principal) have in addition to subject matter knowledge [is] teaching know-how. The Buffalo Creek staff's special expertise has three themes. First, every one of the success indicators is primarily a function of the staff's ability to relate to the children, the parents and each other. Second, the staff shares a common ideology of why the school exists, what is supposed to happen to the children, and their role as teachers (principal) to make it happen. Third, the Buffalo Creek staff is gifted at relationship skills and this is key. Studying Buffalo Creek leads to the conclusion that children in poverty must have teachers who can connect with them. The teachers' desire—and ability, to want to live with the children all day, every day, is prerequisite to children learning.[34]

In his study, Haberman identified all seven relational dispositions among the 29 teachers. By the end of the first year of operation, BCES was designated by the Texas Education Agency (TEA) as "recognized" and 97 percent of the school's low-income English language learners had passed the state test.

Nicholas D. Hartlep, Christopher M. Hansen, Sara A. McCubbins, Guy J. Banicki, and Grant B. Morgan completed a 2017 study, "Teaching in the "Windy" City: A Mixed Method Case Study of Seven Star Teachers in Chicago," using Haberman's Star Teacher framework.[35] The objective of the study was to determine whether the diverse elementary, middle, and high school teachers identified by the district as effective displayed the ideologies and core beliefs of Star Teachers. The seven Star Teachers in the study were persistent, demonstrated fallibility, and tended to blame themselves rather than their at-risk students for any underachievement. The researchers concluded that dispositional information strengthens the teaching staff by helping them understand their strengths and weaknesses and to guide professional development needs.[36]

Although additional research is needed to understand the role relational dispositions play in teacher quality, Haberman's groundbreaking research does point out that only teachers can positively affect student achievement, suggesting that professional development on dispositions should be offered to novice and inservice teachers. Understanding the beliefs or mindsets of Star Teachers may be the linchpin for identifying effective teaching behavior in the classroom.

How This Book Is Organized

Each of the seven main chapters of *What Makes a Star Teacher* focuses on one of Haberman's seven dispositions of Star Teachers, exploring the mindsets and behaviors of Star Teachers in depth. Every chapter includes the following elements:

- **Learning Outcomes:** Learning goals are clearly introduced at the beginning and revisited at the end of each chapter.
- **InTASC Standards:** Relevant InTASC standards for teacher practice are highlighted. Haberman's relational dispositions are not meant to replace technical dispositions such as those outlined in these standards but to fully address the moral dimension of teacher ideology and behavior. Star Teachers possess both technical and relational dispositions.
- **Key Words:** Readers are introduced to important terms that are boldfaced and defined in the body of each chapter.
- **Extension Exercises:** Additional questions and activities related to the disposition in question.
- **Going Further:** A list of resources such as internet sites, videos, and readings for more advanced study.

Chapter 1, **Teacher Persistence,** is about Star Teachers' never-ending pursuit of instructional strategies to support struggling learners. Persistence is driven by two major actions: problem solving and inventive effort. The goal is for no student's academic needs to be overlooked. Star Teachers never give up on trying to engage every student.[37]

Chapter 2, **Protecting Learners and Learning,** discusses how to ensure that students' active participation in meaningful learning experiences outweigh inflexible school curricula and policies. Star Teachers realize all the ways in which large school organizations encroach on teachers and students but find strategies to preserve learning above all else.[38]

Chapter 3, **Putting Theory into Practice,** explains how Star Teachers transform theory and research into commonsense instructional habits. This dimension foretells an educator's receptiveness to professional development activities and likelihood to grow in the profession.[39]

Chapter 4, **Approaching Learners Who Are at Risk,** explores Star Teachers' beliefs about and behaviors toward students categorized as being at risk for failure. Star Teachers point to inadequate teaching and curricula as the chief reasons for students' underachievement. They also shoulder the responsibility for student learning, despite the fact that they cannot control all in-school and out-of-school influences on their students.[40]

Chapter 5, **Orienting to Learners: Professional Versus Personal,** examines the ways in which Star Teachers rely on preparation rather than personal feelings to meet their students' academic or emotional needs. Unlike Pre-Stars, Star Teachers expect students to misbehave and to have bad days but remember to maintain respect and care for them when they do.[41]

Chapter 6, **Surviving in a Bureaucracy,** discusses Star Teachers' skills at navigating burdensome school systems without burning out or leaving the profession. Teachers who hold naïve expectations of working in school systems are most likely to become the victims of those systems.[42]

Chapter 7, **Accepting and Admitting Fallibility,** is about Star Teachers' willingness to admit mistakes and correct them in front of students, thus modeling and setting expectations for how students should respond to their mistakes in the process of learning.[43]

Chapter 8, **Am I a Star Teacher? Developing Dispositions That Support Student Learning,** offers a step-by-step guide to identifying goals and action steps for developing the dispositions of Star Teachers.

Were he alive today, Haberman would be thrilled to see his research converted into practical strategies to help new and seasoned teachers become better at their craft. Haberman had an unbridled passion for all teachers; he was the biggest cheerleader for those who went the extra mile and shined. We give him the last words in this introduction:

> Because one must have a strong commitment to this undergirding ideology it is not possible to translate what [S]tars do into 10 easy steps for anyone to follow. To do what [S]tars do requires sharing the beliefs and values they use as guidelines for making the countless decisions

they make daily. To try to imitate what [S]tars do, without believing as they do, leads to merely going through the motions of teaching and having very little influence on students' learning. For those who accept [S]tars' ideology, these functions can be brought to life; they can become a source of insight and a guide to effective teaching.[44]

Endnotes

1. Haberman, M. (2010). *Star Teachers: The ideology and best practice of effective teachers of diverse children and youth in poverty* (1st ed.). Houston, TX: Haberman Educational Foundation.

2. Haberman, M. (2002). Selecting Star Teachers for children and youth in poverty. *Phi Delta Kappan, 76*(10), 777–781.

3. Haberman, M. (2004). Can Star Teachers create learning communities? *Educational Leadership, 61*(8), 52–56. (p. 53)

4. Dewey, J. (1997). *How we think: A restatement of the relation of reflective thinking to the educative process.* Mineola, NY: Dover.

5. Dottin, E. S. (2010). *Dispositions as habits of mind: Making professional conduct more intelligent.* Lanham, MD: University Press of America. (p. 4)

6. Wasicsko, M. M., Callahan, C. J., & Wirtz, P. (2004). Integrating dispositions into the conceptual framework: Four a priori questions. *KCA Journal, 23*(1), 1–8. Retrieved from http://mynkuhelp.nku.edu/content/dam/coehs/docs/dispositions/resources/four_a_priori_questions.pdf

7. Haberman (2002, p. 777).

8. Haberman (2002, p. 777).

9. Haberman (2002, p. 777).

10. Council of Chief State School Officers (CCSSO). (2011). *InTASC Model core teaching standards: A resource for state dialogue.* Washington, DC: Author. Retrieved from www.ccsso.org/Documents/2011/InTASC_Model_Core_Teaching_Standards_2011.pdf

11. Council for the Accreditation of Educator Preparation (CAEP). (2013). *CAEP Commission on Standards and Performance Reporting.* Retrieved from http://www.caepnet.org/~/media/Files/caep/standards/caep-standards-one-pager-061716.pdf?la=en

12. Diez, M. (2006). Assessing dispositions: Five principles to guide practice. In H. Sockett (Ed.), *Teacher dispositions: Building a teacher education framework of moral standard* (pp.49–60). Washington, DC: AACTE Publications.

13. Jacob, A. (2012). Examining the relationship between student achievement and observable teacher characteristics: Implications for school leaders. *International Journal of Educational Leadership Preparation, 7*(3), 1–13. (p. 11)

14. Osguthorpe, R. D. (2008). On the reasons we want teachers of good disposition and moral character. *Journal of Teacher Education, 59*(4), 288–299. (p. 296)

15. Diez, M., & Murrell, P. (2010). Dispositions in teacher education: Starting points for consideration. In P. C. Murrell, Jr., M. E. Diez, S. Feiman-Nemser, & D. L. Schussler (Eds.), *Teaching as a moral practice: Defining, developing, and assessing professional dispositions in teacher education* (pp. 7-26). Cambridge, MA: Harvard Education Press.

16. Haberman (2010).

17. Haberman (2002, p. 777).

18. Haberman (2010).

19. Haberman, M., & Hill-Jackson, V. (2017). Gentle teaching in a violent society: A postscript for the 21st century. In V. Hill-Jackson & D. Stafford (Eds.), *Better teachers, better schools: What Star Teachers know, believe, and do* (pp. 13–30). Charlotte, NC: Information Age Publishing.

20. Haberman, M. (2002, p. 780).

21. Williams, L. A. (2017). The lifeguard: Confessions of a novice Star Teacher of children in poverty. In V. Hill-Jackson & D. Stafford (p. 110).

22. Ahnert, L., Harwardt-Heinecke, E., Kappler, G., Eckstein-Madry, T., & Milatz, A. (2012). Student-teacher relationships and classroom climate in first grade: How do they relate to students' stress regulation? *Attachment & Human Development, 14*(3), 249–263.

23. Christenson, S. L., Reschly, A. L., & Wylie, C. (Eds.). (2012). *Handbook of research on student engagement.* New York: Springer.

24. Sabol, T. J., & Pianta, R. C. (2012). Recent trends in research on teacher-child relationships. *Attachment & Human Development, 14*(3), 213–231.

25. Cornelius-White, J. (2007). Learner-centered teacher-student relationships are effective: A meta-analysis. *Review of Educational Research, 77*(1), 113–143.

26. Stronge, J. H., & Hindman, J. L. (2006). *The teacher quality index: A protocol for teacher selection.* Alexandria, VA: ASCD.

27. Clark, D. (1993). *Teacher evaluation: A review of the literature with implications for educators.* [Unpublished manuscript]. Long Beach: California State University at Long Beach.

28. Vogt, W. (1984). Developing a teacher evaluation system. *Spectrum, 2*(1), 41–46.

29. Orlich, D. C., Harder, R. J., Trevisan, M. S., Brown, A. H., & Miller, D. E. (2016). *Teaching strategies: A guide to effective instruction.* Boston: Cengage Learning.

30. Darling-Hammond, L. (1990). Teaching and knowledge: Policy issues posed by alternate certification for teachers. *Peabody Journal of Education, 67*(3), 123–154.; Ferguson, P., & T. Womack, S. (1993). The impact of subject matter and education coursework on teaching performance. *Journal of Teacher Education, 44*(1), 55–63.; Scheerens, J., & Blömeke, S. (2016). Integrating teacher education effectiveness research into educational effectiveness models. *Educational Research Review, 18*, 70–87.

31. Olson, C. O., & Wyett, J. L. (2000). Teachers need affective competencies. *Education, 120*(4), 741.

32. Nespor, J. (1987). The role of beliefs in the practice of teaching. *Journal of Curriculum Studies, 19*(4), 317–328.

33. Baskin, M., & Ross, S. (1992). *Selecting teacher candidates via structured interviews: A validation study of the urban teacher interview.* Memphis, TN: Memphis State University.; Baskin, M. K., Ross, S. M., & Smith, D. L. (1996). Selecting successful teachers: The predictive validity of the urban teacher selection interview. *Teacher Educator, 32*(1), 1–21.; Haberman, M. (1993). Predicting the success of urban teachers: The Milwaukee trials. *Action in Teacher Education, 15*(3), 1–5.; Rockoff, J. E., Jacob, B. A., Kane, T. J., & Staiger, D. O. (2008). *Can you recognize an effective teacher when you recruit one?* Cambridge, MA: National Bureau of Economic Research.

34. Haberman, M. (2017). Victory at Buffalo Creek: What makes a school serving low-income Hispanic children successful? In V. Hill-Jackson & D. Stafford (Eds.), *Better teachers, better schools: What Star Teachers know, believe, and do* (pp. 137–160). Charlotte, NC: Information Age Publishing.

35. Hartlep, N. D., Hansen, C. M., McCubbins, S. A., Banicki, G.J., & Morgan, G. B. (2017). Teaching in the "Windy" City: A mixed method case study of seven Star Teachers in Chicago. In Hill-Jackson & Stafford (pp. 160–176).

36. Hartlep et al. (2017).

37. Hill-Jackson & Stafford (2017).

38. Hill-Jackson & Stafford (2017).

39. Hill-Jackson & Stafford (2017).

40. Hill-Jackson & Stafford (2017).

41. Hill-Jackson & Stafford (2017).

42. Haberman (2002). For more on these specific dispositions, please refer to page 780.

43. Haberman (2002). For more on these specific dispositions, please refer to page 780.

44. Haberman (2010, p. 131.).

1

Teacher Persistence

Persistence is reflected in an endless search for what works best with each student. Indeed, Star Teachers define their jobs as asking themselves constantly, "How might this activity have been better—for the class or for a particular individual?"

Learning Outcomes

Upon completion of this chapter, you will be able to

- Define *teacher persistence.*
- Explain why teacher persistence is the key disposition of Star Teachers.
- Analyze the ways in which Star Teachers think about their commitment to learners and their efficacy as teachers.
- Explore the classroom environments and problem-solving approaches of Star Teachers.

Interstate New Teacher Assessment and Support Consortium (InTASC) Standards

Standard #2: Learning Differences

The teacher uses understanding of individual differences and diverse cultures and communities to ensure inclusive learning environments that enable each learner to meet high standards.

Standard #4: Content Knowledge

The teacher understands the central concepts, tools of inquiry, and structures of the discipline(s) he or she teaches and creates learning experiences that make the discipline accessible and meaningful for learners to assure mastery of the content.

Standard #5: Application of Content

The teacher understands how to connect concepts and use differing perspectives to engage learners in critical thinking, creativity, and collaborative problem solving related to authentic local and global issues.

Standard #6: Assessment

The teacher understands and uses multiple methods of assessment to engage learners in their own growth, to monitor learner progress, and to guide the teacher's and learner's decision making.

Standard #8: Instructional Strategies

The teacher understands and uses a variety of instructional strategies to encourage learners to develop deep understanding of content areas and their connections, and to build skills to apply knowledge in meaningful ways.

★ ★ ★ ★ ★ ★ ★ ★ ★ ★ ★

Defining *Persistence*

What pushes some people to keep trying, to never give up, even when the conditions suggest defeat? **Persistence**, also known as tenacity or **grit**, is defined as continuing to strive toward a goal in the face of challenges. It is perseverance with a passion for attaining long-term goals. Persistence is a noncognitive dimension of a person's character, a disposition or a habit of mind operationalized through problem solving.

Though the terms *resilience* and *persistence* are often used interchangeably, they in fact have different meanings. As Grotberg explains, *resilience* is the "human capacity to face, overcome, and even be strengthened by experiences of adversity."[1] Highly resilient individuals are reactive to setbacks in their personal or everyday life, but come out of them as more efficacious people. By contrast, persistence is a *proactive* personal attribute linked to professional action and goal setting. (We will delve more into teacher resilience in Chapter 6: Surviving in a Bureaucracy.)

We need only look at the inspirational quotes plastered on so many office walls—"Patience, persistence, and perspiration make an unbeatable combination for success" (Napoleon Hill); "Success is the result of perfection, hard work, learning from failure, loyalty, and persistence" (Colin Powell)—to understand how desirable a quality persistence is. Most of us can point to instances in our everyday lives of skilled individuals who seem to have an especially high level of *stick-with-it-ness* in their chosen field, exercising persistence to achieve goals despite extraordinary odds.

Persistence has long been tied to success in the workplace. Business literature with titles like *Executive Toughness* and *Stick with It* highlight persistence as key to professional success. It takes persistence to evolve, acquire competencies, and explore opportunities that develop over time. In comparison with individuals who give up easily when they face hardships, people who persist at any effort further refine their skills and develop expertise.

Kelley, Matthews, and Bartone examined the predictive power of grit and hardiness among a cohort of 1,558 West Point cadets, finding these noncognitive characteristics to be major factors in attrition: the less gritty and hardy the cadets, the likelier they were to drop out. Specifically, the authors found grit to be a differentiating factor between cadets who left West Point early ($M = 3.98$) and those who persisted through graduation ($M = 4.08$) (see Figure 1.1). "Conceptually, grit has an obvious link with the demands required for successful performance at West Point," they wrote. "Grit, or 'firmness of character,' is synonymous with fortitude or courage and is the essence of what the Academy sustains and builds in its cadets and graduates."[2] These findings suggest that cadet officers, who develop as professionals through trial and error, may be readily identified by their grit scores.

Teacher Persistence

An online search of the phrase *teacher persistence* leads to innumerable studies on teacher attrition, teacher retention, and job satisfaction—but few studies on teacher persistence. We define *teacher persistence* as a disposition manifested in the day-to-day actions of a teacher pursuing an outcome directly related to improving student achievement. This is in line with Haberman's definition of *persistence in teaching* as the mindset and behavior of a teacher who continues to support learners in a committed way through creative problem solving.[3] For Haberman, persistence is at the heart of the seven dispositions of Star Teachers, helping to maintain and actualize the other six (see Figure 1.2). Persistence determines whether the teacher can sustain fallibility and be vulnerable with students; protect student learning regardless of cost; retain practices that reflect sound theory; preserve a healthy approach to students identified as being at risk; maintain a professional orientation toward student-teacher relationships; and avoid burnout. If learners are to achieve their full potential, teachers must exhibit persistence even in the face of repeated instructional failures, never giving up on their learners.

Figure 1.1 **Grit as a Predictor of Graduation Among West Point Cadets**

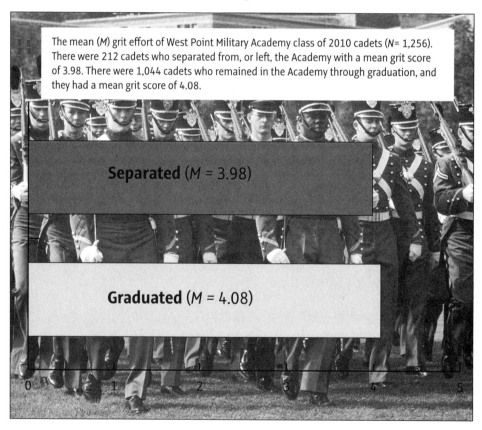

The mean (*M*) grit effort of West Point Military Academy class of 2010 cadets (*N*= 1,256). There were 212 cadets who separated from, or left, the Academy with a mean grit score of 3.98. There were 1,044 cadets who remained in the Academy through graduation, and they had a mean grit score of 4.08.

Separated (*M* = 3.98)

Graduated (*M* = 4.08)

Figure 1.2 **Haberman's 7 Dispositions of Star Teachers**

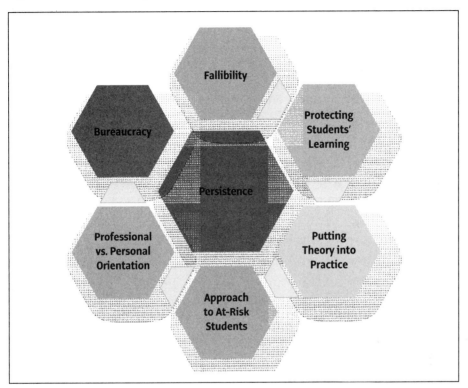

★ 1-1

Are you a persistent teacher? Complete Angela Duckworth's online survey at https://angeladuckworth.com/grit-scale/. Complete the survey before moving on to the next section.

Persistence and Teacher Quality

According to the Every Student Succeeds Act (ESSA),[4] all children in the United States are to be taught in the core academic subjects by "effective" teachers. Among many others, Wheatley suggests that persistence is crucial to teacher effectiveness because it "may promote high expectations for students, development of teaching skills, teachers' reflectiveness, responsiveness to diversity, teaching efficacy, effective responses to setbacks, and successful use of reformed teaching methods."[5]

Substituting *grit* for *persistence,* Robertson-Kraft and Duckworth[6] analyzed two longitudinal studies of nearly 500 novice teachers assigned to elementary, middle, and high schools in low-income districts, measuring factors such as grit, leadership, academic credentials, and teacher performance. Their findings show that novices who demonstrated sustained passion and perseverance in activities prior to becoming teachers were more likely to stay in the profession and prove effective during their first year on the job. The authors defined effective teachers as those who make, on average, "a year's worth of progress according to published norms" and less effective teachers as those for whom "student progress falls short of the target."[7] In their study, the mean grade-point average (GPA) of students with effective teachers (3.59) was nearly identical to that of students with less effective teachers (3.60). Scholastic Aptitude Test (SAT) scores were also close to equivalent, with an average of 1332.78 for students of effective teachers compared to 1327.65 for those with less effective teachers. Similar variables such as "interview ratings of leadership potential and demographics failed to predict retention or effectiveness."[8]

The effective teachers in this study were most readily identified by their grit ratings rather than by the GPA or SAT scores of students. Effective middle school teachers (i.e., those most likely to stay in their jobs) possessed a significantly higher mean grit rating (3.98) than their less effective counterparts (2.79). As Figure 1.3 shows, differences between effective and less effective teachers are more evident when noncognitive characteristics are evaluated.

In another study, Duckworth, Quinn, and Seligman[9] asked 390 novice teachers in low-income districts to complete questionnaires assessing their grit, optimism, and satisfaction with life prior to the first day of school. All three of these characteristics individually predicted some measure of teacher effectiveness for student academic gains over the school year. Further, when the three characteristics were measured collectively, only the combination of grit and life satisfaction was determined to be highly predictive of teacher effectiveness. For this reason, Haberman[10] advises administrators to examine observable and measurable

Figure 1.3 **Grit and GPA as Predictors of Teacher Effectiveness**

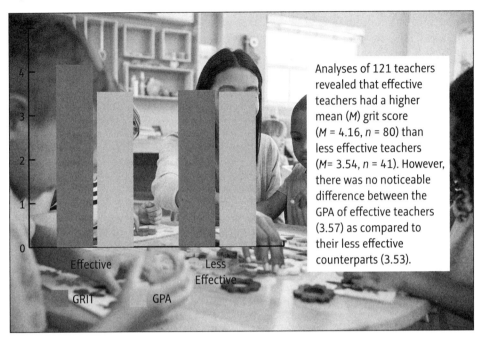

Analyses of 121 teachers revealed that effective teachers had a higher mean (*M*) grit score (*M* = 4.16, *n* = 80) than less effective teachers (*M*= 3.54, *n* = 41). However, there was no noticeable difference between the GPA of effective teachers (3.57) as compared to their less effective counterparts (3.53).

Source: Data from "True Grit: Trait-Level Perseverance and Passion for Long-Term Goals Predicts Effectiveness and Retention Among Novice Teachers," by C. Robertson-Kraft and A. L. Duckworth, 2014, *Teachers College Record, 116*(3), pp. 1–27.

personality factors like persistence among teacher candidates—before they are hired as teachers.

The Mindset of Persistent Star Teachers

We can best understand Star Teachers by appreciating how they (1) perceive the nature of the learner and (2) comprehend their personal sense of efficacy. Haberman notes that Star Teachers express deep and abiding beliefs about the potential of diverse learners, the nature of the teaching role, and the reasons they and their students are in school. They are relentless in their efforts to ensure that every learner, regardless of ability, gender, ethnicity, or social class, experiences success. Star Teachers exhibit determination in seeking instructional methods to support all learners as well as optimism that the methods will succeed.

Star Teachers take their roles as educators seriously. They have an uncommon belief about the abilities of their learners, for whom they hold high expectations, and feel a deep responsibility for helping learners to do their best. Haberman states that this mindset is "a clear reflection of what they believe the daily work of the teacher should be."[11] Star Teachers who exhibit persistence doggedly communicate through their actions that students are

- Central to their work as educators.
- Growing both cognitively and affectively and may require individualized attention.
- Not allowed to fail—no excuses.
- Preparing for lifelong learning.
- Held to very high standards.

Tomlinson offers additional insight into the convictions of persistent teachers:

> The persistent teacher also models the steady but relentless quest for excellence. The persistent teacher generously acknowledges the distance a student has come academically, but also makes clear the distance each student has yet to go. That teacher helps students realize that the quest for quality never ends. If the quest ends, quality ends with it—and so does the growth of the individual. . . . The persistent teacher not only points out that learning has no finish line for students but lives according to that principle as well. That teacher fights "success ego," never succumbing to the sense that she is "good enough" to be exempt from the need to change. "We're all on a journey," the persistent teacher believes, "none of us is ever through striving."[12]

Persistent teachers convey these messages daily to students because they feel responsible for creating an engaging learning environment and helping their students to develop mastery over content. Their mindset prevents them from being overwhelmed by challenges or buckling under setbacks. Persistent teachers' "students first" philosophy is mirrored in their classrooms, which typically enjoy a strong spirit of community, positive teacher-student relationships built on trust, and ample student affirmation. Learners in such classrooms feel supported and often think of their teachers as among the few adults in their lives with their own best interests at heart.

Teacher Efficacy

The concept of **self-efficacy** was originally developed by Albert Bandura and has been defined as the personal belief that one is capable of performing in an appropriate and effective manner to attain certain goals. As such, self-efficacy is a system that controls most personal activity, including suitable use of professional knowledge and skills.[13] **Teacher efficacy** is a similar idea with significant implications for learner achievement. It is a teacher's judgment of his or her capability to promote student engagement and learning even among challenging or unmotivated students. As Tschannen-Moran and Woolfolk Hoy note,

> Efficacy affects the effort [teachers] invest in teaching, the goals they set, and their level of aspiration. Teachers with a strong sense of efficacy tend to exhibit greater levels of planning and organization. They also are more open to new ideas and are more willing to experiment with new methods to better meet the needs of their students. . . . Efficacy beliefs influence teachers' persistence when things do not go smoothly and their resilience in the face of setbacks. Greater efficacy enables teachers to be less critical of students when they make errors and to work longer with a student.[14]

In a large-scale analysis of 43 studies representing 9,216 teachers, Klassen and colleagues[15] explored the connections among teachers' senses of competence, personality, and effectiveness. Their findings revealed a significant positive relationship between a teacher's sense of competence (i.e., self-efficacy) and effectiveness in the classroom. In another study, Jerald[16] noted persistence among the characteristics of teachers with a stronger sense of efficacy. Teachers who have high expectations for learners and who try a new approach when an old one is not working are more likely to have students who learn. Further, Guo and colleagues studied the impact of teacher efficacy, educational level, and teaching experience on the reading outcomes of 1,043 5th grade students.[17] The researchers concluded that teacher efficacy is not positively related to years of experience but that "teacher efficacy was a significant and positive predictor of fifth grade literacy outcomes."[18]

Teachers who set ambitious goals and have a high sense of efficacy are more likely to persist in helping learners to achieve desired outcomes. These teachers model persistence not only in their interactions with students, but also in their own professional development. Research confirms that persistent teachers are curious learners who take professional learning into their own hands.

Teachers with a low sense of efficacy make comments like "When you have students from that part of town, there is nothing you can do as a teacher to help improve their scores on the state exam. What does the district expect from us when the parents are missing in action?" Such teachers are complacent, believing there is nothing they can do to change academic outcomes for learners. They don't feel they have the wherewithal to develop strategies to support learners on their own; their teaching toolbox is empty. When faced with student setbacks, teachers with low efficacy do not exert any additional effort or develop the skills needed to support learners.

By contrast, teachers with a high sense of efficacy do not make excuses for student failure and place the prospect for improved student achievement squarely on their own shoulders: "It will require more effort and coaching, but if I try really hard I can find a way to support the students who are struggling." These optimistic and persistent teachers do not believe inadequate efforts to support learners are necessarily permanent. As Carol Dweck reminds us, it is a teacher's sense of efficacy, not his or her teaching skills, that best predicts whether he or she will become a gritty teacher during tough times who sticks with established learning goals.[19] Persistent teachers will go to the ends of the Earth to make learning happen for all learners; their motto could be "What do I do next?"

Robert Klassen and colleagues explored the connection among teachers' sense of competence, personality, and effectiveness in a large-scale analysis of 43 studies representing 9,216 teachers.[20] The results of their comprehensive evaluation revealed a significant positive relationship between a teacher's sense of competence, or self-efficacy, and effectiveness in the classroom. In a report for the Center for Comprehensive School Reform and Improvement, Craig Jerald[21] noted several behaviors common to teachers with a stronger sense of efficacy, including persistence: teachers who have high expectations for learners and who try another approach when the one they're using is not working are more likely to have students who learn.

In a 2012 study, Guo and colleagues reported that teacher efficacy had a greater influence on the reading outcomes of 5th grade students than teacher experience or teacher education.[22] The study examined teachers' classroom practices to understand whether student outcomes were directly or indirectly associated with teacher characteristics. The investigators found that teachers with a higher sense of self-efficacy provided more support for student learning and created a more positive classroom environment. They noted that their study "establishes that teacher self-efficacy predicts teachers' practices, which in turn predict student literacy outcome over and above the influence of teachers' experience and teachers' education, when controlling for students' previous literacy skills and their social and economic status."[23] The results indicate clearly that teacher efficacy is predicated as much on teacher characteristics and behaviors as on their qualifications.

Star Teachers understand that a small amount of student underachievement may seem insignificant, but over time, curricular content not met in one subject or grade has a cumulative negative effect on individual learners. A Tennessee study titled *Cumulative and Residual Effects of Teachers on Future Academic Achievement* found that teachers have an aggregate effect on student achievement.[24] After three years of ineffective teachers, students scored less than half as well as their peers who had benefited from more effective teachers. When pre-Star Teachers boast a 70 percent pass rate for learners, the persistent teacher wonders, "What happened to the other 30 percent?" Stars are never content when students do not grasp the content. "What do I do next?" is not a passive quip, but the foundation for a professional and personal model of instructional inquiry. Therefore, Star Teachers who are persistent will try another teaching strategy when one strategy is not working.

The Behaviors of Star Teachers Who Are Persistent

Star Teachers who are persistent make extraordinary instructional efforts; they are doers and find creative strategies for acting on their beliefs about supporting student learning. Star Teachers think deeply about the instructional experiences in their classroom and use innovative techniques to bring their ideas to life. The behavior of persistent teachers is best manifested in the ways in which they make the classroom an interesting place to learn and seek to resolve instructional setbacks to find "what works" for their learners.

Persistent Teachers Create Stimulating Classroom Environments

Star Teachers view the classroom as a student-centered environment that inspires creativity, and they work as purposely at maintaining an inviting atmosphere for learning as they do at designing curriculum or implementing instruction.[25] The classroom of a Star Teacher is a wonderland most learners long to visit, with murals and learning centers setting the stage for joyful learning. Steven Wolk captures the convictions of persistent teachers about stimulating spaces when he notes that "the hearts and minds of children and young adults are wide open to the wonders of learning and the fascinating complexities of life"[26] and that "as educators, we have the responsibility to educate and inspire the whole child—mind, heart, and soul."[27]

The classroom of a Star Teacher is designed to embrace the following fundamentals:

Climate: It is ideal to provide an atmosphere for learners with images and sounds that invite creative thinking, such as by placing inspirational quotes around the room or sharing music that excites, winds down, or transitions learners from one activity to the next. A teacher providing a warm welcome to each student sets a positive vibe for the day. It is important to greet learners at the door using their names and with a smile. We all have seen the viral video in which the young male teacher greeted each student with a personalized handshake. A simple gesture like this one sends a message that each learner is a valued member of the classroom and lets them know you "see" them and cannot wait to learn with them.

Organization: Learners should be able to easily move around the various parts of the classroom. Teachers should think through sight lines for items of interest, and traffic flow around the room. The reading nook and class library, the literacy center, the computer area, small- and large-group areas, and so on should be thoughtfully planned out. It is critical to avoid visual clutter and to provide blank or visually quiet spaces that give the eye a place to rest. Supplies, tools, furniture, and books should be stored, not left in full display.

Community: Because Star Teachers believe that learning is highly social, they employ tables to make collaborative learning easy. Students should be able to quickly work with a small group simply by turning their seats. The "simple act of positioning desks can promote positive interpersonal interactions."[28] Learners should feel like they are co-owners of the classroom.

Environmental Conditions: Star Teachers pay attention to air quality and lighting, fully aware that environmental conditions can affect student behaviors and academic performance.[29] Studies have shown that when temperatures are too low or high, the brain will send endless messages to do something about it. Because of the endless intrusions, it then becomes difficult for learners to focus on learning as the body seeks to find a balance in temperature. For example, a 2018 study on grade 9 students demonstrated a direct relationship of classroom temperature to aptitude and attention span of the learners. In regulated temperatures, students performed well. But when the classroom temperature was too hot or too cold, the students' scores were negatively impacted.[30] Since many classroom teachers do not have the ability to control the temperature in their classrooms, it is important to consider how extreme or uncomfortable temperatures affect students' ability to learn, as well as the teacher's ability to teach.[31]

Volume Control: Noise levels can affect learning by prompting students' bodies to release extra cortisol, which weakens the brain's capacity to store short-term memories. Comprehension can be jeopardized, too: The **café effect** is a phenomenon in which the noise of a swirling, bustling classroom compromises the learner's ability to clearly understand speech, especially among elementary-age students.[32] Star Teachers seek to mitigate acoustical problems and increase student focus by installing low-cost sound-absorbing materials like insulation panels in their classrooms.

Seating Arrangement: Does your classroom seating arrangement mirror the rigid columns and rows of the 19th century, or is it flexible and designed to encourage student creativity and engagement? Star Teachers reject the implied hierarchy of traditional seating arrangements that place the teacher at the front of the class, embracing instead formats that flatten the authoritarian order. Their seating arrangements send the message that everyone has a voice and that learning is communal.

Bulletin Boards as Teaching Tools: The classroom walls and bulletin boards of Star Teachers are important learning real estate waiting to be filled with content-related posters, banners, learning centers, and vocabulary word walls. Bulletin boards are opportunities to reinforce concepts, skills, rules, and routines; present exemplary work; and showcase students' photos and awards. The classroom bulletin boards of many pre-Star Teachers often have interesting and eye-catching material that offer little connection to course content or state-mandated teaching standards. By contrast, Star Teachers think of bulletin boards as teaching tools—another chance to visually communicate standards-based content. The best of these bulletin boards also introduce concepts, provide a place for daily review, and offer information about seasonal topics or events that extend lessons in novel and interesting ways.[33] Many Star Teachers will create a concept map on a bulletin board in front of students while introducing a new idea, then invite students to expand the concept map as a way of flexing their critical thinking. The concept map thus becomes a measure of students' comprehension (with the teacher correcting any misconceptions or punctuation errors).

Patricia Marshall offers sound advice: "Whether the students in a class are from the same background or represent a diverse array of racial/ethnic groups, bulletin board displays should include positive and realistic images of individuals from various backgrounds."[34] Marshall adds that bulletin boards can boost students' self-image, advance **cross-cultural competence** and respect, enhance critical and analytical thinking skills, encourage appreciation for different worldviews, and promote diverse orientations to learning.

Persistent Teachers Are Problem Solvers

Student underachievement does not sit well with the persistent teacher, who recognizes that student failure may be a symptom of poor instruction. Star Teachers continually look for ways to find what works and refuse to condemn a student's inability to grasp a concept. When their students are not reaching their benchmarks, persistent teachers don't assume that they cannot learn, but rather that their instructional method is ineffective, and they seek another way to hold the learners' attention. Persistent teachers locate resources to meet individual students' instructional goals by exploiting the latest technology and visiting local libraries, or in some cases establishing connections with social and health services. These educators continually ask themselves, "What do *I* do next to help students learn?"

To make sure that students meet their learning goals, Star Teachers must become problem solvers willing to deeply examine the complexities of learning. **Problem solving** is the process of finding solutions to challenging or complex issues. It is also the mechanism by which persistence becomes operationalized—Star Teachers are not just thinkers, but doers. *Persistence* refers to Star Teachers' tireless and creative pursuit to find instructional solutions to learning problems, whether for the whole class or for a single learner. These highly successful teachers never give up on students and always seek answers when challenges hinder academic progress.

Persistent Teachers Adopt Strategies to Surmount Instructional Setbacks

Instructional setbacks occur when student mastery of course content is hindered or delayed. Every educator will face instructional setbacks in his or her professional career, and persistent teachers assemble a repertoire of strategies to surmount them. Here are some common examples:

- **Flipped classrooms,** which offer learning experiences like lectures and discussions outside the classroom and devote class time to exploring what is learned.
- **Project-based learning,** a highly experiential strategy whereby students initiate projects that are connected to course content.
- **Learning communities** where students collaborate in small groups to meet shared academic goals.
- **Simulated learning and games** that engage and motivate players through direct experiences exploring phenomena, testing hypotheses, and constructing objects.[35]
- **Field trips and guest speakers,** including virtual field trips and online visits with experts or special guests.

Robert J. Marzano, Debra J. Pickering, and Tammy Heflebower propose initiating friendly controversy, presenting unusual information, and questioning to increase responses and student interest.[36] Haberman suggests "project method, peer tutoring, independent study, inquiry training, demonstrations, creative activities, and scientific experimentation"[37] to make classrooms more engaging for learners.

Problem-solving teachers are constantly refining a vast range of strategies that will reach every type of learner they encounter, employing a nimble pedagogical style to find what works for learners in ways that are equitable and meet their students where they are in that moment.

Differentiated Instruction

Because persistent teachers do not believe the myth that students are all the same due to their chronological age, many of them employ **differentiated instruction** (see Figure 1.4) to tailor their teaching to the specific talents and learning styles of individual students. Though a great deal of effort is necessary for a differentiated approach to work, the return—comprehension and mastery of a lesson's content by every student in the class—is worth it.

An extensive inventory of differentiated teaching strategies exists, appealing to a wide array of learners. As Parsons, Dodman, and Burrowbridge note, effective teachers carefully revise their instruction to meet the diversity of needs for their students.[38] Teaching more challenging content to more diverse learners requires K–12 teachers to deeply understand the effects of context and learner variability on teaching and learning.

Differentiated instruction is a set of unique instructional choices that bring learning to life for all students who are working at, below, or above grade level by providing them with multiple paths for accessing new information. Differentiation also allows learners to process and express ideas in ways that makes sense for their individual needs. As Haberman notes, "This form of teaching requires a high level of teacher with-it-ness, i.e. the teacher's ability to sense what is going on everywhere in the classroom, with all of the children, at all times."[39] Practices such as meaningful or respectful tasks, flexible grouping, and ongoing assessments help to guide the process.

Persistent teachers engaged in differentiated instruction consider it to be a mindful and explicit exercise during which they continually ask themselves the following questions:

Figure 1.4 **Differentiation of Instruction**

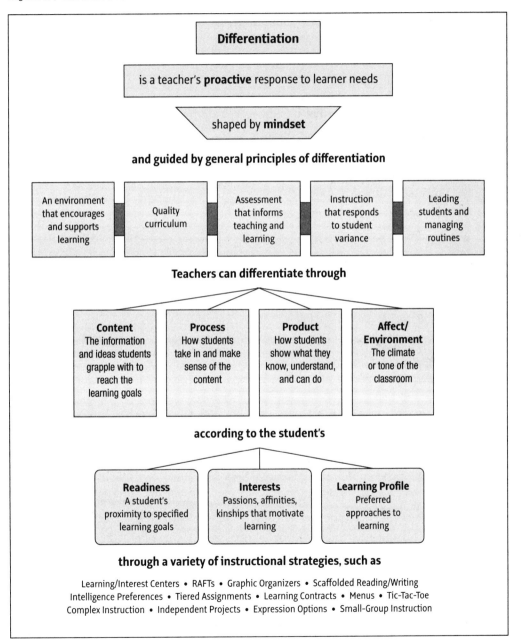

Source: From *The Differentiated Classroom* (p. 20), by C. A. Tomlinson, 2014, Alexandria, VA: ASCD. Copyright 2014 by ASCD.

- How are my efforts advancing or hindering student learning?
- What did I learn about my students' individual learning styles that can help me refine my lessons now and in the future?
- How can I vary my teaching strategies to meet the needs of individual learners?
- What can I do next?

Star Teachers believe that it is their obligation to seek multiple ways to engage all their students in learning. To them, "using only direct instruction would be like having a tool belt with only a hammer in it."[40] This type of heterogeneous teaching can be carried out by adapting content (materials), changing the process (manner or approach), altering the products or outcome of instruction, or modifying the learning environment.

★ 1-2

Divide your professional learning community (PLC) into smaller subject-matter or grade-level groups. In each small group, teachers share different techniques for teaching the same type of lesson or content, explaining where and how they learned each one, and collaborate to answer the following question: "What is the value of teachers collaborating in small groups on instructional matters?" Each group elects a spokesperson to report findings to the larger PLC.

Differentiating Content: Adapting Lessons for Levels of Understanding

A well-designed lesson is composed of learning objectives that should be explicitly conveyed to learners. Simply saying the objectives aloud or writing them on your board will not guarantee learning. How often do teachers hear the question "Do we need to know this for the test?" Students with diverse learning styles and talents need to have learning experiences that both meet them where they are and engender higher forms of thinking by way of creating, investigating, and analyzing. Instructional instruments for accessing depth of comprehension such as Bloom's taxonomy can help teachers create learning objectives and experiences that promote elevated modes of thinking over rote memorization.

Adapting content objectives to suit diverse learning needs is one proven differentiation strategy. Tiered performance levels allow learners to link learning to specific indicators or behaviors. Figure 1.5 shows an 8th grade earth science objective taken from the Texas Essential Knowledge and Skills (TEKS) Standards that is tiered in such a way. Adapted content objectives should be made visible for learners so they can be empowered to improve their own learning.

Star Teachers take great pains to explain these ladders of comprehension to students. "Too often, students want to know how many points they need to get the next letter grade," notes Stephens. "These clearly defined levels of understanding shift the focus from point chasing to knowledge seeking. Without gaining understanding, student learning plateaus or plummets."[41]

Differentiating Process: Adapting Independent Practice for Levels of Understanding

After students' individual levels of proficiency have been ascertained, it is appropriate to identify opportunities for them to demonstrate various levels of comprehension and help them to grow in proficiency. Here are some resources Star Teachers put in place that allow students to choose the learning strategies that suit them best:

Learning Centers: Learning centers are areas of the classroom that are designed for students to interact with instructional materials in an exciting way, individually or alongside peers, as they practice meeting the learning objectives presented in the classroom. Centers are designed for students to deepen their comprehension of content, hone related skills, or develop positive attitudes. They are useful when introducing course material but especially helpful when learners need additional practice with course concepts. Imagine a literacy learning center in a 4th grade class that offers several opportunities for students to practice the concept of idioms and features several activities for each level of performance. Jack, who is struggling academically, may begin his practice at the developing stage and progress to higher levels, while Kerra, a precocious learner who has already achieved some success at the advanced stage, is working toward mastery.

Learning Menus: A list of learning options offers students various selections for learning through purposeful practice. Also known as *choice boards*, **learning menus** present students with several options for producing a final product. Each selection should be rigorous and take approximately the same amount of time to complete. Some teachers literally present the options in the form of restaurant

Figure 1.5 **Example of Differentiating Content by Performance Levels**

8th Grade Science Objective: The student knows that climatic interactions exist among Earth, ocean, and weather systems.

Level: Basic

Indicator:

- Recognize that the Sun provides the energy that drives convection within the atmosphere and oceans, producing winds and ocean currents.

Level: Developing

Indicators:

- Investigate the role of oceans in the formation of weather systems including hurricanes.
- Label the gyres: Indian Ocean, North Pacific, South Pacific, North Atlantic, and South Atlantic.

Level: Proficient

Indicator:

- Use a three-dimensional model to represent the energy that drives convection within the atmosphere and oceans, producing winds and ocean currents.

Level: Advanced

Indicators:

- Relate the interactions of the Earth, ocean, and weather systems to our climate.
- Connect today's climate to the political discussions on climate change, coal jobs, and renewable energy.

Level: Mastery

Indicators:

- Create a booklet to show how the Sun provides energy that drives convection within the atmosphere and oceans.
- Show the role of the oceans in the formation of weather systems such as hurricanes.

Source: From "Levels of Understanding: Learning That Fits All," by C. Stephens, 2015. *Edutopia.* Copyright 2015 by Charity Stephens. Adapted with permission.

menus (i.e., students must select one "entrée" and two "side-dish" experiences, with an option to complete the enriching "dessert").[42]

Anchor Activities: These are exercises that are accessible to learners once they have completed all their classwork. Teachers can offer goal-aligned **anchor**

activities at selected learning centers in the classroom. To encourage delibera-
tion and introspection, Star Teachers require students to articulate their choice
of activities.[43] Some teachers curate digital files with hyperlinks for students to
practice navigating the internet, and several sophisticated platforms use adaptive
analytics to meet individual students' specific academic needs. For example, a
teacher creates pre-tests that determine students' background knowledge. As the
student engages the online assessments, this adaptive analytic scaffolds the content to become more rigorous and relevant in order to meet the specific needs of
the student. These innovative technology solutions "allow learning to be personalized to students' interests, abilities, and preferences in order to provide assistance when needed, and present instruction that is understandable, engaging,
and situated in the context of what is important to learners."[44]

Differentiating Products: Adapting Formative and Summative Assessments

Student appraisals can also be tiered for levels of understanding. **Formative
assessments** are low-stakes ways to measure performance and provide feedback
while students are engaged in learning and should build from basic to advanced
levels of understanding to guide instruction and practice. These types of assessments can be either formal (quizzes) or informal (discussion groups, exit slips,
thumbs up or down) and allow teachers to assess where students are in the learning process and make attendant instructional choices.

Summative assessments are used to evaluate student learning, skill acquisition, and academic achievement at the conclusion of a specific instructional
period (e.g., a project, unit, course, semester, program, or school year). These
types of assessments should embrace all levels of understanding to present a clear
picture of student performance. Figure 1.6 shows examples of product choices
for learners that teachers can include in a learning center, learning menu, or
anchor activity.

Star Teachers build creative rubrics that can be adapted to effectively and efficiently assess student learning regardless of the final product. It is the responsibility of Star Teachers to continually search for "what works" by tailoring learning
experiences to students' needs.

Figure 1.6 **Examples of Product Choices**

• Video	• Slideshow presentation	• Mock trial
• Demonstration	• Travel brochure	• Letter to the editor
• Reenactment	• Song	• Exhibit
• Diagram	• Poem	• News Report
• Advertising campaign	• Puppet Show	• Written Report
• Photo essay	• Map	• Diorama
• Play	• Poster	• Skit
• Creative writing project	• Webpage	

Data-Driven Instruction

Data from classroom and state-level assessments reveal students' proficiency levels, showing who is on target and who may need extra support. While Star Teachers appreciate these methods for taking the academic temperature of students, they also are not overly obsessed by them. What they are is **data literate,** able to read, comprehend, and interpret data to support instruction.[45] Star Teachers approach student data strategically, using the information to better understand student learning, find solutions to problems, and reflect on teaching practices. In *Why Teachers Must Become Data Experts,* Jennifer Morrison explains that effective teachers undergo three attitude shifts that help them to appreciate data. They

1. Realize that data include more than end-of-year standardized test scores.

2. View data collection as a way to investigate the many questions about students, teaching practices, and learning that arise for any committed teacher.

3. Talk with one another about what data reveal and how to build on those revelations.[46]

Data-literate teachers also engage in **data scooping** (see Figure 1.7) by reviewing accessible student data to learn more about individual or classwide academic performance. There are four basic steps to the practice of data scooping:

1. *Data collection* from the most relevant sources (e.g., state records, report cards, formative and summative assessments, conversations with learners). Teachers may also engage in **kidwatching** (i.e., simply observing and recording children's development over time).[47]

2. *Data organization,* which ensures that the collected student data are properly arranged in each learner's individualized portfolio.

3. *Data analysis and interpretation* to better understand and diagnose individual learners' roadblocks to learning. (Adding reflection logs to every student's portfolio is one helpful way to track instructional strategies used.)

4. *Data application,* or using student data to plan curriculum and instruction tailored to the individual strengths and needs of their learners.

Figure 1.7 **Four Steps of Data Scooping**

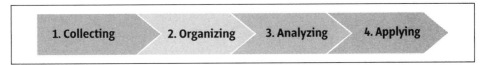

If a learner habitually scores below basic and exhibits other signs of struggling, the Star Teacher will seek opportunities to work one-on-one with him or her, provide peer support, or offer new product choices based on the student's learning style. If students new to the district score lower on a school benchmark than their peers, the Star Teacher will examine assessment data to better understand and address learning gaps. Put simply, Star Teachers exploit student data to understand what works, what does not work, and what instructional approaches may need modifying to support learners' academic achievement.

Teachers must be adaptive to the changing needs of diverse classrooms. As Figure 1.8 shows, today's students are no longer primarily white, middle class, monolingual, or Christian. With every decade the U.S. student body becomes more diverse; by 2025, nearly 6 in 10 students will be nonwhite. Effective teachers must implement strategies that appeal to increasingly heterogeneous classrooms filled with students who learn at faster or slower rates than their peers, speak English as a second language, have unique physical or learning needs, and live in poverty or violent neighborhoods. The tendency for students in some of these groups and others to score lower on tests than their peers is known as the **achievement gap**. Other factors known to affect the achievement gap include students' race or ethnicity, parents' education level, access to high-quality pre-school instruction, school funding, peer influences, teachers expectations, and curricular and instructional quality.[48] Star Teachers do not shy away from multi-cultural education or see it as an obstacle to overcome but rather embrace diversity as an opportunity to find new ways for students to learn.

Figure 1.8 **Projected Student Diversity in K–12 U.S. Classrooms in 2025**

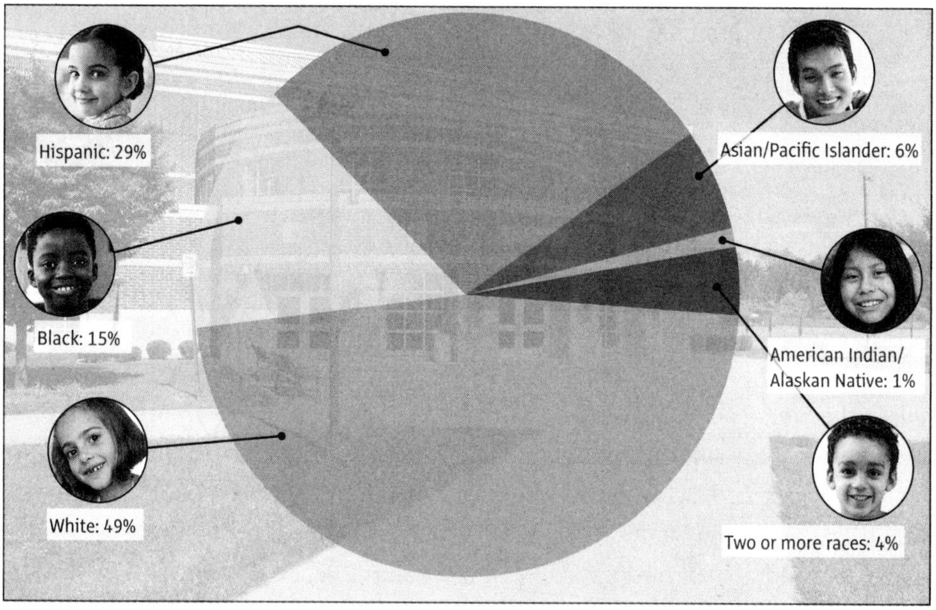

Hispanic: 29%

Asian/Pacific Islander: 6%

Black: 15%

American Indian/ Alaskan Native: 1%

White: 49%

Two or more races: 4%

Source: Data from *State Non-Fiscal Survey of Public Elementary* and *Secondary Education, 2002–03 and 2012–13;* and *National Elementary and Secondary Enrollment Projection Model, 1972 through 2025,* by the U.S. Department of Education, National Center for Education Statistics, Common Core of Data, n.d., Washington, DC: U.S. Department of Education.

Summary

Persistence is manifested in the day-to-day actions of Star Teachers eager to improve student learning who are constantly searching for "what works." These teachers make the classroom an interesting place to learn for students and embrace creative problem solving. Resolute in their quest for student success, they are willing to try different strategies to solve classroom setbacks, implement differentiated instruction, and engage in data scooping to better understand and address their students' academic needs.

Key Words

achievement gap	anchor activity	café effect
cross-cultural competence	data literate	data scooping
differentiated instruction	formative assessment	grit
instructional setback	kidwatching	learning center
learning menu	motivation	persistence
persistence in teaching	problem solving	self-efficacy
setback	summative assessment	teacher efficacy
teacher quality		

Extension Exercises

1. Review this story: It is 6 p.m. on a sweltering Wednesday in Texas, and Lynn is still at school grading her 6th graders' science benchmark exam. She notices that, while many did really well on other parts of the exam, nearly 60 percent of the students did not understand the earth science concepts of rotation and revolution. This is Lynn's fourth year as a teacher, and she thought she had developed a great three-day module to deliver these ideas using strategies like demonstrations, videos, small groups, and direct instruction. What happened? Did Lynn prepare for the inevitable instructional setbacks in her classroom to meet the needs of every learner? Should Lynn keep moving in her lesson? What would you say to advise or coach Lynn?

2. Review your grit score from Star Tracker 1-1 (p. 23). How did you do? In 250–300 words, please explain whether you believe your results to be correct. Do they indicate that you are a persistent teacher? Why or why not? What could you do to develop yourself as a teacher to improve your grit?

3. Sketch the current layout of your classroom space. Next, rethink your classroom design based on the suggestions in this chapter. What classroom design changes can you do that support learning? Create a new classroom design that honors the three fundamentals for the classroom environment.

4. Check out templates for bulletin boards on social media and online sources. What can you do to enhance the visual appeal of the bulletin boards in your classroom? Create a list of six to eight ideas and share with colleagues.

5. Is there an achievement gap issue in your classroom, school, or district among different ethnic groups? Use the four-step data-scooping process to analyze your state's achievement data online and obtain the data specific for your discipline and grade level. Next, create a bar graph of your findings. What teaching strategies do the data suggest that could help you assist learners in your classroom?

Going Further

Web Resources

- "Believing and Achieving," an issue brief posted by the Center for Comprehensive School Reform and Improvement, integrates an overview of research on teacher efficacy with a discussion of educators' responsibility for student learning. www.centerforcsri.org/files/ centerissueBriefJan07.pdf.

- "Teacher Efficacy: What Is It and Does It Matter?" is a short research report by the National Association for Elementary School Principals. Author Nancy Poetheroe does a superb job explaining the link between teacher efficacy and student learning. Check it out at www.naesp.org/resources/1/ Principal/2008/M-Jp42.pdf.

- The website *All Things Assessment* provides various ideas, strategies, and resources to improve educators' proficiency in appraising student work, which may lead to gains in student learning. http://allthingsassessment .info/about-the-center/.

- Earn 3.0 professional development hours in differentiated instruction from the Iris Center at Vanderbilt University. This online module contains strategies for organizing the classroom, suggestions for building differentiated tests and assessments, and audio interviews from leaders with firsthand experience with differentiation in the classroom such as Carol Ann Tomlinson, professor of educational leadership at the University of Virginia. https://iris.peabody.vanderbilt.edu/.

- The site www.teach-nology.com offers many teaching resources (articles, rubrics, and worksheets) to support educators who are interested in building classrooms that support students' voices and choices.

Additional Readings

- In 2014, researcher Felicia Dixon and her colleagues examined differentiated instruction, professional development, and teacher efficacy in the following article: Dixon, F. A., Yssel, N., McConnell, J. M., & Hardin, T. (2014). Differentiated instruction, professional development, and teacher efficacy. *Journal for the Education of the Gifted, 37*(2), 111–127.
- In "Teaching in the Fast Lane: How to Create Active Learning Experiences," Suzy Pepper Rollins tells how to facilitate a highly engaged classroom with ideas to accommodate different levels of learners by using learning centers and group learning "to foster students' critical thinking and confidence" and help them become self-directed learners. See more at www.ascd.org/Publications/Books/Overview/Teaching-in-the-Fast-Lane.aspx.
- This book is based on Martin Haberman's seven dispositions of Star Teachers as outlined in the following article: Haberman, M. (2002). Selecting Star Teachers for children and youth in poverty. *Phi Delta Kappan, 76*(10), 777–781. Page 779 is extremely enlightening.

Endnotes

1. Grotberg, E. H. (1997). *The international resilience research project.* Retrieved from http://files.eric.ed.gov/fulltext/ED417861.pdf (p. 13)
2. Kelly, D. R., Matthews, M. D., & Bartone, P. T. (2014). Grit and hardiness as predictors of performance among West Point cadets. *Military Psychology, 26*(4), 327–342.
3. Haberman, M. (2010). *Star Teachers: The ideology and best practice of effective teachers of diverse children and youth in poverty.* Houston, TX: Haberman Educational Foundation.
4. Every Student Succeeds Act (ESSA) of 2015, Pub. L. No. 114-95 (2015).
5. Wheatley, K. (2002). Teacher persistence: A crucial disposition, with implications for teacher education. *Essays in Education, 3.* Available at www.usca.edu/essays/vol32002/wheatley.pdf

6. Robertson-Kraft, C., & Duckworth, A. L. (2014). True grit: Trait-level perseverance and passion for long-term goals predicts effectiveness and retention among novice teachers. *Teachers College Record, 116*(3), 1–27.

7. Robertson-Kraft & Duckworth (2014, p. 16).

8. Robertson-Kraft & Duckworth (2014, p. 21).

9. Duckworth, A. L., Quinn, P. D., & Seligman, M. E. P. (2009). Positive predictors of teacher effectiveness. *Journal of Positive Psychology, 4*(6), 540–547.

10. Haberman (2010).

11. Haberman (2010, p. 139).

12. Tomlinson, C. (2003). Deciding to teach them all. *Educational Leadership, 61*(2), 6–11.

13. Gavora, P. (2010). Slovak pre-service teacher self-efficacy: Theoretical and research considerations. *The New Educational Review, 21*(2), 17–30.

14. Tschannen-Moran, M., & Hoy, A. W. (2001). Teacher efficacy: Capturing an elusive construct. *Teaching and Teacher Education, 17*(7), 783–805. (pp. 784-785)

15. Klassen, R. M., Tze, V. M., Betts, S. M., & Gordon, K. A. (2011). Teacher efficacy research 1998–2009: Signs of progress or unfulfilled promise? *Educational Psychology Review, 23*(1), 21–43.

16. Jerald, C. D. (2007). Believing and achieving: Issue brief. *Center for Comprehensive School Reform and Improvement*. Retrieved from https://files.eric.ed.gov/fulltext/ED495708.pdf

17. Guo, Y., Connor, C. M., Yang, Y., Roehrig, A. D., & Morrison, F. J. (2012). The effects of teacher qualification, teacher self-efficacy, and classroom practices on fifth graders' literacy outcomes. *Elementary School Journal, 113*(1), 3–24.

18. Guo et al. (2012, p. 4).

19. Dweck, C. (2014). Teachers' mindsets: Every student has something to teach me. *Educational Horizons, 93*(2) 10–15.

20. Klassen et al. (2011).

21. Jerald (2007).

22. Guo et al. (2012).

23. Guo et al. (2012, p. 20).

24. Sanders, W. L., & Rivers, J. C. (1996). *Cumulative and residual effects of teachers on future student academic achievement.* Research Progress Report. Knoxville: University of Tennessee Value-Added Research and Assessment Center.

25. Haberman (2010).

26. Wolk, S. (2009). Joy in schools. In M. Scherer (Ed.), *Engaging the whole child: Reflections on best practices in learning, teaching, and leadership* (pp. 3–14). Alexandria, VA: ASCD.

27. Wolk (2009, p. 4).

28. Marshall, P. (2002). *Cultural diversity in our schools.* Belmont, CA: Wadsworth. (p. 260)

29. Dorman, J. P. (2001). Associations between classroom environment and academic efficacy. *Learning Environments Research, 4*(3), 243–257.

30. Perez, J., Julio Montano, J., & Perez, J. (2018). *Healthy schools as a learning tool.* Retrieved from https://healthyschools.cefpi.org/temperature.html

31. Eo, I. S., & Choi, K. Y. (2014). Study on the effects of learning by changing the color-temperature LED lamp. *International Journal of Multimedia and Ubiquitous Engineering, 9*(3), 309–316.

32. Wålinder, R., Gunnarsson, K., Runeson, R., & Smedje, G. (2007). Physiological and psychological stress reactions in relation to classroom noise. *Scandinavian Journal of Work and Environmental Health, 33,* 260–266.; Whitlock, J., & Dodd, G. (2006). Classroom acoustics—controlling the café effect. . . is the Lombard Effect the key? In *Proceedings of Acoustics 2006: Noise of Progress.* Christchurch, New Zealand.

33. Bafile, C. (2010). From "pretty" to practical: Using bulletin boards to teach. *Education World.* Retrieved from www.educationworld.com/a_curr/profdev/profdev089.shtml

34. Marshall, P. (2002). *Cultural diversity in our schools.* Belmont, CA: Wadsworth. (p. 261)

35. Prensky, M., & Prensky, M. (2007). *Digital game-based learning* (Vol. 1). St. Paul, MN: Paragon.

36. Marzano, R. J., Pickering, D. J., & Heflebower, T. (2011). *The highly engaged classroom.* Bloomington, IN: Marzano Research Laboratory.

37. Haberman (2010, p. 118).

38. Parsons, S. A., Dodman, S. L., & Burrowbridge, S. C. (2013). Broadening the view of differentiated instruction. *Phi Delta Kappan, 95*(1), 38–42.

39. Haberman (2010, p. 114).

40. Haberman (2010, p. 118).

41. Stephens, C. (2015). *Levels of understanding: Learning that fits all.* Retrieved from www.edutopia.org/blog/levels-of-understanding-learning-fits-all-charity-stephens (para 5)

42. IRIS Center. (2010). Learning menus: Examples of product choices. In *Differentiated instruction: Maximizing the learning of all students.* Retrieved from https://iris.peabody.vanderbilt.edu/module/di/cresource/q2/p07/di_07_link_menus/#content

43. Haberman (2010, p. 114).

44. Walkington, C., & Bernacki, M. L. (2014). Motivating students by "personalizing" learning around individual interests: A consideration of theory, design, and implementation issues. In S. A. Karabenick & T. C. Urdan (Eds.), *Motivational interventions: Advances in motivation and achievement* (pp. 139–176). Bingly, West Yorkshire, England: Emerald Group. (p. 139)

45. Stevenson, H. (2017). The "datafication" of teaching: Can teachers speak back to the numbers? *Peabody Journal of Education, 92*(4), 537–557.

46. Morrison, J. (2009). *Why teachers must become data experts.* Retrieved from www.ascd.org/publications/educational-leadership/dec08/vol66/num04/Why-Teachers-Must-Be-Data-Experts.aspx (para. 4)

47. Owocki, G., & Goodman, Y. (2002). *Kidwatching: Documenting children's literacy development.* Portsmouth, NH: Heinemann.

48. Reardon, S. F. (2013). The widening income achievement gap. *Educational Leadership 70*(8), 10–16.

2

Protecting Learners and Learning

"Protecting learners and learning" refers to making students' active involvement in productive work more important than curriculum rigidities and uneven school rules. Effective teachers not only recognize all the ways in which large school organizations impinge on students but find ways to make and keep learning their highest priority.

Learning Outcomes

Upon completion of this chapter, you will be able to

- Evaluate Haberman's concept of teachers "protecting learners and learning."
- Recognize the ideology of Star Teachers who protect learners and learning.
- Identify the intentional behaviors Star Teachers use to protect students and learning and explain their applications to K–12 teaching.

Interstate New Teacher Assessment and Support Consortium (InTASC) Standards

Standard #3: Learning Environments

The teacher works with others to create environments that support individual and collaborative learning and that encourage positive social interaction, active engagement in learning, and self-motivation.

★ ★ ★ ★ ★ ★ ★ ★ ★ ★ ★

Defining *Protecting Learners and Learning*

For Star Teachers, the most important school value, which must be safeguarded at all costs, is learning. "Protecting learners and learning" can be defined as ensuring that children are active and involved in productive work regardless of curriculum rigidities or even school and district rules. Star Teachers effectively protect their students' learning from the realities of a **bureaucratic** school environment, where many of the most important policy and curriculum decisions are unfortunately made at a far distance from students. Students are shortchanged by school bureaucracies, which tend to "apply a one-size-fits-all mentality to teaching."[1]

What are teachers to do when the bureaucracy interferes with their teaching and their students' learning? What are they supposed to do when higher-ups tell them to teach in such a way that contradicts their ideology? How can teachers protect learners and learning in an effective and professional way? Before we explore answers to these questions, let's examine how and why Star Teachers find it important to protect their students' learning time in school.

The Mindset of Teachers Who Protect Learners and Learning

The need to protect learning and learners for Star Teachers stems from their desire to make every minute of student time count in the classroom. Star Teachers understand how school bureaucracy contributes to classroom interruptions. They also understand the value of noninstructional time and how to best use it. This mindset pushes Star Teachers to be guardians of learners and learning.

The Behaviors of Star Teachers Who Protect Learners and Learning

Effective teaching in bureaucratic schools is challenging, but certainly possible. Protective and vigilant teachers are the most important factor in ensuring that students succeed academically. The typical teacher employs instructional methods that honor and feed bureaucratic school structures, neglecting to capture the imaginations of disengaged learners. Haberman summarizes the basic menu of bureaucratic teaching behaviors found in many unsuspecting classrooms as follows:

- Giving information
- Asking questions

- Giving directions
- Making assignments
- Monitoring seatwork
- Reviewing assignments
- Giving tests
- Reviewing tests
- Assigning homework
- Reviewing homework
- Settling disputes
- Punishing noncompliance
- Marking papers
- Giving grades[2]

These teaching behaviors, taken together, and to the systematic exclusion of inspiring instruction, become the predictable drudgery for many K–12 learners. These **low-pedagogy** behaviors constitute "business-as-usual" instruction that is driven by **high-stakes testing**, defined by learning experiences set on cruise control and dictated by textbooks, devoid of authentic learning experiences, and is passive as opposed to active. These instructional behaviors form a **"pedagogy of poverty"** that influences what students expect of their teachers.

By contrast, Star Teachers protect student learning by incorporating creative teaching approaches that constitute **high-pedagogy** instruction, such as the following:

- Cooperative learning
- Peer tutoring
- Individualized instruction
- Computer-assisted learning
- Behavior modification
- After-school programs
- Use of student contracts
- Media-assisted instruction
- Flipped classrooms
- Scientific inquiry

- Lecture/discussion
- Tutoring by specialists or volunteers
- Problem-solving units

In their research on Star Teachers in Chicago Public Schools, Nicholas D. Hartlep and his colleagues found that teachers protect students and learning by being empathetic, being institutionally aware, and having personalized relationships with students.[3] Their findings align with those of Haberman, who states that Star Teachers protect student learning by coping with the bureaucracy and creating student ownership in their learning.[4] The behaviors of Star Teachers shield learners from the school bureaucracy to protect the learning process.

Star Teachers Shield Learners from the School Bureaucracy

Star Teachers protect learners and learning by recognizing the myriad ways in which school is irrationally organized and impinges on student success. They protect learners in two fundamental ways: (1) by making every moment count and (2) by shielding the learner from harsh encounters.

Making Every Instructional Minute Count

When it comes to learning, one of our most precious resources is time. Some propose extending the school day or year, but it is our belief that teachers have all the time they need. Star Teachers know that schools that serve high-poverty and English language learners (ELLs) tend to have more lost learning time than schools that are more affluent.[5] Interruptions are often imposed on the classroom from outside, such as via intercom announcements, requests for students from the front office, or unannounced drop-ins from outside teachers (to name just a few examples). Star Teachers do everything in their power to reduce these interruptions, understanding that they must literally make every minute count in their classroom. According to Leonard, "Limiting the number of intrusions into the classroom setting is essentially protecting the *learning environment* (venue in which instruction and learning occurs) from potential negative effects."[6]

Lost learning time refers to time that could have been used on schoolwork but was otherwise squandered. Teachers have enough time; they just must use it more wisely. Understanding why teachers lose time and what they can do about it is key.[7] As Howard Nelson has noted, "60 to more than 110 hours per year [are lost] in test prep in high-stakes testing grades."[8] To make every minute count, teachers must work to reduce interruptions to teaching and learning. There are two primary culprits of lost learning: (1) noninstructional use of classroom time and (2) externally imposed classroom interruptions.[9]

Here are some examples of daily events that contribute to lost learning time:

- Transitions from lesson to lesson
- Water breaks
- Bathroom breaks
- Taking attendance
- Responding to student outbursts
- Recess
- Trips to the nurse
- Free time
- Daily routines

Done inefficiently, these events can drain precious instructional time. For example, a teacher who has his students take a quick recess without considering the time it takes to transition out of and back into class is harming students if they then run out of time to complete the post-recess lesson. Were this to happen regularly, an incredible amount of time would be lost during a school year.

Instead of complying with bureaucratic policies and practices, Star Teachers have the mindset and ability to maximize their students' **time on task** (i.e., classroom time spent actively engaged in learning). Star Teachers will sometimes hang a sign on the door to the classroom to deter interruptions and protect the learning environment. Consider the example of veteran 5th grade Star Teacher Chad Weagie, who will occasionally place a sign on his door that reads "Testing. Please Do Not Enter," whether a test is in progress or not. Mr. Weagie has also been known to disable the intercom in his classroom, as otherwise it drones on and interrupts class incessantly. Instead, when the front office needs him, someone must call his phone, which he sometimes leaves off the hook. He remarks, "If they really need me, then they send someone down to my room, Pod A. I don't want them interrupting my class. The best place for my students to be is with me."

Mr. Weagie is a student of bureaucracy. He observes how the school operates and views things through a historical lens. Leaders in his school have left and been replaced quite regularly. In his 15 years at the school, 13 principals have come and gone. The current principal will be the longest serving in the school's history if he stays his third year. Mr. Weagie could easily get frustrated by the lack of consistent leadership, but he doesn't. He has more knowledge of the school than all his colleagues and the newly hired administrators, but he has no desire to move up the ranks and become principal (despite already having a master's degree and the required credentials).

"I just want to 'stay low and keep firing,'" he tells us. "I am a teacher first, and I just want to have my kids with me so I can teach them to the best of my abilities."

Mr. Weagie's lack of interest in becoming an administrator speaks to his true desire: to teach. As Haberman notes, "Stars will not necessarily assume leadership roles . . . because they focus on their students."[10] Having experienced the coming and going of administrators, Mr. Weagie is not persuaded to change what is working for his students.

"I know what works for my students," he says. "If a new principal tells me to try something new, I really don't listen to him or her. For many years I have mentored the new teachers who are hired. I have stayed in contact with many of them. Some have left the teaching profession, while others have transferred schools. St. Matthews is considered a 'hard-to-staff' school. We are a Title I school. Many of our students are facing challenges that many people never consider."

Mr. Weagie's ability to survive St. Matthews's bureaucracy has improved over his years of teaching.

"When it gets too hectic, I pull out my 'Testing. Please Do Not Enter' sign, which helps me to protect my students' learning. I don't want my students leaving my classroom because depending where they go in St. Matthews, they may experience chaos and not be supported by some of my peers. But I know that in Pod A we are positive all of the time."

What gives Mr. Weagie the most joy is being with his students and delivering engaging lessons. He has clearly gone to great lengths to protect himself "from an interfering bureaucracy."[11] His classroom is a bunker and he does all that he can to never leave it. He also does all that he can to prevent disruptions that cause his students from leaving the security of the bunker, and he does all that he can to avoid outsiders entering it.

Most organizations and institutions, including schools, rely on bureaucratic systems, breaking their daily operations down into smaller, more manageable tasks. But when schools and classrooms become bureaucratized spaces, children are often disserved. As Tony Waters writes, bureaucratic schools track students in ways that reinforce inequity and strengthen stratification.[12] Star Teachers work to shield their students from policies and practices that are inequitable. Although grouping students by ability may make teaching easier (and certainly more bureaucratic), Star Teachers place their students in mixed-ability groups. As Haberman says, "Whenever students are actively involved in heterogeneous groups, it is likely that good teaching is going on."[13]

Shielding Learners from Harsh Encounters

Star Teachers take responsibility when their colleagues "push students out" due to classroom management difficulties. Take Mr. Smith, for example, a 4th grade teacher in the Milwaukee Public Schools.

"My classroom is like a secret cave," he says. "You can form such a supportive community, kids won't drop out."

One of Mr. Smith's fellow 4th grade teachers was once having a challenging time with a student, Keaty. The teacher would yell at Keaty, making him feel as though he wasn't liked. When Mr. Smith found out about the situation, he spoke with Keaty's mother and had the student transferred into his classroom. What a world of difference that made. Keaty had a temper, and by personalizing his instruction, Mr. Smith helped him feel as though he wasn't alone; he told his students that when he was a 4th grader, he had a temper too, and that it got him into a lot of trouble in school.

Mr. Smith understands that protecting his students from harsh disciplinarians and policies is vital—especially for poor and minority students who have an increased risk of being **"pushed out"** of school. (The Kirwan Institute for the Study of Race and Ethnicity at The Ohio State University offers research-based interventions that schools can use to help keep students on an academic track. You can find these here: http://kirwaninstitute.osu.edu/wp-content/uploads/2014/05/ki-interventions.pdf.)[14]

Sometimes Star Teachers must shield students from receiving harsh encounters with other staff and teachers, doing whatever it takes to gain, maintain, and keep the trust of students. Consider the actions and wherewithal of Mrs. Janet, who has been elementary school librarian in the Chicago Public Schools for the past 15 years. One year while teaching a group of 4th graders, Mrs. Janet noticed how unprofessional the students' teacher was. He regularly dropped off his students 10–15 minutes before the scheduled library time and was frequently late picking them up by as much as five minutes. Coming early and leaving late ate into Mrs. Janet's prep time and caused a backup when it came time to check out books and the next scheduled class had already arrived. These issues caused Mrs. Janet great frustration, but she worked as best as she could and never said anything negative about the teacher in front of his students. Her actions exemplify the ideology Haberman shares in his book *Star Teachers: The Ideology and Best Practice of Effective Teachers of Diverse Children and Youth in Poverty*,[15] whereby Star Teachers protect the very individual who may be disrupting the learning environment.

On days when there was no time left to check out books due to the 4th grade teacher being late, Mrs. Janet would say calmly to the class, "Hey, since you couldn't check out books, I'm going to stay after school and you can come check them out if you like." This provided instant relief: they could still check out library books, and because they were doing so after school they would have more time to browse for the "right" book as well as more one-on-one time with Mrs. Janet, who has built a personal rapport with the students. Her willingness to go the extra mile shows how much she prioritizes positive experiences for her students.

The following week, the same 4th grade teacher dropped off his students 10 minutes early for a technology lesson by Mrs. Janet on coding that incorporates students' school-issued laptops. As the students filed into the library, Mateo quietly informed Mrs. Janet that he forgot his laptop in the classroom.

"Can I go back and get it?" he asked.

Mrs. Janet answered with a question of her own. "Is the teacher going to fuss at you? Before I write a pass for you to get back to your class, I need to know."

Mrs. Janet didn't want Mateo's homeroom teacher to get mad at him and not let him return with the laptop. She knew that the teacher had a quick temper and was frequently impatient and unforgiving with students who disrupted him on his "prep" break. This was ironic given his thoughtlessness toward Mrs. Janet's time, although Mrs. Janet never confronted him about it.

Mrs. Janet continued: "I don't want the trip to be negative for you, so that's why I am checking. Will your teacher let you get the laptop? Because if he's going to fuss, I'm not going to send you on that fruitless trip."

Reluctantly, Mateo conceded that his teacher probably wouldn't let him get the laptop. Because she didn't have an extra laptop to give him, Mrs. Janet let Mateo work with a partner who had brought his.

Mrs. Janet understands that people and policy in schools can cause stress for students, and she doesn't want to add to it. She is aware that some of her colleagues respond to students in unproductive ways, but her focus is on controlling what *she* can control: the decisions she makes in her classroom. She does everything she can to protect her students in a school that is often unpredictable and chaotic. In the simplest of ways, she is cool, calm, and collected and seems to have everything under control. You will never hear her be dismissive of fellow teachers or administrators, even if she feels that they have wronged her or her students. The students who check out books or receive technology lessons from her notice that she is always positive toward them. As Haberman points out, "Stars are more concerned that the students do not lose faith in the school than they are in having to take responsibility for a [fellow educator's] bad decision."[16]

★ 2-1 ───

Reflect on and share an instance when you went off script to protect learners. If you are a preservice teacher, imagine what you would do and under what conditions you would deviate from the stated path.

Star Teachers Protect the Learning Process

The importance of protecting the learning process cannot be understated. As Haberman writes, protecting learning "refers directly to this issue of teaching and learning beyond the curriculum that will be tested for."[17] Star Teachers protect the learning process in three primary ways: (1) by being organized, (2) by teaching subversively, and (3) by sharing their passions with their students.

Being Organized

Teachers use their desks daily, so they should organize it in a way that makes sense to them. Mailboxes are also a form of organization, helping save time by making it quick and easy to return student papers when they're not in class.

Star Teachers have extraordinary managerial skills. As Lindsey Pierron writes, "If a teacher plans effectively, stays on top of paperwork, and has a well-designed physical space, the classroom will run more smoothly than one that is lacking organization."[18] According to Haberman, organized classrooms help teachers and students make sense out of and deal with bureaucratic disruptions of the school day by allowing them to multitask efficiently: "they can do several things at once and still perform them at a high level."[19] In his book *Qualities of Effective Teachers,* James Stronge notes that pre-Star Teachers "have more difficulty responding to individual student needs in their planning. They tend to develop a 'one-size-fits-all' approach to planning, whereas more experienced teachers [do not]."[20]

Star Teachers organize their classrooms in ways that address the three Ps of organization: (1) paperwork, (2) planning, and (3) physical space.

Paperwork. Bureaucratic school policy leads to more and more paperwork for teachers. Consider the case of Rick Young, who taught history in Colorado schools for 25 years and eventually quit due to the immense amount of paperwork.[21] Mr. Young's decision to leave the profession as an experienced teacher is more of a rule than an exception: surveys have found that increased paperwork is correlated with experienced teachers leaving the field.[22]

Pat Hadler shares three direct tips to staying organized with paperwork as a teacher:

1. Use binders and folders to keep papers organized (or use whatever method works for you).
2. Commit to doing paperwork every day so that it doesn't stack up on your desk or end up on a to-do list.
3. Use technology: many apps, templates, and platforms exist that can save you time and energy.[23]

Planning. Star Teachers are good at both short- and long-term planning of engaging learning activities using lesson plans and protocols. Lesson plans are especially important, ensuring that the teacher has thought about students before they even come to school. When students don't understand what is expected of them because a lesson is disjointed, students may drift and become anxious or talkative. Haberman writes that Star Teachers' "planning is primarily focused on how to interest and involve the students in seeing value in learning and becoming involved with the particular subject matter."[24] He goes on to say that Star Teachers "know that when they are able to motivate students learning skyrockets and teaching becomes less stressful."[25] In addition to planning daily, weekly, and monthly lessons, Star Teachers plan for things that happen only occasionally, such as keeping a folder that lays out the lesson plan and classroom procedures for substitute teachers.

★ 2-2 ───

Read the Scholastic Teacher *article "100 Classroom Organizing Tricks" by Dana Truby and Megan Kaesshaefer (available here: www.scholastic.com/teachers/articles/teaching-content/100-classroom-organizing-tricks/). Name and describe one trick from the article you can use to help you plan better in the classroom.*

Physical space. According to Haberman, "What ordinary teachers might regard as too much activity or even chaos, Star Teachers can manage as a normal level of activity."[26] In their pathbreaking study of **environmental chaos,** Lieny Jeon, Eunhye Hur, and Cynthia Buettner found that when (or if) teachers feel they are in a chaotic environment beyond their control, they may feel unpleasant emotions that interfere with their ability to problem solve and protect their students' learning.[27] Teacher organization helps minimize environmental chaos.

There are different types of chaos in the classroom, and not all of them are negative. For example, a classroom that is loud and messy but where students are excited about learning and the teacher is well prepared reflects **organized chaos.** Organized chaos may not appear positive to an outsider, but Star Teachers understand that it is authentic, meaningful, and maximizes student engagement. When students are engaged, chaos is okay. As Andrew Pass writes, "A situation that can accurately be described as 'organized chaos' is one in which an outsider cannot see any specific pattern by which to describe the events transpiring. However, the individual actors within the situation clearly understand what is happening. These individual actors are doing something that is organized and meaningful."[28]

Subversive Teaching

Consider the story of Mr. Michaels, a fourth-year 6th grade language arts teacher with a passion for building and riding bicycles. Mr. Michaels used his hobby to engage his students and inform his lessons, and his students were learning the curriculum-mandated lesson content. One day in the teachers' lounge, the principal told Mr. Michaels to stop using biking and bike maintenance to teach his lessons, ordering him "to stick with the curriculum as it's written." But Mr. Michaels did not do as the principal demanded, because his students were interested in building and maintaining bicycles. Instead of teaching using worksheets and the standard curriculum that his principal requested, Mr. Michaels continued to supplement the curriculum by engaging his students' interests and minds. He was confident that what he was doing benefitted his students because they were doing well academically.

As Arnold Dodge writes, "Good teachers are not good soldiers."[29] Mr. Michaels's response to his principal shows the keen insight of Star Teachers. He understood that building a relationship with administrators is important for his students' learning, so he did not feel awkward responding honestly to the principal. He explained how biking and biking maintenance were being used to enhance students' engagement with the language arts curriculum. His approach was respectful and he assured the principal that his lessons were aligned to the Common Core State Standards,[30] Charlotte Danielson's Framework for Teaching,[31] and the priorities and values of the school administration. Mr. Michaels also never spoke negatively about the principal in front of the students, maintaining a sense of **professionalism**.

The principal was unmoved, but as we discussed in Chapter 1, Star Teachers are persistent problem solvers. Mr. Michaels continued to teach his lessons in the same way—unless an administrator was present in the classroom, in which case he taught the lesson more conventionally, without reference to bicycles.

He was upfront with his students. "Hey, listen, this is what I'm supposed to do," he said. "When an administrator walks in the room, she's going to want to see this, this, and this. All the fun stuff that we normally do, we're going to keep doing it, but if an administrator walks in, we kind of have to do the boring stuff too—or it will *look* boring to you. But don't worry, we are going to come back to this other stuff again."

Because Mr. Michaels understood how bureaucracy operates in the middle school, he joined the Instructional Leadership Team (ILT), where he worked with administrators to analyze school achievement data. It was a lot of work, but Mr. Michaels's actions were calculated. He wanted to know what the school administrators were valuing when they were performing their walkthroughs, as well as lesson observations. He would then know what his students should be doing when (and if) an administrator came and did a lesson observation.

Mr. Michaels knew the risk he took in continuing to teach lessons his way. What would happen if the principal came into his classroom and caught him still talking about bicycles and maintaining bikes? Was his approach worth the risk? He was persistent in coming up with ways to continue doing what was working in his classroom in the face of rules and requests that did not consider the success he was having in his classroom. Mr. Michaels was committed to teaching language arts in a way that effectively engaged his students. As Haberman states, for "Star Teachers the ultimate value to be preserved is learning."[32]

Star Teachers Protect Students from Hidden, Null, and Narrowed Curriculum

Star Teachers teach explicitly. They are aware of hidden ways that norms, values, beliefs, and modes of thought and behavior are taught indirectly. Margaret LeCompte notes that because "teachers are often not aware of the strong normative structure that their management strategies and classroom organization have, these strategies and organizational patterns are said to be 'hidden,' even though they are no less important to a child's learning experience than explicitly cognitive objectives."[33] Star Teachers understand that there is a **hidden curriculum** that some students and their families will not be aware of, which is why they teach about the unseen and untold. As Gail McCutcheon writes, "without realizing it, teachers inadvertently train children such things as to be punctual, to do one's own work, and to be obedient and subservient."[34]

Star Teachers address the hidden curriculum through culturally relevant pedagogy.[35] They impart three types of knowledge to their students: (1) critical (knowledge that critiques the dominant culture), (2) classical (abstract knowledge), and (3) communal (indigenous, community, or "insider" knowledge). Eric Gutstein refers to these as the "three Cs," noting that *critical knowledge is* knowledge about the sociopolitical conditions of one's immediate and broader existence,"[36] "*classical knowledge* generally refers to formal, in-school, abstract knowledge,"[37] and *communal knowledge* "refers to what people already know and bring to school with them. This includes the knowledge that resides in individuals and in communities that usually has been learned out of school."[38] So community knowledge can be critical, but context matters.

In addition to the hidden curriculum, Star Teachers know that there is also a **null curriculum** within schools made up of what teachers don't teach or emphasize.[39] As Eisner notes, "what the curriculum neglects is as important as what it teaches."[40] Indeed, students cannot learn from experiences to which they haven't been exposed. The null curriculum is what makes teachers value expository writing more than creative writing in schools, for example, or claim that Christopher Columbus "discovered" America while ignoring his slaughter of Native Americans.

Similar to the null curriculum is the **narrowed curriculum** that is the outcome of an overriding focus on high-stakes testing. According to the National Council of Teachers of English, "Standardized tests narrow the entire curriculum in many schools, often squeezing out subjects such as music, art, foreign languages, and, especially in elementary grades, social studies, because they are not included in tests."[41]

Star Teachers who expose the hidden, null, and narrowed curriculum protect student learning by being explicit with students about how the system of education works. Culturally responsive teaching mitigates the harm that incomplete curriculum inflicts on students. Star Teachers avoid "teaching to the test," instead opting for lessons that deepen student understanding of content.[42]

Star Teachers Share Their Passions to Support Learning

Sharing passions can be a subversive way to protect students from the hidden curriculum. **Passion** can be defined as an insatiable thirst for knowledge about something—an itch that doesn't go away. In their book *Teaching as a Subversive Activity*, Neil Postman and Charles Weingartner write that "children enter school as question marks and leave as periods."[43] Passionate teachers don't allow their students to become periods; they want their students to be question marks, curious about the world.

Passion and enthusiasm are vital for student learning. One study on secondary teachers discovered that "teacher enthusiasm positively relates to students' interest, conceptualized as enjoyment and intrinsic value."[44] According to the researchers, "enthusiastic teachers help instill in their students positive subject related affective experiences and a sense of the personal importance of the subject."[45] Christopher Day notes that "enthusiastic teachers (who are knowledgeable and skilled) who have a sense of vocation and organizational belonging work harder to make learning more meaningful for students, even those who may be difficult or unmotivated."[46] Day's research finds that teacher commitment and passion are correlated with teacher enthusiasm.

Peter Benekos examined the characteristics of good teachers and found that "passion" was most common.[47] He writes that "passion for teaching includes the ability to teach students how to learn and to instill enthusiasm and interest in learning."[48] The passion that Star Teachers have for learners and learning is contagious and has a positive effect on students.

According to Furnham, "Passion takes a teacher from being merely good to great."[49] Unfortunately, traditional teaching is divorced from passion. The teachers most likely to be considered "good" are those who simply cover the curriculum. But Star Teachers view their students, and not the curriculum, as being of primary importance. And in personalizing their approach, Star Teachers will often bring their hobbies and passions into the classroom. In his book *The Passionate Teacher: A Practical Guide,* Robert Fried writes that "[w]e must show our students what it means to be passionate learners as well,"[50] and sharing our passions with students is a great way to do this while also encouraging a sense of wonder, exploration, and innovation.[51] As Haberman writes, Star Teachers "are typically involved in some life activity that provides them with a sense of well-being and from which they continually learn."[52]

Fourth grade teacher Mr. Gaines is guided by the principle that "the best teachers are those who show you where to look, but don't tell you what to see."

"I don't share that I love to run long distances so that my students all become long-distance runners like me—although if they do, that's fine," he says. "I share my passion for running because I cannot hide my passion. Running is much like teaching—it is a long race and it requires determination and dedication. Teaching requires mental toughness. My students know that I love to run—I've told them, and my classroom has photos of me after finishing marathons."

Mr. Gaines uses his passion for running to teach mathematical concepts such as distance to his 4th grade students.

"Given that there are 5,280 feet in a mile," he asks, "how many times would we need to run around the track to run a mile?"

"Four times, Mr. Gaines," answers Miguel.

"That is correct, Miguel."

The students then run four times around the school's quarter-mile track. They have a lot of energy—it's May, and they're anxious for summer. Mr. Gaines intentionally plans his math lesson outdoors because he wants his students to be engaged, excited, and involved with learning mathematical competencies like calculating distance, estimating time and speed, and graphing and calculating ratios and fractions.

"At first, I didn't think it could be fun to run, but Mr. Gaines is so energetic," says Mr. Gaines's student Susanna. "He has caused me to want to run long distances like him."

Consider a teacher who loves reading the classics and brings them into her classroom to engage her learners; or who enjoys yoga in his spare time and uses it to re-center young learners after long days on the playground; or who is passionate about food scarcity and discusses her community service work with students to ignite their sense of agency; or who, because he loves cooking, creates a lesson entitled "Cooking Up Fractions."

Tina Barseghian has this to say about passion: "A passion-driven teacher is a model for her students. Teachers must be able to lead in the areas that they're passionate about (whether this be in the classroom or after school). They must demonstrate that they have lives outside of school and that they are well balanced people. Being transparent with students and building relationships with them beyond the classroom can help drive learning—students work harder with people who matter to them."[53]

★ 2-3 —————————————————————————————

Take Anne Dranitsaris's Find Your Passion quiz (available here: www.qzzr.com/c/ quiz/187599/6a4bb3d9-4299-4dbf-876e-9d9092417f9c). Do you think your results are accurate? Why or why not?

Summary

Bureaucracy impedes learning in school, and protecting learners from it is one of the things that makes Star Teachers extremely effective in the classroom. When doing what is in the best interest of students conflicts with the demands of the school bureaucracy, Star Teachers attempt to "resolve their struggles with bureaucracy patiently, courteously, and professionally"[54] by (1) being organized (and helping students to organize themselves), (2) teaching subversively (in defiance of hidden or null curriculum), and (3) sharing their passions with their students.

As the vignettes in this chapter illustrate, the positive impact that teachers like Mr. Michaels and Mrs. Janet have on their students is far reaching. Star Teachers are resilient problem solvers who are passionate and effective, who model lifelong learning for students, and who behave professionally and respect the objectives of school administrators, but who are not afraid to challenge the status quo, if student learning is not protected. They are passionate about their vocation and they model lifelong learning. Their passion is contagious, making learning exciting for students and increasing both motivation[55] and achievement.

Key Words

bureaucratic	encouragement	environmental chaos
hidden curriculum	high pedagogy	high-stakes testing
lost learning time	low pedagogy	narrowed curriculum
null curriculum	organized chaos	passion
pedagogy of poverty	praise	professionalism
"pushed out"	school-to-prison pipeline	subversive teaching
time on task		

Extension Exercises

1. Subversive Teaching Activity: Subversive teaching often comes about when teachers ask clarifying questions about how they teach (e.g., "In what ways do I allow my biases to get in the way of my selection of lessons or classroom materials?"). Name two subversive questions that you could pose for yourself.

2. Examine this PDF: www.jimwrightonline.com/pdfdocs/engagedTime.pdf. Write down your daily and weekly classroom schedule and plans. Where could you maximize time for student learning? How will you accomplish more student learning within your schedule?

3. Share Your Passion Activity: Conduct an online search for "5 Ways to Share Your Passion for Learning" published on *Teach Hub*. See www.teachhub.com/5-ways-share-your-passion-learning. Read the article, then select one of the five strategies and share your passion with someone.

4. Rudolf Dreikur's understanding of classroom management suggests that encouragement is better than praise. Read this document that distinguishes between the two: www.positivediscipline.com/sites/default/files/praise_and_encouragement.pdf. Think of some responses you may make in the classroom. Assess whether they are forms of praise or encouragement. If you find yourself praising more than encouraging, reflect on your practice and try shifting the balance.

5. Passion Discovery Activity: Take the Interest Profiler online at www.mynextmove.org/explore/ip. What are your results? Read about each interest type: realistic, social, investigative, enterprising, artistic, and conventional. What did you learn about your interests? How do your interests align with what you are most passionate about?

6. Kitchen Math: Go to YouTube and search for the videos "Kitchen Math" by the Twice as Good Show at www.youtube.com/watch?v=wszRf0A3btk and "Cooking Up Fractions Series" by HumanRelationsMedia available at www.youtube.com/watch?v=DCqYoL1a3a4. After viewing the two videos, create a list of the possible interests that you could bring into the classroom to teach mathematics. For example, LEGO bricks can be used to

teach fractions. After you create your list, share your list with someone and review theirs. What did you discover?

7. Subversive Exercise: Find a copy of Postman and Weingartner's 1969 book *Teaching as a Subversive Activity*. Turn to page 61. What do you see? After, search YouTube for the video titled "Teaching Teachers as a Subversive Activity" by Scott Schwister, www.youtube.com/watch?v=VhUylbuHNyY. What do you think about teaching subversively? Why is it difficult to do it?

Going Further

Web Resources

TED (www.ted.com) contains videos that address the idea of "Protecting Learners and Learning." Specifically, check out Christopher Emdin's "Teach Teachers How to Create Magic": www.ted.com/talks/christopher_emdin_teach_teachers_how_to_create_magic.

Additional Readings

- Anyon, J. (1980). Social class and the hidden curriculum of work. *The Journal of Education, 162*(1), 67–92. Anyon's famous article "discusses examples of work tasks and interaction in elementary schools in contrasting social class communities. She illustrates differences in classroom experience and curriculum knowledge among schools and assesses student work in social settings through a theoretical approach to social class analysis. Anyon suggests that a hidden curriculum is at play" and articulates implications for educational theory and practice.

- Flinders, D. J., Noddings, N., & Thornton, S. J. (1986). The null curriculum: Its theoretical basis and practical implications. *Curriculum Inquiry, 16*(1), 33–42. In this essay, Flinders, Noddings, and Thornton examine the concept of "null curriculum"—what schools do not teach. According to the authors, "although the notion of null curriculum cannot be defined in precise terms, it does have worthwhile application in certain practical areas of curriculum development and evaluation." Their essay provides a primer on the null curriculum for teachers who may be unfamiliar with the concept.

- King, S. E. (1986). Are you doing inquiry along these lines? Inquiry into the hidden curriculum. *Journal of Curriculum and Supervision, 2*(1), 82–90.

This article is authored by a high school guidance counselor. The article is timeless and offers many helpful pieces of information regarding the hidden curriculum. The article will help inservice and preservice teachers consider how the hidden curriculum affects student learning.

- Haberman, M. (1991). Pedagogy of poverty versus good teaching. *Phi Delta Kappan, 73*(4), 290–294. Haberman's seminal article discusses what he labels as a "pedagogy of poverty." Haberman unpacks why the "pedagogy of poverty" does not protect student learning. This short article is a valuable resource for both preservice and inservice teachers because they may believe that they are actually being effective as a teacher and protecting their students' learning, but the opposite actually may be taking place.

Endnotes

1. Breault, D. A., & Allen, L. A. (2008). *Urban education: A handbook for educators and parents.* Westport, CT: Praeger. (p. 25)

2. Haberman, M. (1991). The pedagogy of poverty versus good teaching. *Phi Delta Kappan, 73*(4), 290–294. (p. 291)

3. Hartlep, Nicholas D., & Associates. (2014). *What makes a Star Teacher? Examining the dispositions of PK–12 urban teachers in Chicago.* Normal: Illinois State University, Department of Educational Administration and Foundation.

4. Haberman, M. (2004). Can Star Teachers create learning communities? *Educational Leadership, 68*(1), 52–56.

5. Rogers, J., & Mirra, N. (2014). *It's about time: Learning time and educational opportunity in California high schools.* Los Angeles: UCLA IDEA. Retrieved from https://idea.gseis.ucla.edu/projects/its-about-time/Its%20About%20Time.pdf

6. Leonard, L. J. (2001). From indignation to indifference: Teacher concerns about externally imposed classroom interruptions. *The Journal of Educational Research, 95*(2), 103–109. (p. 105)

7. Daniel, K. (2007). Take action now to prevent lost time for classroom instruction. Here's how. Retrieved from www.kdfiredup.com/uploads/1/8/8/4/18849178/msta_article_on_time.pdf

8. Nelson, H. (2013). Testing more, teaching less: What America's obsession with student testing costs in money and lost instructional time. Washington, DC: American Federation of Teachers. Retrieved from www.aft.org/sites/default/files/news/testingmore2013.pdf (p. 3)

9. Leonard, J. (2001). From indignation to indifference: Teacher concerns about externally imposed classroom interruptions. *The Journal of Educational Research, 95*(2), 103–109.

10. Haberman (2004).

11. Haberman, M. (1995). Selecting "Star" Teachers for children and youth in poverty. *Phi Delta Kappan, 76*(10), 777–781. Retrieved from http://files.eric.ed.gov/fulltext/EJ1110301.pdf. (p. 780)

12. Waters, T. (2012). *Bureaucratizing the child: The manufacture of adults in the modern world*. New York: Palgrave Macmillan.

13. Haberman, M. (1991). The pedagogy of poverty versus good teaching. *Phi Delta Kappan, 92*(2), 81–87. (p. 86)

14. Contractor, D., & Staats, C. (1991). Interventions to address racialized discipline disparities and school "push out." Retrieved from http://kirwaninstitute.osu.edu/wp-content/uploads/2014/05/ki-interventions.pdf

15. Haberman, M. (2010). *Star Teachers: The ideology and best practices of effective teachers of diverse children and youth in poverty*. Houston, TX: Haberman Educational Foundation.

16. Haberman (2010, p. 153).

17. Haberman, M. (2005). Selecting and preparing urban teachers. Retrieved from www.habermanfoundation.org/Articles/Default.aspx?id=32 (para. 22)

18. Pierron, L. (n.d.). Teacher organization tips. Retrieved from http://study.com/academy/lesson/teacher-organization-tips.html#lesson

19. Haberman (2004, p. 114).

20. Stronge, J. H. (2007). *Qualities of effective teachers* (2nd ed.). Alexandria, VA: ASCD. (p. 58)

21. Brundin, J. (2016, September 4). After 25 years, this teacher says it's all the paperwork that made him quit. *NPR*. Retrieved from www.npr.org/sections/ed/2016/09/04/485838588/after-25-years-this-teacher-says-its-all-the-paperwork-that-made-him-quit

22. Benham, B., & O'Brien, L. (2002). Why are experienced teachers leaving the profession? *Phi Delta Kappan, 84*(1), 24–32.

23. Hadler, P. (2015, December 10). 3 ways to deal with special ed paperwork: Conquering the mountain. Retrieved from http://geiendorsed.com/blog/tips/3-ways-to-deal-with-special-ed-paperwork-conquering-the-mountain/

24. Haberman, M. (2010). *Star Teachers: The ideology and best practice of effective teachers of diverse children and youth in poverty*. Houston, TX: Haberman Educational Foundation. (p. 119)

25. Haberman (2010, p. 119).

26. Haberman (2010, p. 114).

27. Jeon, L., Hur, E., & Buettner, C. K. (2016). Child-care chaos and teachers' responsiveness: The indirect associations through teachers' emotion regulation and coping. *Journal of School Psychology, 59*, 83–96.

28. Pass, A. (2014, March 20). Organized chaos: A characteristic of an awesome classroom. Retrieved from www.apasseducation.com/blog/organized-chaos-a-characteristic-of-an-awesome-classroom (para. 2)

29. Dodge, A. (2014, August 27). Teaching as a subversive activity. *The Huffington Post*. Retrieved from www.huffingtonpost.com/arnold-dodge/teaching-as-a-subversive-_b_5724706.html

30. Kendall, J. (2011). *Understanding Common Core State Standards*. Alexandria, VA: ASCD.

31. Danielson, C. (2007). *Enhancing professional practice: A framework for teaching*. Alexandria, VA: ASCD.

32. Haberman (2010, p. 139).

33. LeCompte, M. (1978). Learning to work: The hidden curriculum of the classroom. *Anthropology & Education Quarterly, 15*(1), 22–37. (p. 23)

34. McCutcheon, G. (1981). On the interpretation of classroom observations. *Educational Researcher, 10*(5), 5–10. (p. 6)

35. Ladson-Billings, G. (1995). But that's just good teaching! The case for culturally relevant pedagogy. *Theory into Practice, 34*(3), 159–165. Retrieved from www.outdoorfoundation.org/pdf/CulturallyRelevantPedagogy.pdf

36. Gutstein, E. (2007). Connecting community, critical, and classical knowledge in teaching mathematics for social justice. *The Montana Mathematics Enthusiast Monograph*, 1–10. Retrieved from www.educ.fc.ul.pt/docentes/jfmatos/areas_tematicas/politica/Gutstein.pdf (p. 2)

37. Gutstein (2007, p. 3).

38. Gutstein (2007, p. 2).

39. Flinders, D. J., Noddings, N., & Thorton, S. J. (1986). The null curriculum: Its theoretical basis and practical implications. *Curriculum Inquiry, 16*(1), 33–42. Retrieved from http://wp.vcu.edu/hhughesdecatur/wp-content/uploads/sites/1868/2013/01/Null-curriculum.pdf

40. Eisner, E. (1994). *The educational imagination: On the design and evaluation of school programs* (3rd ed.). New York: Macmillan College Publishing. Retrieved from http://people.cehd.tamu.edu/~pslattery/documents/EducationalImagination.pdf

41. National Council of Teachers of English. (2014). How standardized tests shape—and limit—student learning. Retrieved from www.ncte.org/library/NCTEFiles/Resources/Journals/CC/0242-nov2014/CC0242PolicyStandardized.pdf

42. Popham, W. J. (2001). Teaching to the test? *Educational Leadership, 58*(6), 16–20.

43. Postman, N., & Weingartner, C. (1969). *Teaching as a subversive activity*. New York: Dell. (p. 60)

44. Keller, M. M., Goetz, T., Becker, E. S., & Morger, V. (2014). Feeling and showing: A new conceptualization of dispositional teacher enthusiasm and its relation to students' interest. *Learning and Instruction, 33*, 29–38. (p. 34)

45. Keller et al. (2014, p. 34).

46. Day, C. (2012). New lives of teachers. *Teacher Education Quarterly, 39*(1), 7–26. (p. 9)

47. Benekos, P. J. (2016). How to be a good teacher: Passion, person, and pedagogy. *Journal of Criminal Justice Education, 27*(2), 225–237.

48. Benekos (2016, p. 228).

49. Furnham, A. (2001, January). Insight: Passion takes a teacher from being merely good to great. *The Telegraph*. Retrieved from www.telegraph.co.uk/finance/2906525/Insight-Passion-takes-a-teacher-from-being-merely-good-to-great.html

50. Fried, R. L. (2001). *The passionate teacher: A practical guide*. Boston: Beacon.

51. Bilgin, A., & Balba, M. Z. (2016). Personal professional development efforts scale for science and technology teachers regarding their fields. *Acta Didactica Napocensia, 9*(2), 67–78.

52. Haberman (1995).

53. Barseghian, T. (2011, July 13). Nine tenets of passion-based learning. *KQED*. Retrieved from https://ww2.kqed.org/mindshift/2011/07/13/nine-tenets-of-passion-based-learning/

54. Haberman (1995).

55. Patrick, B. C., Hisley, J., & Kempler, T. (2000). What's everybody so excited about? The effects of teacher enthusiasm on student intrinsic motivation and vitality. *Journal of Experimental Education, 68*(3), 217–236.

3

Putting Theory into Practice

Theory into practice refers to the teacher's ability to put theory or research into practice. Conversely, it also refers to the teacher's ability to understand how specific teaching behaviors support concepts and ideas about effective teaching. In addition, this dimension predicts the teacher's ability to benefit from professional development activities and grow as a professional practitioner.

Learning Outcomes

Upon completion of this chapter, you will be able to

- Define *theory into practice*.
- Analyze the mindset of Star Teachers who embrace the theory into practice dimension.
- Analyze the various behaviors of Star Teachers who can bridge theory and practice.
- Use Gibbs's Reflective Teaching Cycle to challenge instructional ideas, improve your teaching, and support student learning.

Interstate New Teacher Assessment and Support Consortium (InTASC) Standards

Standard #4: Content Knowledge
The teacher understands the central concepts, tools of inquiry, and structures of the discipline(s) he or she teaches and creates learning experiences that make the discipline accessible and meaningful for learners to assure mastery of the content.

Standard #5: Application of Content
The teacher understands how to connect concepts and use differing perspectives to engage learners in critical thinking, creativity, and collaborative problem solving related to authentic local and global issues.

Standard #7: Professional Learning & Ethical Practice
The teacher plans instruction that supports every student in meeting rigorous learning goals by drawing upon knowledge of content areas, curriculum, cross-disciplinary skills, and pedagogy, as well as knowledge of learners and the community context.

★ ★ ★ ★ ★ ★ ★ ★ ★ ★ ★

Defining *Theory into Practice*

Since the early 20th century, the field of teacher education has wrestled with how to balance **theory** (generalizations of principled knowledge) and **practice** (classroom instruction). In 1908, for example, John Dewey offered a balanced perspective, arguing that professional instruction of teachers is not exclusively theoretical but involves a certain amount of practical work as well.[1] The craft knowledge uncovered by research must somehow be converted into practical strategies if it is to help teachers make sound decisions about instruction. And teachers must have a clear understanding of how theory (or "ideal") can inform practice (the "real") (Figure 3.1).

There is reciprocity between theory and practice. On one hand, theory offers insight into practice by defining, labeling, or offering practical solutions to problems. On the other hand, practice, through experiences and illustrations, can establish, explain, dismiss, or show relationships to theory. Teachers must be

Figure 3.1 **Reciprocity of Theory and Practice**

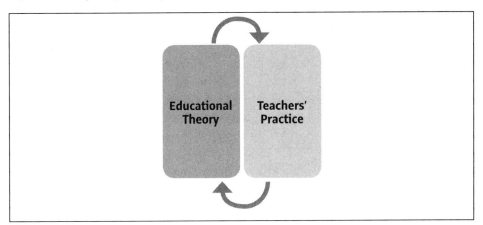

open to new knowledge claims and theories of practice to improve instruction and proactive about discarding stale ideas to reshape instruction.

In the age of information, both the practice of education and its underlying knowledge base change so rapidly that teachers must engage in continuous professional learning throughout their careers. In 1986, educational psychologist Lee Shulman remarked that learners need teachers who are more than experts on their subjects.[1] There are three types of teachers' knowledge for which Shulman advocates: (1) content or subject matter knowledge; (2) general pedagogical knowledge, with special reference to broad principles and strategies of classroom management and organization that transcend subject matter; and (3) knowledge of learners and their characteristics. Shulman refers to the combination of these three knowledges as **pedagogical content knowledge,** or **PCK** (see Figure 3.2).

According to Shulman, PCK "represents the blending of content and pedagogy into an understanding of how particular topics, problems, or issues are organized, represented, and adapted to the diverse interests and abilities of learners, and presented for instruction."[2] What we call teachers' content knowledge essentially consists of generalizations or theories grouped into disciplinary studies of history, mathematics, chemistry, literature, reading, and so on. The first three years in a four-year teacher preparation program (TPP) are devoted to learning theories in the university classroom, ranging from the art of teaching to

Figure 3.2 **Pedagogical Content Knowledge (PCK)**

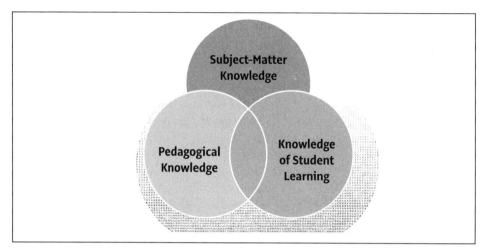

Source: Adapted from the work of Lee S. Shulman. Used with permission.

the scientific concepts that drive subject-matter expertise. The last year of the TPP is spent in the field learning how to apply what they've learned in ways that make sense to students. This long-standing design aims to ensure that teachers can apply years of theory to real classroom practice.

Both theoretical and practical knowledge are important for teachers' subject matter and development. For example, it was not until the 1840s that reading comprehension as a theory to be studied took root, as students in the United States started being assessed on their reading accuracy and fluency. By the 1890s, reading instruction began to be dominated by basal readers, such as the McGuffey Readers, based squarely on then-contemporary theories of reading comprehension. Shortly thereafter, teacher manuals for science-based basal reading instruction were designed to teach fluency, vocabulary, comprehension, and phonemic awareness. Today, reading theory and practice are so integrated that researchers and teachers can barely see the sunlight between them.

The Theory-Practice Gap

The gap between theory and practice is well known but misunderstood. In 1974, progressive educators Chris Argyris and Donald Schon suggested that there were two types of pedagogical theories: "theories-of-action" (i.e., those which teachers champion but, when faced with the realities of the classroom, don't incorporate into classroom practice);[3] and "theories-in-use" (i.e., theories that teachers put into practice because they address specific classroom issues).[4] Among the most common questions teachers have about education theory is "Yeah, but how do I apply it in my classroom?" For many educators, there is a disconnect between real situations in the classroom and the ideal conditions proposed by theorists.

In his book *The Reflective Practitioner,* Donald Schon discusses the enduring mistrust between theorists and practitioners.[5] Many practitioners scoff at theories that they claim have little relevance to practical situations. For example, teachers learning principles of constructivism may find the ideas difficult to implement in a climate of high-stakes testing. Many teachers complain that what they learn in TPPs or professional development courses is not applicable to the classroom. At the same time, many theorists spend considerable resources developing broad theories of effective instruction that they doubt practitioners are heeding.

The relationship between educational theory and practice is often described in top-down terms, with academics dominating discussion and generating, building on, and testing the theories that determine practice. The result of this hierarchy, with theory valued more than practice, is a "crisis in confidence in professional knowledge" known as the **theory-practice gap**.[6]

Every encounter that a teacher has with a learner should be a unique opportunity to draw on craft knowledge, a unique combination of ideas and experience. Many teacher advocacy and accreditation agencies (e.g., the Interstate New Teacher Assessment and Support Consortium [InTASC], Council for the Accreditation of Educator Preparation [CAEP], and National Board for Professional Teacher Standards [NBPTS]) communicate foundational teacher knowledge and skills, supported by research, for all disciplines and grade levels. The chief objective of these organizations is to provide a framework of what all teachers should know and be able to do to support student achievement. Star Teachers are able to carefully examine the standards, which are driven by theories, and translate them into successful practice.

Cross-Stepping: Bridging Theory and Practice

Star Teachers have the uncanny ability to move between theory and practice almost seamlessly using either a deductive or an inductive approach. In a

deductive approach, teachers move from the general (theory) to the specific (practice), using the latter to explain the former. Stars know how to analyze abstract instructional concepts and apply them to real classroom situations. Conversely, in an **inductive** approach, teachers move from the specific to the general by identifying a practice first and then trying to make sense out of it through theory. As Haberman explains, "Without this ability to see the relationship between important ideas and day-to-day practice, teaching degenerates into merely 'keeping school.'"[7] Teachers need to grow throughout their professional careers by continuously moving between theory and practice—a process known as **cross-stepping**. Star Teachers are able to hypothesize about the many possible outcomes of applying a particular theory in the classroom as well as to explain how specific aspects of their practice connect to broad theories or concepts. Without cross-stepping, rather than having 30 years of experience at the end of their careers, teachers can be said to have had one year of experience 30 times.[8]

★ 3-1

Do you know how to cross-step? Share a recent example of a common instructional practice you perform in your classroom, and articulate the principle, concept, or knowledge base that supports it.

Theory to Practice

Effective teaching requires teachers to construct, develop, apply, discard, and reconstruct theories of learning and teaching. According to Haberman, sound theories are not merely "common sense" but rather carefully crafted instructional approaches acquired from years of experience and comprehensive inquiry.[9] These theories are most beneficial to learners when teachers test them out in the classroom, listen to colleagues' critiques, and remain abreast of current research. Star Teachers who are asked to give concrete examples of ways they've put some teaching principle they believe in into practice, they can cite clear, observable cases.

Patrick Haymes, a 3rd grade teacher with about 14 years of teaching under his belt, engages in cross-stepping from theory to practice when he explains why he uses learning communities with young students even though the strategy typically requires higher-order cognitive skills.

"My students are learning to read for comprehension," he says. "I use learning communities to tease out the big ideas from reading passages. I also use
a technique called 'seats up, heads together,' which allows students to work
together to solve the questions from the reading passages. Learning communities
can work for learners at any stage—you just need to edit the approach to meet
them where they are."

Patrick is a Star Teacher able to transform an abstract theory into a specific
set of classroom activities. He is also able to deal with gradations of meaning, recognizing that phenomena do not always exist as absolutes by adjusting a higher-
order strategy for use with younger learners. He understands that the theoretical
underpinning of the learning community strategy is flexible, and that theories
should direct rather than dictate teacher behavior.

Practice to Theory

Most experienced teachers understand that they operate according to commonly accepted knowledge and beliefs, or theories, that have been proven over
time. The art of teaching and learning is guided by theories about what will and
will not work for our students. Some of these theories are learned informally
and implicitly through practice, while others are acquired formally and explicitly
through TPPs and professional development opportunities. As Haberman writes,
"Stars can explain what their day-to-day work adds up to; they have a grasp not
only of the learning principles that undergird their work but also of the long-
term knowledge goals that they are helping their students achieve."[10]

Anna, a grade 8 Star science teacher, cross-steps from practice to theory as
she allows students to engage in problem-based learning around issues of their
choosing.

"We don't have a traditional classroom," she says. "It is possible to use
problem-based learning and teach to the state's accountability standards. Our
classroom practices are based on the constructivist philosophy to teaching and
learning, so students create the meaning for their own learning.

"This doesn't mean free reign by any means. After I consult with the department head and other grade-level teachers, we decide on the topics to teach
during particular times. I don't always like lessons from the textbook. I took a
graduate science course a year ago and learned how to align students' needs to

state mandates within problem-based instruction. All it means is I have to be a little more creative by generating guidelines for my students' projects, facilitating the proper environment, and using the science standards as my teaching objectives."

We tell Anna that her approach sounds like a great deal of work.

"Funny thing is, we can't go back," she says. "My students' achievement scores are up since I turned our classroom into a constructivist space."

Our classroom?

"I couldn't do this without them. They know that their voices and ideas matter, that they own the space too, and that we're in this together. I'm not the sage on the stage, just the guide on the side."

As Anna's example shows, practice allows us to test theory within our laboratory or classroom. Star Teachers learn how to respond to the needs of students by committing themselves to classroom strategies while exploring the theoretical knowledge base to find solutions for instructional problems.

Star Teachers Are Lifetime Learners: The Mindset of Star Teachers

It has long been accepted that teaching, as the learning profession, should require educators to continually grow personally and professionally. **Lifelong learning** is defined as "all learning activity undertaken throughout life, with the aim of improving knowledge, skills and competencies within a personal, civic, social and/or employment-related perspective."[11] Teaching is a highly social enterprise, and Star Teachers effectively model how learning works. They question, analyze, and create solutions to professional and personal problems.

In addition to displaying a thirst for learning, both novice and veteran teachers need to be able to combine their knowledge of pedagogy and subject matter into sound instruction by experimenting with curricula and learning programs.

Teachers as Self-Directed Learners

According to Malcolm Knowles, **self-directed learning** is a process by which individuals extend their learning in new contexts; identify human and material resources for learning, choosing, and implementing appropriate learning strategies; and take the initiative, with or without the assistance of others, in diagnosing their own learning needs and formulating personal learning goals.[12] It is crucial that teachers not leave their learning needs in the hands of the principal or school district.

In his work, Knowles made the following assumptions about adult learners that we believe also hold true for Star Teachers:

- They use the knowledge they already possess to understand the structure of new information.
- They move from dependency to increasing self-directedness as they mature and can direct their own learning.
- They're ready to learn when they assume new social or life roles.
- They're problem-centered and want to apply new learning immediately.
- They're motivated to learn by internal rather than external factors.[13]

Self-directed learning is an essentially independent process defined by the learner's autonomy regarding decisions about professional learning. Star Teachers seek out a diverse array of professional development sources to enhance their cross-step competencies, and they take ownership of their learning by determining their needs, setting goals, identifying resources, implementing a plan to meet their goals, and evaluating outcomes.[14]

Professional Learning Opportunities

Available professional learning opportunities for educators have expanded greatly over the last 30 years. There are three primary types of professional development for educators: job-embedded learning, professional activities, and formal education (see Figure 3.3). Teacher learning is usually focused on subject-matter content, instructional methods, and classroom management.

State and local school districts typically require teachers to complete between 150 and 175 hours of professional development units (PDUs), clock hours, or continuing education units (CEUs) over five years.[15] Star Teachers crave all types of learning and view professional development as empowering rather than compulsory, helping them to develop agency and hone their craft.[16] A 62-year-old who takes a course in computer coding to help stay current with her middle schoolers; a 15-year veteran who joins up with a Hispanic community organization to learn more about his school's increasingly diverse study body; a sharp novice teacher who joins a professional social media platform to stay on top of educational reform issues—all of these are examples of continuous learning experiences that Star Teachers embrace.

In his essay "Teacher as a Learner," Leonard Kaplan proposes that effective teachers seek to learn about (1) themselves and their commitment to learners; (2) others, including diverse peers and parents; (3) and the profession.[17] They also need to acquire a deep understanding of the unique classroom contexts within which teaching and learning occur.

Figure 3.3 **Professional Learning Opportunities for Teachers**

Job-embedded or workplace learning: Joining inservice training; shadowing or observing teachers; reflecting on practice; doing peer reviews; attending peer conferences; setting up and reviewing professional portfolios; participating in professional learning communities.

Professional activities: Mentoring; joining and participating in membership organizations; participating on a committee; planning and delivering workshops; reading journals and articles; joining book clubs, online forums, or discussions groups; participating in list-servs; reviewing books or articles; and reviewing education-focused podcasts.

Formal education: Attending and participating in conferences or workshops; writing articles; taking distance learning classes or enrolling in graduate education.

★ 3-2

Are you an intellectually curious person? You and your peers should work together as a team to search online for the phrase "intellectually curious" and for a related quiz from a credible site. What do your results say about you as a classroom leader or as a lifelong learner? Discuss your quiz results with your peers.

Growth Mindset

Carol Dweck explains in her groundbreaking book *Mindset: The New Psychology of Success* that our outlook, or mindset, determines our likelihood to take risks to be successful.[18] Star Teachers have a **growth mindset** because they are committed to growing as lifelong learners, which in turn helps their students succeed.

Research increasingly shows that when teachers shift from a mindset of professional development to one of professional learning, they start to see themselves as active rather than passive learners confident in their ability to improve their practice.[19] These highly effective teachers believe that intelligence is malleable and that they are always able to learn and improve; are not afraid to meet instructional challenges head-on; seek and value feedback from administrators, peers, and students to improve their practice; and view instructional setbacks as teachable moments as well as opportunities to learn from their standards. By contrast, pre-Star Teachers with a **fixed mindset** seek professional development to "check the box" and are uninterested in learning new teaching innovations (see Figure 3.4).

Star Teachers recognize that professional learning is not only a matter of keeping pace with craft knowledge, pedagogy, and technology, but also of reflecting on practice so they can infuse it with new knowledge. Stars approach each class, year after year, looking to learn something new about their students, their profession, or even themselves. The successes of Star Teachers reveal what is working, and each new failure, when viewed as a learning opportunity, helps them refine their practice to support learners in new ways.

Teacher Learning = Student Learning

What good is teacher learning if it does not lead to changes in teaching behavior? Professional growth is crucial to teachers' job performance and focused on experiences that directly affect student achievement.[20] Teacher learning helps educators link theory to practice, showing them how to decipher their own behaviors to improve instruction. As Linda Darling-Hammond writes,

> Growing evidence suggests that this kind of professional development not only makes teachers feel better about their practice, but it also reaps learning gains for students, especially in the kinds of more challenging learning that new standards demand. Creating a profession of teaching in which teachers have the opportunity for continual learning is the likeliest way to inspire greater achievement for children.[21]

The most effective professional learning opportunities are job-embedded, can be applied in the moment to teachers' classrooms, and are flexible;[22] they are also content-focused, active, collaborative, coaching-infused, reliant on feedback and reflection, and sustained over time.[23]

Figure 3.4 **Fixed Versus Growth Mindset for Teachers**

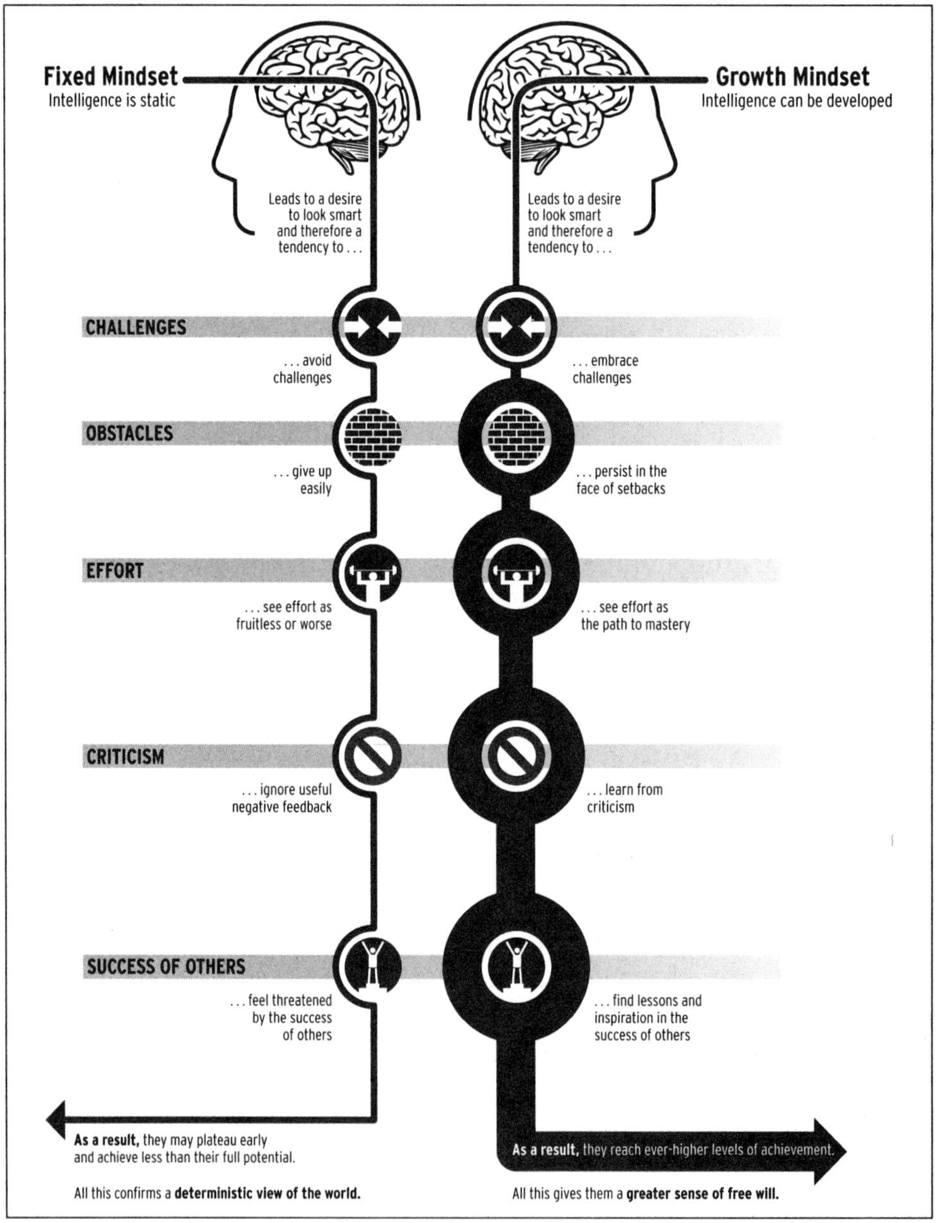

Fixed Mindset
Intelligence is static

Growth Mindset
Intelligence can be developed

Leads to a desire
to look smart
and therefore a
tendency to . . .

Leads to a desire
to look smart
and therefore a
tendency to . . .

CHALLENGES
. . . avoid
challenges

. . . embrace
challenges

OBSTACLES
. . . give up
easily

. . . persist in the
face of setbacks

EFFORT
. . . see effort as
fruitless or worse

. . . see effort as
the path to mastery

CRITICISM
. . . ignore useful
negative feedback

. . . learn from
criticism

SUCCESS OF OTHERS
. . . feel threatened
by the success
of others

. . . find lessons and
inspiration in the
success of others

As a result, they may plateau early
and achieve less than their full potential.

As a result, they reach ever-higher levels of achievement.

All this confirms a **deterministic view of the world.**

All this gives them a **greater sense of free will.**

Source: Image designed by Nigel Holmes. Copyright 2006 Carol Dweck. Used with permission.

In conjunction with 17 professional education associations, the National Staff Development Council (NSDC) identified 12 standards for teacher learning, organized around three themes of content, context, and process, and that provide meaningful experiences for educators and student achievement.[24] These standards draw upon a growing bank of studies that describe the three major attributes of effective professional development:

1. The *content* of professional learning is most effective when it emphasizes specific teaching tasks, assessment, observation, and reflection in addition to student learning;

2. The *context* of professional learning should be a larger, coherent, standards-based, and collaborative approach to bridging the theory-practice gap; and

3. The *process* should include opportunities for active learning or "sense-making" to practice and reflect on new strategies, which should be sustained and intense.[25]

Professional Development as an Opportunity to Learn

Professional development conjures up images of teachers sitting in oversized conference spaces, drinking bad coffee, and listening to so-called experts. It is required to retain certification, and pay increases are tied to it. Often they are organized as one- to two-day "sit and get" seminars. Seldom are these types of activities connected to the realities of the classroom, and rarely do they result in changes in teacher behavior. Professional development must be a natural extension of a teacher's practice.

A study by the U.S. Department of Education of 221 4th grade teachers engaged in a 93-hour content-intensive professional development program found that the process had a positive effect on teacher instruction.[26] The research describes a typical lesson and the amount of time that an average teacher devotes to each of the three mathematical quality instruction (MQI) dimensions of instructional quality: (1) *Richness of mathematics,* which emphasizes the conceptual aspects of math, such as the use and quality of mathematical explanations; (2) *student participation in mathematics,* which focuses on student explanations and reasoning; and (3) *errors and imprecision,* which centers on incorrect, unclear, and imprecise use of math. Lower error and imprecision scores are desirable and indicate fewer content errors and less imprecision than higher scores.[27] On average, the teachers who completed the professional development program scored 21 percentile points higher than those who did not.

In another study, Leigh Parise and James Spillane found that formal and job-embedded learning were highly predictive of instructional growth among teachers of elementary math and English language acquisition.[28] Yet another study concluded that teachers in Canada, China, and Singapore experience professional learning that is pivotal to their instruction and "not something done on Friday afternoons or on a few days at the end of the school year."[29] In order for this to happen, the study authors write, "teachers must be able to take principles and concepts from a variety of sources (i.e., courses, workshops, books, and research) and translate them into practice."[30]

Linda Darling-Hammond advocates for new models of professional development that include the following elements:

> mentoring for beginners and veterans; peer observation and coaching; local study groups and networks for specific subject matter areas; teacher academies that provide ongoing seminars and courses of study tied to practice; and school-university partnerships that sponsor collaborative research, interschool visitations, and learning opportunities developed in response to teachers' and principals' felt needs.[31]

While there are some notable examples of school districts that have boldly begun to incorporate these elements in their professional learning programs, Star Teachers recognize that they often need to seek professional development on their own, which suits their individual needs.

Star Teachers as Reflective Practitioners

Everyone learns best from prior experience. **Reflection** is the ability to go through an experience, think about it deeply, and grow from it. When teachers investigate the effects of their teaching on student learning and take the time to reflect on theory, they become sensitive to instructional variation and more aware of what works for what purposes in what situations. Training in reflection also helps teachers learn how to see the world from multiple perspectives and use what they learn to reach every student.

Reflection has been a highly valued component of education since the turn of the 20th century. John Dewey defined **reflective thinking** as an "active, persistent, and careful consideration of any belief or supposed form of knowledge in the light of the grounds that support it and the further conclusions to which it tends."[32] For Dewey, reflective thinking was a means for educators to circumvent routine, in-the-moment thinking. He outlined the following criteria for an effective process of reflection:

1. The issue upon which the teacher reflects must occur in the social context where teaching occurs.
2. The teacher must be interested in the problem to be resolved.
3. The issue must be "owned" by the teacher; that is, derived from his/her own practice.
4. Reflection on the issue involves problem solving from the teaching situation in which the teacher is located.
5. Ownership of the identified issue and its solution is vested in the teacher.
6. The teachers' ideas need to be tested through the practice of teaching.
7. Ideas about teaching, once tested through practice, must lead to some course of action.
8. Hence, reflective actions may be transformed into new understanding and redefined practice in teaching. Tested practice must lead to some kind of action resulting in change.
9. Reflective actions should cause new understanding and changes in teaching.[33]

Over time, interest in **reflective practice** as a form of professional development has grown among educators.[34] Reflective practice is associated with learning from experience,[35] solving instructional dilemmas, improving student academic achievement, stimulating personal and professional growth,[36] and closing the gap between theory and practice.[37] Instructional growth is both a reflective and an active process—a combination of teacher thinking (reflection) and classroom experiences (action). Linda Finlay explains that reflective practice is

> understood as the process of learning through and from experience towards gaining new insights of self and/or practice. This often

involves examining assumptions of everyday practice. It tends to involve the individual practitioner in being self-aware and critically evaluating their own responses to practice situations. The point is to recapture practice experiences and mull them over critically in order to gain new understandings and so improve future practice.[38]

According to Donald Schon, educators who use reflective practice examine their actions in the form of *reflection-in-action* and *reflection-on-action*. Reflection-in-action involves thinking about problems while they're occurring, whereas reflection-on-action is thinking about them after the fact.[39] Consider, for example, a science teacher who notices that her students are still puzzled as she explains mitosis for the second time and realizes, on the spot, that she needs to engage the visual learners. Unplanned, she reaches for some modeling clay and conducts a spontaneous demonstration. This teacher's realization and shift in teaching strategy during the lesson constitutes reflection-in-action. By contrast, if she were to ponder the challenge of how to get mitosis across to her students and decide upon next steps after the class was over, she would be engaging in reflection-on-action.

Most professional standards and credentialing processes require educators to engage in some kind of reflective practice. For example, Proposition 4 of the National Board for Professional Teaching Standards (NBPTS) proposes that "teachers think systematically about their practice and learn from experience."[40]

Overcoming Barriers to Reflective Practice

Unfortunately, many educators consider reflection to be little more than advanced daydreaming—likely because few have been trained to do so.[41] The four key barriers to teacher reflection are lack of time, curriculum demands, unsupportive school leaders, and fear of engaging in the process incorrectly.

Barrier 1: Time. Teachers have endless demands on their schedules both inside and outside the classroom. Many educators have little time to exchange understandings with peers or to grade students' work with the detail and feedback they would prefer. Persistent teachers understand that classrooms are fast-paced and unpredictable places where student learning is dictated by schedules and mandates, but they do not allow the swirl of educational theater to distract them from their educational goals.

Conversations, critical analysis, and student portfolios are some of the ways teachers engage in reflective practice. Though some teachers practice reflection out loud, the preference for most practitioners is still to write, usually in reflection journals. Written reflection helps teachers to deepen and personalize their learning as well as to integrate theory with practice. Journals and portfolios run the gamut from highly structured to entirely free-form and have been used to improve learning in virtually every subject area.[42]

Mobile apps, such as One Note, Taskade, Notability, and Easy Voice Recorder, are helping teachers with the platforms to create a structured system to write reflective journals while protecting their time. It is important for teachers to use these reflection instruments properly, moving through the intended stages of reflection to inform their instruction. A variety of reflection formats exist to help teachers abandon the idea that reflection is a burdensome act.

Barrier 2: Curriculum Demands. The rigidity and inflexible nature of the district's canned curriculum is another barrier to reflective practice. When teachers have so much content to cover in so little time, they tend to focus on covering the material rather than on reflection about instruction.

Two opposing perspectives of classroom instruction, the transmission approach and the constructivist approach, help us to understand teacher efficacy. In the transmission approach, teachers rely exclusively on teacher-proof materials such as the school district's curriculum manual for directions and assessment suggestions. Pre-Star Teachers find comfort in this style, but it reinforces the kind of unpredictable and unexamined instruction that stifles teacher growth, "guided primarily by impulse, tradition, and authority."[43]

To overcome this obstacle to teacher development, teachers must adopt a growth mindset of classroom instruction. Star Teachers are reflective and refuse to blindly follow instructional routines or work on impulse in the classroom. Rather, Stars embrace a constructivist philosophy to teaching and learning that recognizes all stakeholders as active participants and students become empowered to engage in their own meaning making for their learning experiences. In this way, Stars plan lessons methodically—based on the personalities, interests, and learning acuity of their students. In constructivism, the students become partners in learning and are prompted to engage in personalized learning projects. Because they are confident in their professional judgments, Stars can forego packaged curricula and concentrate on their lessons of their own design that reach every learner. This type of teaching requires an adaptive, bright, skillful, and open-minded teacher with a capacity to grow. Teachers with a growth mindset or high sense of teacher efficacy are reflective about events in the classroom and carefully plan lessons based on what students currently know and what they need to learn.

Barrier 3: Unsupportive School Leaders. If the leaders of a school do not encourage reflective thought or provide the resources for staff to engage in it, teachers are unlikely to feel empowered enough to practice reflection on their own. If the leaders in your school aren't supportive of reflection, you might ask yourself, "What's the point of me teaching if I am not trusted to make decisions on behalf of my learners?"

In the essay "What Teachers Say About Reflection," Christine Canning reminds us that teachers resist reflection because they have been discouraged to do so.[44] Many teachers lose their autonomy to please their professors and school leaders. Canning explains that many novice teachers do not know their own voices and often "defer to professors and supervisors for good grades and positive evaluations" because they've "developed internal patterns on focusing on what they felt they were *supposed* to say."[45] Reflection lets teachers regain their own voice and develop the confidence to make their own instructional decisions in the classroom. While teachers may not have the power to change instruction at the district or school level, they can, through a model of inquiry, improve on the choices they make in their own classrooms.

Barrier 4: Fear of Reflection. Learning the art of reflective problem solving must begin in TPPs and continue throughout every teacher's career. Teachers resist reflection because it has never been explained or taught to them in a systematic way that links teacher thinking to real results for student achievement. Emily Hayden and Ming Chiu suggest that novice teachers who use reflection to engage in more problem exploration were better suited to adapt their instructional practices and solved more instructional problems than their peers.[46]

To move beyond the fear of reflection, teachers must think of instructional problems as opportunities to test academic theories. Neil Haigh suggests that learning through reflection is more effective if the learner understands the various structures or categories for composing reflections.[47] In a 1995 study, Hatton and Smith identified four types of reflective writing:

1. *Descriptive writing,* which is not considered deep thinking or analysis, but merely restates events or ideas;
2. *Descriptive reflection,* which is analytical;
3. *Dialogic reflection,* or internal dialogue that connects to evidence or documentation, much like a portfolio, for tracking one's journey; and
4. *Critical reflection,* which is an advanced form of decision making framed within a larger historical, social, or political landscape.[48]

Teachers must be willing to investigate each type of reflection and select the one that best matches their subject area and teaching style.

The Reflective Teaching Cycle

There are several reflection frameworks that can be used to systematically guide reflective problem solving for teachers. One of the first and most cited processes is David A. Kolb's four-stage experiential learning theory, which proposes that a learner moves through a spiral of immediate experience that leads to observations and reflections, and is then followed by the development of ideas and culminates in testing ideas in practice.[49] Graham Gibbs's Reflective Teaching Cycle integrates Kolb's experiential learning theory with Schon's ideas of reflection-on-action (see p. 86) and is made up of the following six steps: description, feelings, evaluation, analysis, conclusion, and action (see Figure 3.5).[50]

Step 1: Description of the Instructional Challenge or Problem. The first step of the Reflective Teaching Cycle is pinpointing the problem you want to answer. When you observe a gap between practice and theory, identify the instructional goal you want to achieve and be sure to write it down. Too often teachers forget about a problem they encounter because they haven't written it down. This simple act forces the teacher to reflect on the issue. Teachers who are not reflective will seek simple solutions to defining an instructional problem without determining the depth of the problem, or they may avoid instructional challenges altogether. Stars spend a great deal of time identifying the instructional challenge before they set out to get an answer because they understand that naming the issue is equally as important as solving it.

Figure 3.5 **Gibbs's Cycle of Reflective Teaching**

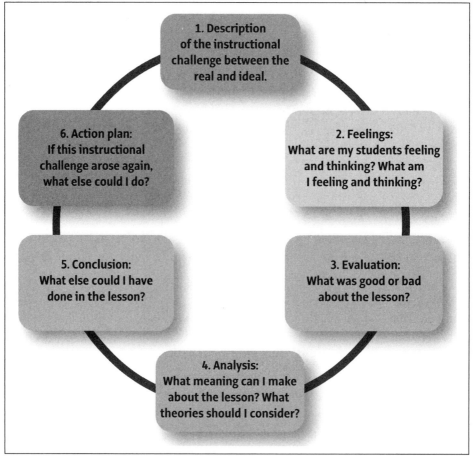

Source: From *Learning by Doing* (p. 46), by G. Gibbs, 1988, Oxford, UK: Further Education Unit, Oxford Polytechnic. Copyright 1988 by G. Gibbs. Adapted with permission.

Step 2: Feelings of Students and Teachers. Unlike many other models, the Gibbs Reflective Teaching Cycle takes into account students' and teachers' emotions regarding instruction.[51] Star Teachers listen to their students, peers, and administrators in addition to themselves and discuss their emotions authentically and in a conversational tone. Remember that paying attention to the feelings of the stakeholders is meant to be an instructive piece of reflective journaling, so avoid being too verbose, personal, or off topic.

Step 3: Evaluation of the Lesson. In this step, the educator describes the entire lesson from the beginning and identifies which element of the lesson led to the problem being considered. This step involves authentic critique of instruction and ensures that adequate time is spent assessing lesson elements.

Step 4: Analysis of the Lesson. In this step, the teacher discusses and interprets the instructional problem and related theory with colleagues, who share their own insights. Because reflective journaling is a professional activity, be sure to include references of scholarly sources in your writing. During this step, it is a good idea to revisit the evaluation phase in Step 3 and reconfirm that your definition of the problem is still valid. Following their reflective work, educators frequently discover that the problem they really want to answer is very different from the one they initially had in mind.

Step 5: Conclusion. In this step, you write down what you are going to do next to possibly solve the problem using creative strategies that will work with all affected learners. When writing about a lesson that did not go as planned, try to consider all possible solutions.

Step 6: Action Plan for Future Problems in the Lesson. This is the step that separates pre-Star Teachers from Star Teachers. Many teachers stop the process after Step 5, but Star Teachers go on to reflect on deeply held beliefs that may be adversely affecting our work. Reflective practice pushes us to confront theories or practices that are detrimental to student learning.

Researchers who have studied how reflective teachers and nonreflective teachers solve problems have found obvious differences in the quality of the decision making at each stage of the process.[52] Nonreflective teachers make instructional decisions on the spot that may or may not result in achievement gains for learners. By contrast, reflective educators make thoughtfully considered instructional decisions that result in observable academic growth for learners.

Summary

Some teachers engage in best practices but can't explain why; others can explain best practices well but are unable to engage in them. Star Teachers can do both, connect theory to practice and practice to theory. Teachers with a growth mindset who commit to continuous learning throughout their careers learn how to translate theory into action. Reflection enables educators to be more cognizant of their instructional decisions and judgments; make the best use of the knowledge available; challenge and develop the existing professional knowledge base; avoid instructional mistakes; and maximize opportunities for student learning. Reflective practice is cyclical, with teachers continually monitoring, evaluating, and revising their practice. By closely following the six stages of Gibb's Reflective Teaching Cycle, teachers become more confident about cross-stepping between theory and practice.

Key Words

cross-stepping	deductive	disconnect
fixed mindset	growth mindset	inductive
lifelong learning	pedagogical content knowledge (PCK)	practice
reflection	reflective practice	reflective thinking
self-directed learning	theory	theory-practice gap

Extension Exercises

1. Name and describe three to five instructional theories that guide your instructional habits. Over the last five years, has the number of items on this list increased, decreased, or remained the same? What does this say about you as an instructor?

2. Identify a scholar who writes about an instructional theory that you use in your teaching. Try using Google Scholar to locate an academic article. In what ways does the scholar get it right, and how might this theory be reconsidered in the classroom?

3. Go to www.mindsetonline.com and take the Mindset Test. What are your results? Do you agree or disagree with the results? Why or why not?

4. List the professional learning activities you have undergone in the last year. For each one, write whether it changed your behavior or instructional practices. Please elaborate and explain why or why not.

5. Identify a lesson that you struggled with implementing in your classroom, and apply Gibbs's Reflective Teaching Cycle to determine where any

roadblocks to students' learning arose. Did you identify instructional ideas and behaviors that need to be removed or adapted?

6. Review the four barriers to teacher reflection identified in this chapter. Name and describe the two barriers that prevent you from engaging in reflective practice to solve problems in the classroom. Next, develop two ideas for each barrier that you can implement to reduce or remove obstacles and become a more reflective educator.

7. Each educator should have a professional development plan to further develop professionally. The chart in Figure 3.6 can help you identify several professional learning opportunities to expand your pedagogical knowledge, content knowledge, and knowledge about learners. To complete this chart, check your district's professional development offerings and search the internet.

Figure 3.6 **Professional Learning Opportunities for Teachers**

Job-embedded and workplace learning: taking inservice training; shadowing or observing colleagues; using reflective practices; participating in peer reviews and peer conferences; creating portfolios; joining professional learning communities.

Professional activities: joining professional membership organizations; mentoring; participating in related committees and workshops; reading journals and articles; attending book clubs; participating in online forums, discussions groups, and list servs; reviewing books and articles.

Formal education: attending conferences and workshops; participating in distance learning; attending graduate education.

8. Invite a peer who is well versed in teaching your content area or grade level to videotape you in action giving a lesson that puts theory into practice. Then, watch the video together to compare the theory with your actions. Name areas where you successfully cross-stepped and one or two areas that may need improvement.

Going Further

Web Resources

- Check out the ASCD podcast "Reflective Teachers Are More Effective: Improvement Doesn't Happen by Accident" here: http://inservice.ascd.org/

resources-to-help-you-build-teachers-capacity/. Listen as ASCD authors Alisa Simeral and Pete Hall and teacher Kim Price explore how teachers can develop their capacity for success through self-reflection for greater student learning.

- Review *Educational Leadership*'s list of seven points to ponder about lifelong learning here: www.ascd.org/ASCD/pdf/journals/ed_lead/el201603_take-aways.pdf.

Additional Readings

- "Believing and Achieving," an issue brief posted by the Center for Comprehensive School Reform and Improvement, integrates an overview of research on teacher efficacy with a discussion of educators' responsibility for student learning: www.centerforcsri.org/files/ centerissueBriefJan07.pdf.
- "Teacher Efficacy: What Is It and Does It Matter" is a very short research report by the National Association for Elementary School Principals. Author Nancy Poetheroe does a superb job explaining the link between teacher efficacy and student learning. Check it out at www.naesp.org/ resources/1/Principal/2008/M-Jp42.pdf.
- In *Teaching in the Fast Lane: How to Create Active Learning Experiences,* author Suzy Pepper Rollins explains how to balance autonomy and structure in an active classroom.

Endnotes

1. Shulman, L. S. (1986). Those who understand: Knowledge growth in teaching. *Educational Researcher, 15*(2), 4–14.
2. Shulman, L. S. (1987). Knowledge and teaching: Foundations of a new reform. *Harvard Educational Review, 57*(1), 1–22. (p. 8)
3. Argyris, C., & Schon, D. A. (1974). *Theory in practice: Increasing professional effectiveness.* San Francisco: Jossey-Bass.
4. Argyris, C. (1976). Single-loop and double-loop models in research on decision making. *Administrative Science Quarterly, 21*(3), 363–375.
5. Schon, D. (1983). *The reflective practitioner.* New York: Basic Books.
6. Nuthall, G. (2004). Relating classroom teaching to student learning: A critical analysis of why research has failed to bridge the theory-practice gap. *Harvard Educational Review, 74*(3), 273–306.

7. Haberman, M. (2002). Selecting Star Teachers for children and youth in poverty. *Phi Delta Kappan, 76*(10), 777–781. (p. 780)

8. Haberman (2002, pp. 779–780).

9. Haberman, M. (1985). Can common sense effectively guide the behavior of beginning teachers? *Journal of Teacher Education, 36*(6), 32–35.

10. Haberman (2002, p. 780).

11. *Lifelong learning* definition, Wikipedia.

12. Knowles, M. S. (1975). *Self-directed learning: A guide for learners and teachers*. New York: Association Press.

13. Knowles (1975).

14. Garrison, D. R. (1997). Self-directed learning: Toward a comprehensive model. *Adult Education Quarterly, 48*(1), 18–33.

15. Every Student Succeeds Act (ESSA) of 2015, Pub. L. No. 114–95 (2015).

16. Smylie, M. A. (2014). Teacher evaluation and the problem of professional development. *Mid-Western Educational Researcher, 26*(2).

17. Kaplan, S. (1987). The teacher as a learner. In G. L. Bissex & R. H. Bullock (Eds.), *Seeing for ourselves: Case study research by teachers of writing* (pp. 41–58). Portsmouth, NH: Heinemann.

18. Dweck, C. S. (2016). *Mindset, the new psychology of success: How we can learn to fulfill our potential*. New York: Random House.

19. Easton, L. B. (2008, June). From professional development to professional learning. *Phi Delta Kappan, 89*(10), 755–761.

20. Desimone L. (2009). How can we best measure teacher's professional development and its effects on teachers and students? *Educational Researcher, 38*(3), 181–199.

21. Darling-Hammond, L. (1998). Teacher learning that supports student learning. *Educational Leadership, 55*(5), 6–11. (p. 10)

22. Blank, R. K. (2013). What research tells us: Common characteristics of professional learning that leads to student achievement. *Journal of Staff Development, 34*(1), 50–53.

23. Darling-Hammond, L., Hyler, M. E., & Gardner, M. (2017). *Effective professional development*. Palo Alto, CA: Learning Policy Institute. Retrieved from https://learningpolicyinstitute.org/sites/default/files/product-files/Effective_Teacher_Professional_Development_REPORT.pdf

24. National Staff Development Council. (2001). *Council standards for staff development* (Revised). Oxford, OH: Author. Retrieved from www.gtlcenter.org/sites/default/files/docs/pa/3_PDPartnershipsandStandards/NSDCStandards_No.pdf

25. National Staff Development Council (2001).

26. Garet, M. S., Wayne, A. J., Stancavage, F., Taylor, J., Eaton, M., Walters, K., Song, M., Brown, S., Hurlburt, S., Zhu, P., Sepanik, S., & Doolittle, F. (2011). Middle school mathematics professional development impact study: Findings after the second year of implementation. NCEE 2011-4024. *National Center for Education Evaluation and Regional Assistance*. Retrieved from http://files.eric.ed.gov/fulltext/ED519922.pdf

27. Garet et al. (2011).

28. Parise, L. M., & Spillane, J. P. (2010). Teacher learning and instructional change: How formal and on-the-job learning opportunities predict change in elementary school teachers' practice. *The Elementary School Journal, 110*(3), 323–346.

29. Jensen, B., Sonnemann, J., Roberts-Hull, K. N, & Hunter, A. (2016). *Beyond professional development: Professional learning in high-performing systems.* Washington, DC: National Center on Education and the Economy. Retrieved from www.ncee.org/wp-content/uploads/2015/08/BeyondPDWeb.pdf 9 (p. 3)

30. Haberman (2002, pp. 779–780).

31. Darling-Hammond, L. (1998). Teacher learning that supports student learning. *Educational Leadership, 55*(5), 6–11. (p. 9)

32. Dewey, J. (1997). *How we think: A restatement of the relation of reflective thinking to the educative process.* Mineola, NY: Dover.

33. Dewey (1997), cited in Rodriguez, S. J. (2008), Teachers' attitudes towards reflective teaching: Evidence in a professional development program (para. 16). Retrieved from www.scielo.org.co/scielo.php?script=sci_arttext&pid=S1657--07902008000200006

34. Beyer, L. E., & Zeichner, K. (1987/2018). Teacher education in cultural context: Beyond reproduction. In T. Popewitz (Ed.), *Critical studies in teacher education* (pp. 298–334). New York: Routledge; Brownlee, L. J., & Schraw, G. (2017). Reflection and reflexivity: A focus on higher order thinking in teachers' personal epistemologies. In G. Schraw, J. L. Brownlee, L. Olafson, & M. Vanderveldt (Eds.), *Teachers' personal epistemologies: Evolving models for transforming practice.* Charlotte, NC: Information Age Publishing; Feucht, F. C., Lunn Brownlee, J., & Schraw, G. (2017). Moving beyond reflection: Reflexivity and epistemic cognition in teaching and teacher education. *Educational Psychologist, 52*(4), 234–241; Isik-Ercan, Z., & Perkins, K. (2017). Reflection for meaning and action as an engine for professional development across multiple early childhood teacher education contexts. *Journal of Early Childhood Teacher Education, 38*(4), 342–354.; Jamil, F. M., & Hamre, B. K. (2018). Teacher reflection in the context of an online professional development course: Applying principles of cognitive science to promote teacher learning. *Action in Teacher Education, 40*(2), 220–236.

35. Feucht et al. (2017); Isik-Ercan & Perkins (2017); Jamil & Hamre (2018).

36. Beyer & Zeichner (1987/2018); Brownlee & Schraw (2017).

37. Brownlee & Schraw (2017).

38. Finlay, L. (2008). Reflecting on reflective practice. *Practice-based Professional Learning Centre, 52,* 1–27. https://pdfs.semanticscholar.org/c128/691f2615de873dfe544fcb5dc902fe812675.pdf (p. 1)

39. Schon (1983).

40. National Board for Professional Teaching Standards. (2002). *What teachers should know and be able to do.* Arlington, VA: Author. Retrieved from www.nbpts.org/sites/default/files/what_teachers_should_know.pdf

41. Rodríguez (2008).

42. Moon, J. (2003). *Learning journals and logs: Reflective diaries*. Exeter, UK: Center for Teaching and Learning. Retrieved from http://racma.edu.au/index.php?option=com_docman&task=doc_view&gid=216 (p. 3)

43. Dewey (1997, p. 9).

44. Canning, C. (1991). What teachers say about reflection. *Educational Leadership, 48*(6), 18–21.

45. Canning (1991, p. 19).

46. Hayden, H. E., & Chiu, M. M. (2015). Reflective teaching via a problem exploration–teaching adaptations–resolution cycle: A mixed methods study of preservice teachers' reflective notes. *Journal of Mixed Methods Research, 9*(2), 133–153.

47. Haigh, N. (2000). Teaching teachers about reflection and ways of reflecting. *Waikato Journal of Education, 6,* 87–97.

48. Hatton, N., & Smith, D. (1995). Reflection in teacher education: Towards definition and implementation. *Teaching and Teacher Education, 11*(1), 33–49.

49. Kolb, D. A. (1984). *Experiential learning: Experience as the source of learning and development*. Englewood Cliffs, NJ: Prentice Hall.

50. Gibbs, G. (1988). *Learning by doing: A guide to teaching and learning methods*. Oxford: Further Education Unit, Oxford Polytechnic.

51. Gibbs (1988).

52. Lee, H. J. (2005). Understanding and assessing preservice teachers' reflective thinking. *Teaching and Teacher Education, 21*(6), 699–715.

4

Approaching Learners
Who Are at Risk

This chapter deals with how teachers approach learners who are at risk—their perceptions of the causes of and cures for students falling behind in basic skills. Star Teachers see poor teaching and rigid curricula as the major causes of unsuccessful learning. Stars are willing to assume personal accountability for their students' learning despite being unable to control all in-school and out-of-school influences on learners and form productive relationships with students to seed educational breakthroughs.

Learning Outcomes

Upon completion of this chapter, you will be able to

- Define *at risk*.
- Identify the behaviors of learners classified as at risk.
- Analyze the ideology or mindset of Star Teachers who teach learners classified as at risk.
- Analyze the various behaviors of Star Teachers who teach learners classified as at risk.
- Assess students' risk factors in your classroom.
- Appraise three keys to building productive teacher-student relationships.

Interstate New Teacher Assessment and Support Consortium (InTASC) Standards

Standard #2: Learning Differences

The teacher uses understanding of individual differences and diverse cultures and communities to ensure inclusive learning environments that enable each learner to meet high standards.

Standard #7: Planning for Instruction

The teacher plans instruction that supports every student in meeting rigorous learning goals by drawing upon knowledge of content areas, curriculum, cross-disciplinary skills, and pedagogy, as well as knowledge of learners and the community context.

★ ★ ★ ★ ★ ★ ★ ★ ★ ★ ★

Defining *At Risk*

There will come a time in our teaching career when we will question our professional competence because we have students who appear to be unmotivated and disengaged from learning. "I am hopelessly stuck!" we say to ourselves. "Some of my students just can't get turned on to learning. I'm worried about not being able to provide them with what they need." Learners who are at risk present educators with the greatest challenges in the classroom. It is heartbreaking to witness some students struggle with course concepts or appear psychologically absent from class while others are whizzing successfully through their assignments. We often look at our failing students and wring our hands in despair, waiting for a **breakthrough** in these students' academic lives. We can all identify a student who is not experiencing success in our classroom and who we fear is at risk of failing. Who is the student at risk in your classroom?

★ 4-1 ─────────────────────────────

The term at risk *evokes a great deal of emotions and imagery. If you were to draw a portrait of an at-risk learner, what would he or she look like? What conversations do the at-risk students in your classroom have with their peers and with you? What behavior do they exhibit in school?*

In their book *At-Risk Students: Reaching and Teaching Them,* Richard Sagor and Jonas Cox describe **at-risk students** as those who are unlikely to graduate on schedule with the skills and self-esteem needed to exercise meaningful options in the areas of employment, leisure, civic affairs, and both inter- and intrapersonal relationships.[1]

Haberman considers *at risk* to be a dangerous label used too often to imply that students are somehow deficient or culturally deprived.[2] And because those placed in the at-risk category are disproportionately students of color, the term has become a not-so-clever euphemism for referring to black or Latinx students. Haberman's research predates the work of Sagor and Cox and describes at-risk students as those who

- Have low academic scores;
- Become teenage parents;
- Are frequently absent;
- Have moved frequently;
- Are from low socioeconomic backgrounds;
- Are frequently disciplined or suspended;
- Come from fragile homes;
- Have language struggles;
- Are victims of crime, physical abuse, and chemical addiction;
- Are of color;
- Have sensitive physical, mental, or emotional conditions; and/or
- Come from non-English-speaking backgrounds.[3]

Both Sagor and Cox's and Haberman's definitions of at-risk students are broad and encompass all types of learners, and new scholarship confirms that students categorized as at risk come from every geographic region, socioeconomic level, ethnic background, language competency, mental health identity, and ability group.[4] The causes that give rise to learners being considered at risk can surface within and outside the school environment. Students are not born at risk but **classified as at risk**[5] due to circumstances thrust upon them over which they often have no control. Consider the following statistics related to **in-school risk factors**:

- Thirteen percent of the school-age population has some form of a learning disability.[6]
- Nearly one in five students enter school with an undiagnosed learning disability.[7]
- Black and Latinx children are overrepresented in the learning disability category.[8]
- One in five students speak a language other than English at home.[9]
- Gifted learners are underidentified[10]—especially learners of color, who are underrepresented in gifted education classrooms.[11] As a result, gifted learners may not receive the support they need in mainstream classrooms and thus not reach their full potential, leading them to sometimes drop out of school.[12]
- High-quality preK education increases students' readiness to learn, making them less susceptible to academic failure.[13]
- One out of every three school-age students is physically, verbally, or emotionally bullied in school,[14] creating a barrier to learning.[15]
- Students of color are more likely to be taught in poor schools with little resources and a low-level curriculum,[16] creating a nationwide achievement gap between the haves and have-nots.[17]

In addition to these in-school factors, many **out-of-school risk factors** exist that, although not expressly academic, indirectly affect student learning (see Figure 4.1). Here are some examples:

- Thirteen million children live in households without enough nutritious food, and 3.9 million of them live with the threat of food scarcity.[18]
- One in five school-age students live in severe poverty[19] and are thus more likely to experience cognitive lags.[20]
- Students with attendance problems may feel disconnected from the school, making them highly vulnerable to failure.[21]
- Students whose families move residences often, including kids from military families, are at an increased risk of falling behind their peers and dropping out of school.[22]

Figure 4.1 **Risk Factors Affecting Student Achievement**

In-School Risk Factors	**Out-of-School Risk Factors**
Low academic scores	Frequent absenteeism
Low scores in basic skills	Frequent residential moves or homelessness
Psychological challenges	Little to no parental or caretaker involvement
Physical challenges	Physical or chemical abuse
Special learning needs	Being an adjudicated delinquent
English spoken as a second language	Low socioeconomic status
Low PreK education or school readiness	Identifying as an ethnic minority
Bullying	Poor nutrition or food scarcity
A poor attitude toward authority	
A poor attitude toward schooling	

Students categorized as being at risk of academic failure are less likely to be fulfilled economically, socially, and personally over time. The economic costs to society of students' lack of preparedness are in the billions of dollars and go to such social services as drug and alcohol rehabilitation, support programs for victims of abuse, psychological services, medical support, incarceration, unemployment compensation, skills retraining, and more.[23]

Ten Characteristics of Discouraged Learners

Teachers often take preemptive measures to identify vulnerable learners. Notes from a prior year's teacher, state achievement tests, and report cards can offer some insight as to which students may be at risk for academic failure. Because student engagement drives student learning, it is the most important sign to look for in students, though the clues may be subtle. Sagor and Cox offer the following 10 traits and actions of disengaged learners that can help you spot them in your class:

1. They are low in self-confidence and have a deeply held sense of personal impotency, helplessness, and lack of self-worth.

2. They avoid school, contact, and classes because it is all deemed as too demanding and/or threatening, or because it is confusing and unresponsive to their needs.

3. They do not have much faith in adult figures who have repeatedly failed them. In order to gain the trust of these mistrusting young people, you must be consistent in their lives and make no promises that you cannot keep.

4. They have no long-term vision for their future due to life circumstances. Effective teachers must find a way to show the long term consequences of short-term assignments.

5. They are behind others in academic skills by middle school. It is by this time that they have lost faith in the school system and in themselves. Their reading, writing, and math abilities are deficient, and they have come to see themselves as unteachable rather than unskilled. The real tragedy is that many adults see them that way too.

6. They may come from unstable homes where the caretakers often share related characteristics: low skilled, low self-confidence, distrustful of institutions, avoidance, suspicious of the future. Teachers who are able to reach these learners have to show real empathy, caring, and respect for the students' home lives.

7. Discouraged learners often have unhealthy peer relationships. The attempts to pull them away from their peers often results in pushing them closer together. For discouraged learners, a healthy self-concept grows as their sense of the future enlarges, and not as a result of disapproval of their friends.

8. They are irritated with the predictable pattern of the classroom routine that they understand to be mundane "drill and kill" activities. Star Teachers capture these learners' short attention spans by providing productive lessons that also help learners overcome academic deficiencies.

9. Discouraged learners have a "practical" learning style. They express themselves best through oral and not through written means.

10. Lastly, discouraged learners do not see a relationship between effort and achievement. Instead, they perceive accomplishment as

occurring by chance or ease of the task. They are "externalizers"— learners who do not have control over their destiny. When they do poorly, it is the result of an impossible task, bad luck, a bad day, or an adult who refuses to help them.[24]

Too many teachers are stymied in their attempts to support at-risk learners, trying approaches that prove ineffective time and time again. The intimidating mission before us as teachers is to create classrooms that will provide at-risk learners with opportunities to become as engaged as other students in class. This task may be easier said than done; nevertheless, Haberman maintains that Star Teachers have the mindset and know-how to help at-risk learners.

★ 4-2

Brianna was diagnosed with a perceptual impairment, a learning disability, when she was in 2nd grade. This learning disability prevents learners from fully understanding content and requires that they develop comprehension strategies. As a result of the learning disability, Brianna is falling behind in every subject except science and is at risk of not being promoted with her classmates.

In language arts class, other students are busily polishing their scripts and practicing their dialogues for next week's oral presentation. Despite the flurry of activity, Brianna takes refuge in her phone and easily fades into the background. The teacher notices that Brianna is yet again withdrawn, but he is focused on helping students fine-tune their projects.

When Brianna arrives at science class, the teacher greets each student and compliments Brianna on the organization of her report on unsung inventors. Brianna eagerly dons a lab coat, which indicates that she's scientist of the week. Brianna's science teacher has introduced her to a computer program that helps build science vocabulary and often asks her to explain passages from the readings in impromptu walkabouts. These learning strategies have helped raise Brianna's scores nearly three letter grades. Explain why you think Brianna is succeeding in science class and struggling in English class.

Teacher Mindset: At Promise Versus at Risk

Teachers' perceptions of at-risk students are the most powerful predictors of student success. Those who perceive the student, parents, and community to be responsible for a students' academic failure embrace a **deficit ideology.**[25] These teachers' perceptions often center on the learner's inability to avoid or overcome at-risk behavior. Teachers who believe success is primarily controlled by the learner are **blaming the victim.**[26] Star Teachers, by contrast, believe that the school, the curriculum, and their own instruction are equally to blame when students don't succeed. Stars flip the label "at risk" on its head and see their students as "**at promise,**"[27] focusing on their potential rather than their circumstances.

Research shows that educators are unbending on the notion that they are not answerable for students' lack of success[28] and often transfer blame for academic failure to family background.[29] This lack of **accountability** is disturbing because teachers relinquish responsibility for teaching at-risk learners due to factors beyond the student's control. To lay the blame for students being categorized as at risk is to forfeit our responsibility as teachers.

When asked to explain the large number of students at risk of failing or dropping out, pre-Stars will go through the same litany of causes as deficit researchers: dysfunctional families, drugs, violence, gangs, lack of health care, poor housing, unemployment, crime, lack of faith in education, lack of role models, physical problems. Pre-Star Teachers do not criticize schools or teachers. They see shortcomings in the victim, his or her family, and community, and they see no need to change what they do in class. These teachers justify their perceptions with such comments as "What am I supposed to do about hunger or child abuse?" or "I'm a teacher, not a nurse or a social worker."

The ideology of Star Teachers is quite different. They know about all the outside factors that place students at risk and the ways in which curricula and teaching methods do the same, and their focus is on the latter. They do not blame the victim, but rather the damaged school structures (irrelevant curriculum, boring teachers, authoritative methods) that keep the student from learning. This is more than a different perspective; it is a different paradigm. Research suggests that the defining question should not be "Is the child at risk of failing?" but rather "Is the school at risk of failing the child?"[30] Star Teachers say, "Look, I exert the most control over what and how I teach. I should be able to find ways of involving my students in learning no matter what their out-of-school lives are like. That's my job—to find activities and projects that turn them on to learning." This does not mean that Star Teachers are insensitive to the family problems and social forces that negatively affect learners, just that they focus on and accept responsibility for students' classroom learning.

The Importance of Productive Teacher-Student Relationships

Many of us can fondly recall special teachers whose classrooms we couldn't wait to visit. These are the educators who remembered our favorite hobbies or specific contributions to the class and who could sense when we were not having a good day. All learners are hardwired to interact socially, and students who are classified as at risk in the classrooms of pre-Stars become at-promise students in the classroom of Stars thanks to positive teacher-student relationships.

There is little debate that students who have a rapport with their teachers are more motivated to learn. It's simple: when students feel acknowledged and affirmed, they are more likely to engage with lessons. In "Student-Teacher Relationships Are Everything," James Ford explains the significance of building rapport in the classroom:

> The relational part of teaching may very well be its most underrated aspect. It simply does not get the respect it deserves. Teachers don't respect relationship-building as an important part of their praxis. When teachers are good at building relationships with students, the skill is seen more as cover for a lack of content knowledge or wherewithal to instruct with rigor.[31]

Nurturing personal bonds with students helps us to better understand how learners function and to further individualize curriculum. Results of a review of 99 studies on teacher-student relationships covering a 20-year period indicate that stronger relationships have a positive effect on student engagement and acheivement.[32] Another study, this one of 690 2nd and 3rd graders classified as at risk, found that students' perceptions of their relationships with teachers were closely associated with motivation and reading and math competence.[33] In positive teacher-student relationships, students are willing to share their ups and downs, ask questions without being made to feel as if their questions are insignificant, and experience a broad collection of positive outcomes ranging from classroom happiness[34] and decreased stress[35] to greater self-efficacy.[36]

Achieving positive teacher-student relationships with learners categorized as at risk is not an easy task, but it is a vital one. For Stars, the goal of these relationships is academic improvement; they understand that success in school can mean the difference between a positive life path (a satisfying career, strong relationships, high self-esteem) and a negative one (teenage pregnancy, dropping out, chemical abuse). Stars understand that short-term academic failure has cumulative effects on learners as they progress from one grade to the next[37] as well as on their long-term life prospects.[38]

Three Keys to Building Productive Teacher-Student Relationships

There is no shortage of advice available for teachers on building better relationships with learners, but too many fall short by being mostly teacher-centered. The focus is almost always on learning experiences, classroom approaches, interests, and objectives of teachers rather than students. The goal is for class to run smoothly without interruptions to teacher management.

By contrast, Stars use student-centered relationship-building strategies that focus on the interests and individual traits of each learner. These teachers don't rely on one-size-fits-all solutions; they do not approach a student who is being bullied, for example, as they would a student who struggles with English. The most successful student-centered relationships include the following three key characteristics that can be tailored to meet individual students' needs: (1) authentic empathy, (2) high expectations, and (3) a sense that "we're all in this together" (see Figure 4.2).

Authentic Empathy

Students who are classified as at risk wrestle with many in- and out-of-school issues that affect their ability to learn, and we need to understand their unique challenges. This requires a degree of **empathy**—the ability to express concern for and adopt the perspective of another. Empathetic teachers can stand in their learners' shoes and see classroom challenges from their point of view. Star Teachers use empathy to improve students' sense of belonging and to encourage their interest in classroom activities. They understand that some students may be too hungry to focus on their math lesson, vicariously take on the frustration of the child who struggles with a learning disability, or consider how bullying can rob the battered child of self-esteem.

Figure 4.2 **Keys to Building Productive Teacher-Student Relationships**

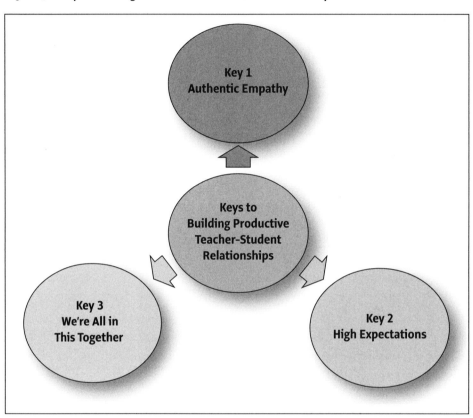

★ 4-3
Share a classroom experience of a breakthrough with a learner classified as at risk.

Many empathetic teachers cannot move beyond wringing their hands in pity for their students. Teachers who transmit **authentic empathy** seek instructional adaptations and support mechanisms to help learners surmount academic barriers. As educators, we must employ empathetic strategies that go beyond feeling sorry for our learners and help them to be successful on their own accord—to exhibit **resilience** by learning to swiftly rebound from adversity. Students who are classified as at risk must be encouraged to maneuver around their circumstances and take ownership of their own learning and futures despite the unfair hand they have been dealt. Star Teachers convey to learners that the factors placing them at risk *are not their fault* and act as students' partners in achieving academic success.

In an ASCD InService blog post, Bryan Harris offers the following strategies for helping students classified as at risk become resilient:

1. **Avoid labeling children as "high risk" or "at risk."** Instead, refer to high-risk environments or situations that present challenging conditions. All children are capable of great things given the appropriate support, and they tend to live up to or down to the expectations we set for them.

2. **The person who delivers the program is more important than the program itself.** There are numerous effective programs available that are designed to increase resiliency in students and loads of research about the effect of teaching students the skills and attitudes of resiliency. However, personal relationships and connections are the foundation of all effective programs.

3. **Sometimes the apple does fall far from the tree.** Students facing challenging situations or difficult home lives need to understand and believe that they can succeed. They need to know, through stories, examples, and role models, that with the right work ethic and commitment they can be successful. They need not be bound solely by their environment, background, or surroundings.

4. **View children not as problems to be fixed but as individuals with strengths, dreams, and opinions.** Traditionally schools have been places where the focus has been on identification, remediation, and correction of *deficits*. Indeed, schools need to know where students are lacking and work hard to help students master important skills and content. However, we also need to use the strengths, abilities, and interests of students for them to truly thrive and overcome adverse situations.

5. **Students must be actively involved in the life of the school and in their own learning.** Resiliency isn't developed being passive. Students need to connect to the people, the content, and the overall learning environment in order to thrive. Challenge students to track their own learning, create goals, and connect to other students with similar interests. In addition, all students should be exposed to challenging curriculum and high expectations.

6. **The stuff of school can be cold and impersonal.** The curriculum, the overreliance on testing, the schedules, and even the instruction can sometimes lead children to believe that school is something that is done *to them*. Take time to make personal connections with students, to laugh with them, and share stories to make school warm, fun, and personal.

7. **Resilience isn't constant in any of our lives.** Resilience tends to ebb and flow throughout our lives based on current situations and challenges. We all have times in our lives where things are going well and times when things are tough. The resilient person is the one who can bounce back, learn, and thrive through the tough times.[39]

Consider the following scenario. David is a quiet 6th grader at risk of failing due to his poor attitude about schooling. Mr. Sachs spends time getting to know about David's background and learns that his itinerant foster-home life is probably a huge factor influencing his outlook. Mr. Sachs imagines what it must be like to pack all your belongings in a trash bag and move on to your next foster family in the dead of night. He refuses to give up on David. This doesn't mean he lets him off the hook, but rather that he insists David join in every lesson and commit to learning. After nearly 22 days and endless requests to engage with his peers during lessons, David finally engages in the classroom activities and completes the makeup assignments that Mr. Sachs created to keep him from falling behind.

Despite the many obstacles (high-stakes testing, large class sizes, extra school duties, etc.),[40] Stars transmit their concern for students classified as at risk and reinforce it through actions aimed at empowering student resilience and, in turn, improving academic performance.

High Expectations

In the late 1960s, scholars Robert Rosenthal and Lenore Jacobson released a study of nearly 300 elementary school students titled "Pygmalion in the Classroom." When the researchers told teachers in the study that their lower-achieving students were actually "growth spurters" with high IQs, the teachers tended to offer them more support, attention, feedback, and encouragement. Data from tests taken before and after the study showed that the students taught by these teachers experienced a rise in IQ scores of between 10 and 30 points.[41]

Rosenthal and Jacobson's study demonstrates a "Pygmalion effect" or **self-fulfilling prophecy**—an academic prediction that proves itself to be true—and remains a flashpoint in the field.[42] Two more recent studies have confirmed the study's findings, concluding that teacher expectations can affect students' current[43] and future academic achievement[44] and may strongly predict college completion.[45] These findings build on decades of research on the influence of teacher expectations on student performance (see Figure 4.3).

Here's an example. Ms. Reynolds has a diverse group of 28 students in her 10th grade English language arts class split 50/50 between white students and students of color. Five students speak English as a second language and two have an Individualized Educational Plan (IEP). Through her expectations and interactions, Ms. Reynolds demands that all students try their best on writing assignments. If they don't, Ms. Reynolds spends time with them, forcing them to write, rewrite, and then write some more until they achieve mastery. This is not a strategy Ms. Reynolds reserves for the English-only speakers or the students whose parents can afford private tutors; she employs it with every learner in her class. The learners who are identified as at risk in Ms. Reynolds's class detect that she cares for them and is giving them the support they need to reach her extraordinarily high expectations.

Figure 4.3 **Self-Fulfilling Prophecy**

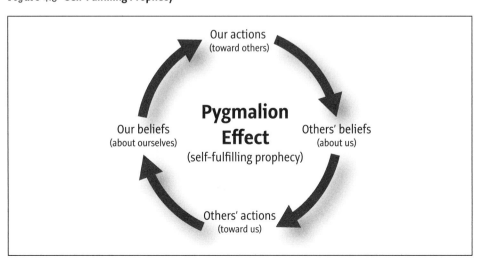

Source: Adapted from "Pygmalion in the Classroom," by R. Rosenthal and L. Jacobson, 1968, *The Urban Review, 3*(1), pp. 16–20.

A Sense That "We're All in This Together"

According to Haberman, Star Teachers "consciously create opportunities to demonstrate to the students 'this is your class, your work, your effort. Whatever happens here that is good and praiseworthy is something that you make happen. I need you and we need you.'"[46] He continues: "The goal of learner independence leads [Star Teachers] to use coaching as their basic means of teaching, and coaches do not merely serve as sources of knowledge."[47] Students are naturally curious people, so why do many who are classified as at risk seem indifferent to learning? The fact is that learning new skills and content is often just not fun for students. Every assignment feels like a burden that they'll never unload, part of a mind-numbing and seemingly unending routine of inflexible curricula. Star Teachers help learners manage these students' feelings of being overwhelmed or bored by nurturing a climate of collaborative learning, incorporating creative ways to share the learning load. Scholars like Sonia Nieto[48] and Nel Noddings[49] advocate creating a classroom environment where students feel unity and a cooperative spirit. A sense of community encourages learners to form positive emotional bonds with their teacher and peers, which in turn improves their attitude and motivation for learning. Community-building strategies include

- The jigsaw approach to student assignments, where the workload is divided among students or teams.
- Visiting or calling students' families with good reports or before issues arise.
- Creating a family atmosphere with inviting work spaces for both individual and group work.
- Making celebrations (of holidays, birthdays, etc.) a key feature of the classroom.
- Modeling respect with an uplifting communication style and acknowledging when students are respectful. For example: "Jaqueline, I just heard you offer some of your paper and pens to April. I appreciate your generosity and I know that April does too. You are a great co-learner, and I am glad you are in this class." This simple and explicit affirmation highlights a student action, encourages peer support, and models praise language. Stars know that other learners are in earshot of their comments.

- Showing up in students' community or extracurricular events. It means a lot to a student for a teacher to attend his or her chess game or a volleyball match. The simple gesture shows that you care, which can ignite engagement in your classroom.
- Knowing students' likes and dislikes.
- Making learning joyful. Goodlad[50] and Wolk[51] both have proposed that joy is missing in our schools. Many students unplug from learning because their classrooms are joyless spaces. By contrast, the classrooms of Star Teachers are happy environments that students clamor to get into and don't want to leave. When students are happily engrossed in learning to the point that everything else can wait, they are experiencing **flow**.[52]

Mrs. Toler has a special bond with her students who are classified as at risk. They know that she will use her lunch break to review basic skills with them, and they like that she assigns peer tutors and organizes her class in learning communities with clearly defined roles and accountability measures. Michael, a normally apathetic learner in his other classes, finds support and sanctuary in Mrs. Toler's class, where everyone is engaged and teams up to conquer the classroom activities. When Mrs. Toler, who teaches math, follows up with Michael on his spelling test, she signals that his entire education is important to her. "We're in this together" is not just a clever adage, but a mindset proven to enrichen classroom relationships and stimulate student learning.

Summary

How teachers approach at-risk learners is the most powerful predictor of their effectiveness and staying power. Both in- and out-of-school factors contribute to students being classified as at risk and test the abilities of the most qualified of teachers. Star Teachers understand that students haven't asked for the factors that have placed them at risk and assume responsibility for providing them with engaging learning opportunities and helping them surmount academic obstacles. Star Teachers also know to establish strong relationships with students and understand the three keys to doing so: profound empathy, high expectations, and a perception that "we're all in this together."

Key Words

accountability	at promise	at-risk students
authentic empathy	blaming the victim	breakthrough
classified as at risk	deficit ideology	empathy
flow	in-school academic risk factors	out-of-school risk factors
resilience	self-fulfilling prophecy	

Extension Exercises

1. Create an action plan for a student classified as at risk using Figure 4.1 as your starting point. Please feel free to add your own list of risk factors if appropriate. List each risk factor and note if it is a low- or high-risk factor. Next, identify instruction that could be used to improve achievement and tactics to improve your relationship with the student, including clear goals and implementation dates. Include prospective community resources that might help to stem or decrease the risks. Use the following list as a guide to create and complete your action plan.

   Action Plan
   - Student name:
   - Risk factor:
   - Low or high risk:
   - In- or out-of-school factor:
   - Teaching tactics:
   - Relationship tactics:
   - School resources:
   - Communities resources:

2. What are the duties in the school environment constraining teachers from conveying empathy to learners? Is it possible for teachers to have too much or too little empathy? Explain your response.
3. Find an online empathy test from a credible website, and complete it. What is your empathy score, and what does it convey about your ability to relate to learners classified as at risk?

4. Identify four key strategies you can use in your classroom to improve a sense of community.

5. List and briefly describe five ways students are rewarded and punished in your classroom. Next, analyze whether these approaches build or tear down the relationship you have with them. If an approach is not a relationship builder, sketch out an alternative approach and discuss it with a peer.

6. Examine one of your lesson plans and identify how you address each of the three relationship-building approaches discussed in this chapter. Overall, how are your relationships with motivated students and learners classified as at risk? Use the following list as a guide to create and complete your self-assessment.

   • Teacher:
   • Grade level:
   • Subject matter:
   • Number of students:
   • Number of students classified as at risk:
   • Lesson objective(s):
   • Key 1. Empathy:
   • Key 2. High Expectations:
   • Key 3. Purpose:

Going Further

Web Resources

   • The 40-year mission of the Communities in Schools organization is well worth reviewing. The group is a "school-based staff partner with teachers to identify challenges students face in class or at home and coordinate with community partners to bring outside resources inside schools. From immediate needs like food or clothing to more complex ones like counseling or emotional support, we do whatever it takes to help students succeed." Learn more about how to join this great cause at www.communitiesin-schools.org/.

   • Service learning is a great pedagogical strategy to support learners classified as at risk. Many lesson plans and programs are available online but the National Youth Leadership Council (NYLC) leads the way in recognizing the contributions that young people are making to change the world and to help prepare them and their adult mentors in reaching their goals. To learn more, visit http://servicelearningconference.org/2017/about.

- YouthChange.org offers innovative online and live professional development opportunities to help engineer breakthroughs for learners classified as at risk. Check them out at www.youthchg.com/products-page/webinar/teaching-at-risk-students-online-professional-development-class/.
- The Center for Research on Education, Diversity, & Excellence (CREDE) created five standards based on an exhaustive literature review on effective instruction for diverse populations across disciplines and grade levels. The standards apply to all students and are proven to demonstrate best practices for supporting learners classified as at risk. Learn more at http://manoa.hawaii.edu/coe/credenational/the-crede-five-standards-for-effective-pedagogy-and-learning/.

Video

- Watch the 13-minute film *Room 26* to see Mr. Smith, a Star Teacher, work with learners who have been classified as at risk due to socioeconomic issues yet are thriving academically. To order a copy of the film, visit www.habermanfoundation.org/Room26.aspx.

Additional Readings

- For great teaching tips, check out the book *Classroom Strategies to Help At-Risk Students* by David R. Snow (ASCD, 2014). The book synthesizes recent research into six effective strategies for teaching at-risk students: whole-class instruction, cognitively oriented instruction, small groups, tutoring, peer tutoring, and computer-assisted instruction.
- Often disadvantaged students are not exposed to the experiences that ignite their intellectual development. In *After-School Prevention Programs for At-Risk Students: Promoting Engagement and Academic Success* (Springer, 2014), Elaine Clanton Harpine shares how after-school opportunities have positive effects on academic performance and social behaviors as well as offering enrichment activities for students classified as at risk.

- In *Fostering Resilient Learners: Strategies for Creating a Trauma-Sensitive Classroom*, Kristin Souers and Pete Hall (2016) explore an urgent and growing issue—childhood trauma—and its profound effect on learning and teaching.

Endnotes

1. Sagor, R., & Cox, J. (2004). *At-risk students: Reaching and teaching them*. New York: Eye on Education.

2. Haberman, M. (1995). *Star Teachers of children in poverty*. Indianapolis, IN: Kappa Delta Pi. (p. 48)

3. Haberman (1995).

4. Armstrong, T. (2018). *Multiple intelligences in the classroom* (4th ed.). Alexandria, VA: ASCD; Domitrovich, C. E., Durlak, J. A., Staley, K. C., & Weissberg, R. P. (2017). Social-emotional competence: An essential factor for promoting positive adjustment and reducing risk in school children. *Child Development, 88*(2), 408–416.; Martin, J. L., & Beese, J. A. (2017). Talking back at school: Using the literacy classroom as a site for resistance to the school-to-prison pipeline and recognition of students labeled "at risk." *Urban Education, 52*(10), 1204–1232.; Rishel, T., & Miller, P. C. (2018). Embracing possibilities for English learners: Inclusion, comfort, and care. Tomlinson, C. A. (2014). *The differentiated classroom: Responding to the needs of all learners*. Alexandria, VA: ASCD.

5. Sanders, M. G. (2001). (Ed.). *Schooling students placed at risk: Research, policy, and practice in the education of poor minority adolescents*. New York: Routledge.

6. https://nces.ed.gov/programs/coe/indicator_cgg.asp

7. National Center for Learning Disabilities. (2014). *The state of learning disabilities* (3rd ed.). New York: Author. Retrieved from www.ncld.org/wp-content/uploads/2014/11/2014-State-of-LD.pdf

8. National Center for Learning Disabilities (2014).

9. McCabe, A., Bornstein, M. H., Guerra, A. W., Kuchirko, Y., Paez, M., Tamis-LeMonda, C. S., Cates, C. B., Hirsch-Pasek, K., Melzi, G., Song, L., Golinkoff, R., Hoff, E., & Mendolsohn, A. (2013). Multilingual children: Beyond myths and toward best practices. *Social Policy Report, 27*(4), 1–21.

10. Mann, R. L. (2004). Gifted students with spatial strengths and sequential weaknesses: An overlooked and under-identified population. *Roeper Review, 27*(2), 91–96.

11. Swanson, J. D. (2006). Breaking through assumptions about low-income, minority gifted students. *Gifted Child Quarterly, 50*(1), 11–25.

12. Renzulli, J. S., & Park, S. (2000). Gifted dropouts: The who and the why. *Gifted Child Quarterly, 44*(4), 261–271.

13. Anderson, L. M., Shinn, C., Fullilove, M. T., Scrimshaw, S. C., Fielding, J. E., & Normand, J. (2003). The effectiveness of early childhood development programs: A systematic review. *American Journal of Preventive Medicine, 24*(3), 32–46.

14. Gladden, R. M., Vivolo-Kantor, A. M., Hamburger, M. E., & Lumpkin, C. D. (2014). *Bullying surveillance among youths: Uniform definitions for public health and recommended data elements, Version 1.0*. Atlanta: National Center for Injury Prevention and Control, Centers for Disease Control and Prevention, and U.S. Department of Education.

15. Rothon, C., Head, J., Klineberg, E., & Stansfeld, S. (2011). Can social support protect bullied adolescents from adverse outcomes? A prospective study on the effects of bullying on the educational achievement and mental health of adolescents at secondary schools in East London. *Journal of Adolescence, 34*(3), 579–588.

16. Goldhaber, D., Lavery, L., & Theobald, R. (2015). Uneven playing field? Assessing the teacher quality gap between advantaged and disadvantaged students. *Educational Researcher, 44*(5), 293–307.

17. Reardon, S. F. (2011). The widening academic achievement gap between the rich and the poor: New evidence and possible explanations. In M. Corak (Ed.), *Generational income mobility in North America and Europe*. Cambridge: Cambridge University Press.

18. No Kid Hungry. (2016). *Hunger devastates children: Facts on childhood hunger in America*. Retrieved from www.nokidhungry.org/pdfs/Fact_Sheet-2016.pdf

19. Children's Defense Fund. (2016). *Child poverty in America 2015: National analysis*. Retrieved from www.childrensdefense.org/library/data/child-poverty-in-america-2015.pdf

20. Jensen, E. (2009). *Teaching with poverty in mind: What being poor does to kids' brains and what schools can do about it*. Alexandria, VA: ASCD.

21. Aucejo, E. M., & Romano, T. F. (2016). Assessing the effect of school days and absences on test score performance. *Economics of Education Review, 55*, 70–87.

22. Astor, R. A., Jacobson, L., & Benbenishty, R. (2012). *The teacher's guide for supporting students from military families*. New York: Teachers College Press.

23. Marchbanks III, M. P., Blake, J. J., Smith, D., Seibert, A. L., Carmichael, D., Booth, E. A., & Fabelo, T. (2014). More than a drop in the bucket: The social and economic costs of dropouts and grade retentions associated with exclusionary discipline. *Journal of Applied Research on Children: Informing Policy for Children at Risk, 5*(2), 17; Alderman, M. K. (2013). *Motivation for achievement: Possibilities for teaching and learning*. New York: Routledge.

24. Sagor & Cox (2004, pp. 8–10).

25. Valencia, R. R. (1997). Introduction. In R. R. Valencia (Ed.), *The evolution of deficit thinking* (pp. ix–xvii). London: Palmer.

26. Lewis, C. W., James, M., Hancock, S., & Hill-Jackson, V. (2008). Framing African American students' success and failure in urban settings: A typology for change. *Urban Education, 43*(2), 127–153.

27. Boykin, A. W. (2000). The talent development model of schooling: Placing students at promise for academic success. *Journal of Education for Students Placed at Risk (JESPAR), 5*(1–2), 3–25; Franklin, W. (2000). Students at promise and resilient: A historical look at risk. In M. S. Sanders (Ed.), *Schooling students placed at risk: Research, policy, and practice in the education of poor and minority adolescents* (pp. 3–17). Mahwah, NJ: Erlbaum; Stuart, T. S., & Bostrom, C. G. (2003). *Children at promise: 9 principles to help kids thrive in an at-risk world*. San Francisco: Jossey-Bass.

28. Lauermann, F. (2014). Teacher responsibility from the teacher's perspective. *International Journal of Educational Research*, *65*, 75–89.

29. Ullucci, K., & Howard, T. (2015). Pathologizing the poor: Implications for preparing teachers to work in high-poverty schools. *Urban Education*, *50*(2), 170–193.

30. Boykin (2000); Franklin (2000).

31. Ford, J. (2017, January 31). Student-teacher relationships are everything. [Blog post]. Retrieved from http://blogs.edweek.org/teachers/teacher_leader_voices/2017/01/relationships_are_everything.html (para. 3)

32. Klem, A. M., & Connell, J. P. (2004). Relationships matter: Linking teacher support to student engagement and achievement. *Journal of School Health*, *74*(7), 262–273.

33. Hughes, J. N., Wu, J. Y., Kwok, O. M., Villarreal, V., & Johnson, A. Y. (2012). Indirect effects of child reports of teacher-student relationship on achievement. *Journal of Educational Psychology*, *104*(2), 350–365. (p. 350)

34. Baker, J. A. (1999). Teacher-student interaction in urban at-risk classrooms: Differential behavior, relationship quality, and student satisfaction with school. *The Elementary School Journal*, *100*(1), 57–70.

35. Yoon, J. S. (2002). Teacher characteristics as predictors of teacher-student relationships: Stress, negative affect, and self-efficacy. *Social Behavior and Personality: An International Journal*, *30*(5), 485–493.

36. Yoon (2002).

37. Walberg, H. J. (1988). Synthesis of research on time and learning. *Educational Leadership*, *45*(6), 76–85.

38. Hanson, T. L., Austin, G., & Lee-Bayha, J. (2003). *Student health risks, resilience, and academic performance*. Los Alamitos, CA: WestEd.

39. Harris, B. (2012, July 18). Building resiliency in struggling students: 7 ideas from research. [Blog post]. Retrieved from http://inservice.ascd.org/building-resiliency-in-struggling-students-7-key-ideas-from-research/

40. Cooper, B. (2004). Empathy, interaction, and caring: Teachers' roles in a constrained environment. *Pastoral Care in Education*, *22*, 12–21.

41. Rosenthal, R., & Jacobson, L. (1968). Pygmalion in the classroom. *The Urban Review*, *3*(1), 16–20.

42. Merton, R. K. (1948). The self-fulfilling prophecy. *The Antioch Review 8*(2), 193–210.

43. Reyna, C. (2008). Ian is intelligent but Leshaun is lazy: Antecedents and consequences of attributional stereotypes in the classroom. *European Journal of Psychology of Education*, *23*(4), 439–458.

44. Rosenthal, R. (2010). Pygmalion effect. In *The Corsini encyclopedia of psychology* (Vol. 3). Hoboken, NJ: Wiley.

45. Boser, U., Wilhelm, M., & Hanna, R. (2014). *The power of the Pygmalion effect: Teachers' expectations strongly predict college completion*. Washington, DC: Center for American Progress.

46. Haberman (1995, p. 84).

47. Haberman (1995, p. 86).

48. Nieto, S. (2010). *The light in their eyes: Creating multicultural learning communities* (10th ed.). New York: Teachers College Press.

49. Noddings, N. (2005). *The challenge to care in schools.* New York: Teachers College Press.

50. Goodlad, J. I. (2004). *A place called school: Prospects for the future* (2nd ed.). New York: McGraw-Hill.

51. Wolk, S. (2009). Joy in schools. In M. Scherer (Ed.), *Engaging the whole child: Reflections on best practices in learning, teaching, and leadership* (pp. 3–14). Alexandria, VA: ASCD.

52. Wolk (2009, p. 11).

5

Orienting to Learners: Professional Versus Personal

The difference between a professional versus a personal orientation to learners lies in whether teachers use instruction to meet their own or their students' emotional needs. Pre-Stars have a different set of expectations than Star Teachers about relating to children, with the latter exhibiting genuine care and respect for them even when the learners do things they personally regard as despicable.

Learning Outcomes

Upon completion of this chapter, you will be able to

- Identify the differences between professional and personal orientation to learners.
- Recognize and adopt the mindsets of teachers with a professional orientation.
- Recognize and adopt the behaviors of teachers with a professional orientation.
- Evaluate your level of sensitivity and modify it when appropriate to maintain respectful relationships with your students.

Interstate New Teacher Assessment and Support Consortium (InTASC) Standards

Standard #8: Instructional Strategies

The teacher understands and uses a variety of instructional strategies to encourage learners to develop deep understanding of content areas and their connections, and to build skills to apply knowledge in meaningful ways.

Standard #9: Professional Learning and Ethical Practice

The teacher engages in ongoing professional learning and uses evidence to continually evaluate his/her practice, particularly the effects of his/her choices and actions on others (learners, families, other professionals, and the community), and adapts practice to meet the needs of each learner.

★ ★ ★ ★ ★ ★ ★ ★ ★ ★ ★

Defining *Professional and Personal Orientations to Learners*

How did you imagine teaching would be? Many of us dreamed of being a great teacher with well-behaved students hanging on our every word, only for reality to set in as soon as we enter the classroom. Students insult each other, they fight, they disrespect the learning space, and they learn where all our buttons are just so they can push them. In response, many teachers turn to books on classroom management and experiment with every philosophy of discipline under the sun, but still no changes occur. Pre-Star Teachers demonstrate a **personal orientation** to learners that is based solely on having their own emotional needs met. By contrast, Star Teachers maintain a **professional orientation** to learners, remaining respectful and focused on student achievement regardless of student behaviors and attitudes. The former is selfish, whereas the latter is selfless.

A Professional Orientation to Learners

Being a professional teacher is a Sisyphean undertaking. You must engage all students in learning while attending to their many unique learning styles, and you must behave ethically and respectfully even when students, parents, and school administrators do not. As the National Education Association's (NEA) Code of Ethics states,

The educator accepts the responsibility to adhere to the highest ethical standards. The educator recognizes the magnitude of the responsibility inherent in the teaching process. The desire for the respect and confidence of one's colleagues, of students, of parents, and of the members of the community provides the incentive to attain and maintain the highest possible degree of ethical conduct. The Code of Ethics of the Education Profession indicates the aspiration of all educators and provides standards by which to judge conduct.[1]

The Association of American Educators (AAE) Code of Ethics for Educators defines teacher professionalism similarly:

The professional educator strives to create a learning environment that nurtures to fulfillment the potential of all students. The professional educator acts with conscientious effort to exemplify the highest ethical standards. The professional educator responsibly accepts that every child has a right to an uninterrupted education free from strikes or any other work stoppage tactics.[2]

Star Teachers exhibit teacher professionalism by remaining true to their calling, passion, and duty to learners. A study by the Bill & Melinda Gates Foundation found that many people become teachers because they want to "give back" to society.[3] (Other reasons include to make a difference, to work with children, and because they love their particular academic subject.[4]) These individuals understood that although they would not get rich in the profession, they would reap other valuable benefits.

It's this commitment to public service that teachers fall back upon when times get tough and they start questioning why they continue working in bureaucratic schools, spending their own money on school supplies, and receiving little recompense.

For Linda Darling-Hammond, teacher professionalism has the most to do with doing what is best for students.[5] Patricia Phelps agrees: "From my perspective," she writes, "teacher professionalism involves a series of commitments. At the base of these essential commitments is a focus on student learning. Our professionalism is most evident when we make students our first priority."[6]

Don't Take It Personally: The Mindset of Star Teachers with a Professional Orientation

Star Teachers expect to have some students in their classrooms they may not necessarily love—and they also expect to be able to teach them. Star Teachers understand that behavior problems among learners are to be expected in every classroom. It is not a question if students will misbehave or act in undesirable ways, but when. This mentally prepares them to handle discipline issues when they arise. By contrast, pre-Stars expect all students to love them, so when they encounter misbehavior they are too frazzled to respond effectively.

Star Teachers also understand that they must be proactive, not reactive, when it comes to behavioral difficulties in the classroom. This means not taking student mischief personally. Star Teachers don't see student behavior as a reaction to anything they have done, but rather as a symptom of larger problems in the student's life. As Haberman writes, "Whatever the reasons for children's behavior—whether poverty, personality, a handicapping condition, a dysfunctional home, or an abusive environment—classroom teachers are responsible for managing children, seeing that they work together in a confined space for long periods, and ensuring that they learn."[7] Haberman also notes that Star Teachers "use such terms as caring, respect, and concern, and they enjoy the love and the affection of students when it occurs naturally. But they do not regard it as a prerequisite for learning."[8]

Like Tina Turner, Star Teachers ask, "What's love got to do with it?" Stars do not expect to "love" their students; rather, as Haberman writes, "genuine respect is the best way to describe the feelings that Star Teachers have for their students."[9] Star Teachers demonstrate a commitment to their learners regardless of how they feel in the moment. Approaching the learner respectfully is an affirmation of the learner's humanity, communicating through words and deeds "I see you" and "You matter." Teaching doesn't require love, but rather obliges us to remain even-keeled and consistent in our conduct, concerned more with doing what is right than what is popular or makes us feel good. Pre-Star Teachers "cannot and do not discriminate between the love of parents for their children and the love of teachers for their students," writes Haberman. "[Pre-Star Teachers] regard love as a prerequisite for any learning to occur."[10]

Research suggests that as teachers progress in their careers, they worry less about themselves and more about their learners.[11] They regard such love as a prerequisite for learning and believe that it should be reciprocated by students. Consequently, it is not uncommon for pre-Stars to become **disillusioned**. When they realize that they cannot love their students as they would their own children, or that their students will never love them as they would a parent, they may wonder if they've chosen the wrong career.

Because many teachers were good students who enjoyed school as kids, they may have trouble relating to students who don't share those same characteristics. Students are naturally volatile; their academic performance and social behaviors are inconsistent, which is absolutely normal for children. The combination of codependent teachers and inconsistent students can cause serious problems in the classroom. These teachers are on a roller coaster: If the kids are behaving and performing and making them feel good, then life is good, but the moment a difficulty arises they are filled with self-doubt and place blame on their students.

Here are five quick signs that you are taking things too personally as a teacher:

1. When student performance is erratic, you are puzzled. You take it to mean that you are doing something incorrectly as the teacher.
2. You feel great when your students are learning, but your mood sinks when your students misbehave. You believe this is their problem, not yours.
3. You find it hard to brush off mean or insensitive comments from students.
4. When your colleagues share nice things their students have done for them, you are jealous. Instead of being happy, you wonder why your students don't behave similarly.
5. If you send home a request for parents to volunteer in your classroom and no one responds, you believe they must not care about the event. You take it as a personal attack and get frustrated with the planning process since no one has stepped up to assist you.

Respect: Behaviors of Star Teachers with a Professional Orientation

If Tina Turner's reflection about love helps to frame our thinking about not taking student behaviors too personally, Aretha Franklin's "R-E-S-P-E-C-T" can guide how we should act as Star Teachers with a professional orientation. Respectful behavior creates a virtuous feedback loop from teacher to student and back again. Star Teachers (1) model respectful behavior, (2) are authoritative rather than authoritarian in the classroom, and (3) and are warm demanders.

Star Teachers Model Respect

"Teachers are role models—but what are they modeling?" asks Angela Lumpkin.[12] According to Phelps, a **role model** is "a person who inspires and encourages us to strive for greatness, live to our fullest potential and see the best in ourselves."[13] Broadly speaking, Star Teachers model the following six items for students: (1) passion and inspiration, (2) values, (3) commitments, (4) empathy and acceptance, (5) lifelong learning, and (6) perseverance.

Haberman writes that students "will model behavior of teachers they respect—teachers who have strong interests, who love to learn, who are always reading something of interest."[14] Star Teachers model how to treat others, especially when others might not deserve our respect because they are being disrespectful themselves.[15] (See "Three Keys to Building Productive Teacher-Student Relationships" on page 107).

As Maya Angelou has said, "At the end of the day people won't remember what you said or did, they will remember how you made them feel."[16] Studies show that teachers who model respect build students' character, morality, and prosocial behavior.[17] Humanity, care, and respect—the unifying themes of Haberman's seven dispositions—are what ultimately distinguish the beliefs and behaviors of Star Teachers and pre-Stars. In *Caring: A Feminine Approach to Ethics and Moral Education*, Noddings shares the following sage words:

> When a teacher asks a question in class and a student responds, she receives not just the "response" but the student. What he says matters, whether it is right or wrong, and she probes gently for clarification, interpretation, contribution. She is not seeking the answer but the involvement of the cared-for. For the brief interval of dialogue that

grows around the question, the cared-for indeed "fills the firmament." The student is infinitely more important than the subject matter.[18]

Haberman writes that "Stars demonstrate their respect for learners in their language, posture, address, the care with which they listen and remember student ideas, and by their willingness to learn about their students' interests."[19] Star Teachers teach unconditionally: They bring their best to the classroom no matter how much students misbehave, how disrespectful they are, or how hard they are to teach. This necessitates responding instead of reacting and developing partnerships with students.

Responding versus Reacting. Reactions are instant[20] and devoid of understanding, whereas responses are imbued with values, core beliefs, thought, and reflection. Jon Mertz says that "responding is guided less by emotion and more by logic."[21] Leo Babauta says a response "is taking the situation in, and deciding the best course of action based on values such as reason, compassion, cooperation, etc."[22]

Here's an example. Let's say Matthew tells his teacher that Jonathan hit Jennifer. A reaction would be, "Jonathan, Matthew said you hit Jennifer, and now she's crying. Go to the principal's office right now!"—impulsive and not seeking to uncover what happened. By contrast, a response would be more measured and focused on understanding the situation: "Jonathan, I noticed Jennifer is crying. Matthew said you hit her. I know you would not want to hurt a fellow student. Can you please tell me what happened from your perspective?"

Research has found that teachers make 1,500 educational decisions over the course of a single school day.[23] It would be convenient if our students fell in line all the time to make these decisions easier and faster, but rarely is that case. Star Teachers are mindful about responding rather than reacting to these students.[24]

Developing Partnerships with Students. Haberman writes that "Stars' ability to relate to children puts them on the same side as the students rather than making them adversaries,"[25] whereas pre-Stars are most concerned with student discipline and classroom management. Star Teachers teach "gently" and do not "manipulate and control students." Haberman, along with one of this book's authors, Valerie Hill-Jackson, developed the following list of "gentle" teaching behaviors that convey respect for students:

- Put students ahead of subject matter. Use students' interests. Generate students' interests.
- Never go through the meaningless motion of "covering" material apart from students' involvement and learning. Never use shame or humiliation. Never scream or harangue.
- Never get caught in escalating punishments to force compliance. Listen, hear, remember, and use students' ideas. Model cooperation with all other adults in the building. Respect students' expressions of ideas. Demonstrate empathy for students' expressions of feelings. Identify student pain, sickness, and abuse, and follow up with people who can help them.
- Redefine the concept of a hero. Show how people who work things out are great. Devise activities at which students can succeed; success engenders further effort. Be a source of constant encouragement by finding good parts of all students' work.
- Defuse, sidestep, redirect all challenges to your authority. Never confront anyone, particularly in public. Use cooperative learning frequently. Create an extended family in the classroom.
- Use particular subject matters as the way to have "fights": science "fights" about rival explanations, math "fights" about different solutions, social studies "fights" about what really happened.
- Never ask students for private information publicly. Don't try to control by calling on children who are not paying attention and embarrassing them. Demonstrate respect for parents in the presence of their children.[26]

Star Teachers prefer cultivating synergy and collective agency to being disciplinarians. Engagement is the end goal, not managing behaviors. Because they understand what good teaching looks like, they teach and manage the classroom in the following ways:

- They involve students with issues they regard as vital concerns;
- They involve students with explanations of human differences;
- They help students see major concepts, big ideas, and general principles and not merely engage in the pursuit of isolated facts;
- They involve students in planning what they will be doing;
- They involve students with applying ideals such as fairness, equity, or justice to their world;

- They involve students directly in real-life experience;
- They involve students in heterogeneous groups;
- They ask students to think about an idea in a way that questions common sense or an assumption accepted as "good" by everyone; or relates new ideas to ones learned previously, or applies an idea to the problems of living;
- They involve students in redoing, re-polishing or perfecting their work;
- They involve students with technology of information access, and;
- They involve students in reflecting upon their own lives and how they have come to believe and feel as they do.[27]

Star Teachers' approach to classroom management relies on **encouragement** more than **praise**. Encouragement is important in all classrooms regardless of grade level because all students wish to feel included and supported. Praise is temporary, whereas encouragement lasts a lifetime. Rudolf Dreikurs's research on student (mis)behavior is elucidating. Dreikurs's social discipline model proposes that students who don't behave in class are seeking to fulfill the following four needs: (1) attention, (2) power and control, (3) revenge, and/or (4) help (see Figure 5.1).

Here's an example that illustrates Dreikurs's model quite well. Mr. Scott has been teaching 5th grade for 13 years. One afternoon, a student named Jolanda enters the classroom and refuses to take her seat. Puzzled, Mr. Scott attempts to deescalate the situation by asking to talk with her out in the hallway. Jolanda refuses and became even more brazen: "Mr. Scott, I am not going out in the hallway to talk to you! If you ask me again, I am going to spit on you!" Mr. Scott doesn't respond to Jolanda's threat with words, but just walks back to his desk. She yells after him, "See, I told you! Go walk back to your desk! There isn't anything you can do to make me sit down!" Instead of misreading Jolanda's behavior as a threat, Mr. Scott waited for her to cool down before speaking to her again in private. This time he learns that there are some things in Jolanda's life that are causing her to act out, and he's a convenient target.

Underlying Jolanda's words and actions are her needs for attention, power and control, and, finally, help—three of the four needs from Dreikurs's model. Mr. Scott could escalate the situation with Jolanda, which would lead to more lost learning time and harm their relationship. Instead, he chooses to respond rather than react.

Figure 5.1 **Dreikurs's Social Discipline Model**

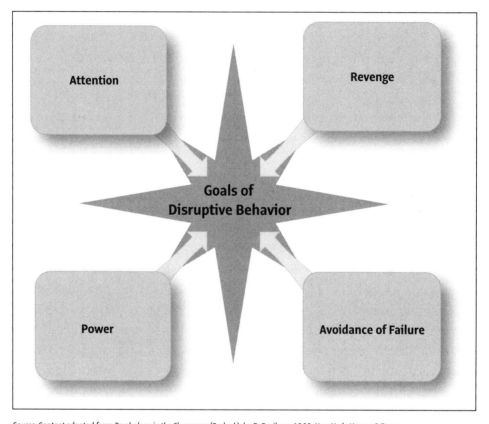

Source: Content adapted from *Psychology in the Classroom* (2nd ed.), by R. Dreikurs, 1968. New York: Harper & Row.

Research has found that misbehavior may be a sign that students are not comprehending the material,[28] which means discipline or student misbehaviors are really unresolved instructional challenges.[29] Whereas most teachers spend their careers engaged in a never-ending battle for control of their classrooms, Star Teachers spend most of their time teaching.

Stars Are Authoritative, Not Authoritarian

Star Teachers do not conceive of their relationships with students in terms of rewards or punishments, but explanations: words like *interest, involvement,* and *participation* are more common to them than motivating students to learn.

They are more likely to be happy for—and with—students who do well than to issue those students a reward. They prefer to share students' feelings of accomplishment than to reinforce behavior. Star Teachers see themselves as working with students, coaching them, and providing them with help. Most of all, they encourage students to want to do the work because of its intrinsic value, not because they will be rewarded for it. In *Motivating Students to Learn*, Jere Brophy distinguishes between **authoritarian** figures, who seek to police children, and **authoritative** figures, who want youngsters to understand the consequences of their actions, by doing the following:

- Accepting the child as an individual;
- Communicating this acceptance through warm, affectionate interactions;
- Socializing by teaching the child prosocial values and behavioral guidelines, not just imposing "discipline";
- Clarifying rules and limits, but with input from the child and flexibility in adapting to developmental advances (e.g., allowing more opportunities for autonomy and choice as children develop greater ability to handle these opportunities responsibly);
- Presenting expectations in ways that communicate respect for and concern about the child, as opposed to "laying down the law";
- Explaining the rationales underlying demands and expectations;
- Justifying prohibitions by citing the effects of children's actions on themselves and others rather than by appealing to fear of punishment or essentially empty logic such as "good children don't do that";
- Teaching desired values and modeling their applications; and
- Continually projecting positive expectations and attitudes: treating children as if they already are, or at least are becoming, prosocial and responsible people.[30]

Star Teachers have the uncanny ability to make every student feel as though he or she matters and is respected by transmitting encouraging messages in the classroom. These teachers are confident, relaxed, and professional as opposed to frenzied or authoritarian. Their ability to relate to students makes them partners rather than adversaries. Star Teachers understand what makes their students tick because they spend time getting to know them. (See Figure 5.2.)

Figure 5.2 **Authoritarian Versus Authoritative Approaches to Discipline**

		Teacher Involvement	
		Low	**High**
Discipline	Weak	Permissive-Neglectful	Permissive-Indulgent
	Strong	Authoritarian	Authoritative

Source: From "Parenting and Teaching: What's the Connection in Our Classrooms?," by D. Baumrind, in *Psychology Teacher Network, 23*(2), p. 2 (copyright © 2013 by Douglas A. Bernstein) as adapted in "Current Patterns of Parental Authority," by D. Baumrind, *Developmental Psychology, 4*(1, Pt.2), pp. 1–103.

According to James Stronge, "teachers spend about 70 percent of their classroom instruction time on the core curriculum. The remaining 30 percent is spent on completing such tasks as collecting money for the school fundraiser and enforcing classroom rules and procedures."[31] He adds that although classroom management consumes a teacher's time, it is very important "if you want learning to occur."[32] In *Primary Sources: America's Teachers on Teaching in an Era of Change*, a survey of more than 20,000 public school teachers on a variety of issues, one elementary teacher notes that "student behavior is the most time-consuming issue in the classroom";[33] another suggests that "new teachers today need ongoing training" to address misbehavior, and that "when a teacher is hired, he or she should be required to attend a class on classroom management as well as receive tips on controlling behavior."[34]

In *One-Minute Discipline: Classroom Management Strategies That Work*, Annie Bianco notes that classrooms with few disruptions have unrelenting teachers who engender a culture of appreciation and positive relationships and exude the joy of learning with students.[35] Haberman's research and observations of discipline problems lead him to conclude that most classroom problems are caused and escalated by the teachers themselves, who are frequently replicating behaviors displayed by their own teachers when they were in school.

Teachers often discipline students using automatic, unthinking reactions to misbehaviors that reflect no knowledge of child development or learning. Other responses include some sort of discipline system they learned in a class or workshop. Unfortunately, these systems only work if the teacher and students have established a positive working relationship—in which case there shouldn't be management problems in the first place. Star Teachers do not follow "systems" of classroom management because there are no responses guaranteed to work with all students in all situations.

As teachers become increasingly proficient at keeping students on task, they will develop the following six skills:

1. **Withitness**—a heightened awareness of everything going on with all the students everywhere in the classroom.
2. **Multitasking**—an increase in the ability to deal with several students' problems simultaneously.
3. **Responding to individual needs**
4. **Avoiding escalation**—stamping out automatic reactions that worsen the misbehaviors.
5. **Professionalizing behavior**—learning to respond in ways that meet students' emotional needs rather than the teacher's personal needs.
6. **Acting decisively** and staying in control of the situation.

One expression of authoritarianism in schools is **zero-tolerance policies,** which have had a disproportionate effect on students of color and from poor socioeconomic backgrounds, creating what is known as the **school-to-prison pipeline** (see Figure 5.3).[36] According to the Anti-Defamation League (ADL), "While black students represent 18% of children enrolled in preschool, they represent 48% of all preschool children receiving more than one out-of-school suspension. In comparison, white students represent 43% of preschool enrollment but 26% of preschool children receiving more than one out-of-school suspension."[37] The ADL also reports that while "black students represent 16% of student enrollment, they represent 31% of students subjected to a school-related arrest. In comparison, white students represent 51% of enrollment and 39% of those arrested."[38] According to the U.S. Department of Education, "Of the 49 million students enrolled in public schools in 2011–2012, 3.5 million students were

Figure 5.3 **School-to-Prison Pipeline for K–12 Learners**

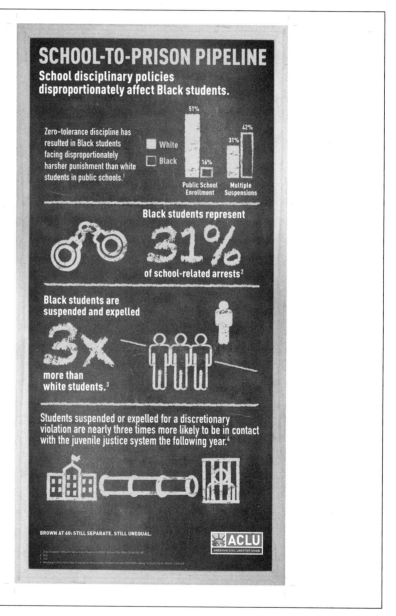

suspended in-school; 3.45 million students were suspended out-of-school; and 130,000 students were expelled."[39] National studies present compelling evidence that discipline is uneven when it comes to race,[40] gender,[41] and (dis)ability status.[42] The National Women's Law Center reports that "In preschools, Black girls are 20% of the girls enrolled but 54% of the girls receiving out-of-school suspensions; in K–12, Black girls are 16% of the girls enrolled but 45% of the girls receiving out-of-school suspensions."[43]

Students don't "drop" out of school, they are pushed out, often by zero-tolerance policies.[44] Star Teachers try to keep them in. As Haberman and Hill-Jackson point out, zero-tolerance policies can lead to students being pushed out of the safety of school and into a world where they may not have caring adults to look out for their safety and welfare.[45] Being pushed out can be a function of not being taught by the most effective teachers. Vulnerable students are placed with ineffective, pre-Star Teachers, based on tracking and school bureaucratic norms. For example, too often, schools assign remedial classes to new and inexperienced teachers when the students could benefit from the experience of veteran teachers. Schools many times have it backward, with the most effective teachers teaching the most advanced students and the least experienced teachers in charge of the classes in highest need of good-quality instruction.

Katie Hogan, a high school English teacher in the Chicago Public Schools (CPS), is known for being one of 12 teachers at Curie Metropolitan High School who publicly refused to give students a test that was part of the No Child Left Behind–mandated state exam.[46] In the end, CPS abandoned the test. No longer at Curie, Ms. Hogan now teaches at Social Justice High School (SOJO).[47] She is fortunate, because SOJO understands the relationship between zero-tolerance policies and high-stakes testing. According to the Advancement Project, the two practices—zero-tolerance policies and high-stakes testing—have become mutually reinforcing and combine to push huge numbers of students out of school.[48] Zero-tolerance policies and high-stakes testing can lead to negative student experiences. If students perform poorly on high-stakes exams, they are labeled by their peers and teachers. Under the high-stakes testing regime, students are merely numbers. Students who disengage, or who have difficulty learning, can quickly become seen as "problems," and when these students become frustrated or act out, they violate rules. Under the zero-tolerance regime, these violations lead to being pushed out of school. Although zero-tolerance policies are supported for their focus on student safety and high-stakes testing practices are supported for their focus on academic rigor and accountability, the argument that they are mutually reinforcing and not in the interest of students is a difficult argument to make to the public.

Star Teachers Are Warm Demanders

Star Teachers behave in ways that encourage mutual respect,[49] including by acting as **warm demanders**—Judith Kleinfeld's term for teachers who affectionately demand that their students learn.[50] In an article about warm demanders, Jacqueline Jordan Irvine shares this example of how such teachers address student misbehavior: "That's enough of your nonsense, Darius. Your story does not make sense. I told you time and time again that you must stick to the theme I gave you. Now sit down."[51] This may seem like a harsh response at first, but on closer inspection, it's a warm demand: Darius knows better, and the teacher knows that. Franita Ware points out that warm demanding "discipline is often misconstrued by people who lack a cultural sensitivity or emic perspective into the authoritarian style of parenting in the African American community."[52] Bondy, Ross, Hambacher, and Acosta shared the following strategies for becoming a warm demander:

- Be very explicit in what you want the child to do but not in a way that is cruel or mean but is very . . . . direct.
- Give an explicit, direct instruction.
- Go over to the student and say this is exactly what I need you to be doing right now, and I expect to see this of you.
- You do not embarrass a child.
- You are not cruel or demeaning about it.
- You explain the why of everything so they at least understand it.[53]

Star Teachers demonstrate respect for their students by learning their names, following through on demands, being consistent with praise and blame, demonstrating integrity and morality, and respecting their students' voices and choices. Students respond to this approach by exhibiting a zeal to learn and showing respect to the teacher in return.

Summary

Star Teachers manifest their professional orientation to learners by committing themselves to the academic success of their students. These teachers don't take classroom misbehavior personally (unlike pre-Stars with a personal orientation, who are hypersensitive to slights from students). Star Teachers model respect, which reduces misbehavior and increases learning; are authoritative rather than authoritarian; form partnerships with learners; and warmly demand high expectations from all students in their classrooms.

Key Words

authoritarian	authoritative personal	disillusioned
encouragement	orientation	personal orientation
praise	professional orientation	role model
school-to-prison pipeline	warm demanders	zero-tolerance policies

Extension Exercises

1. Reflect on your teaching philosophy. How does the ideology shared in this chapter contribute to it?

2. View the five phases of teaching shared in Figure 5.4: (1) anticipation, (2) survival, (3) disillusionment, (4) rejuvenation, and (5) reflection. Based on the current month, reflect on which phase you may be experiencing. What's contributing to what you're experiencing? If you have taught for more than one year, have you noticed changes in your feelings and experiences?

3. Your Personality Type: Search for "personality inventory" online and choose two inventories to complete.
   - http://psych.fullerton.edu/mbirnbaum/web/personalityb.htm
   - www.16personalities.com/free-personality-test

   For each inventory, follow the directions to determine your overall character. What are your results for both inventories? Do you agree with the results?

Figure 5.4 **Phases of First-Year Teachers' Attitudes Toward Teaching**

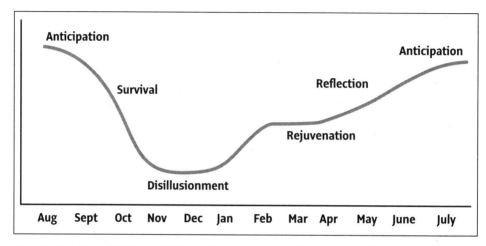

Compare and contrast the results for the two tests. Are you more likely or less likely to take student comments or behaviors personally? How can knowledge of your personality temperament help you become more successful as a teacher?

4. Getting to Know Your Students Activity: Ask your students to answer the following questions, and record their responses on the whiteboard. Aggregate the responses into themes. Analyze the responses to see if patterns emerge.

Elementary
- Describe your family.
- What is something funny, weird, unusual, or special about one person in your family?

Middle School
- Name one thing you could teach someone else how to make or how to do.
- What's your favorite holiday of the year? What makes this holiday your favorite?

High School

- If you had to eat the same meal every day for a month, what would it be?
- What's one thing that you would like to change about your school that would make it a better place for you?

Going Further

Web Resources

- Like Martin Haberman, Robert Marzano has 50 years of educational research experience. Visit his website at www.marzanoresearch.com and click on the "Free Resources" tab, the second from the right on top, for helpful information that you can use in your teaching. Click "Tips from Dr. Marzano" and then click on the Coaching Classroom Instruction book. You will find tips on relationships that complement the information in this chapter.
- The Bad Kids Educator Toolkit is designed for teachers dealing with students classified as at risk. The toolkit is comprised of three parts: a discussion guide, professional development training tools, and lesson plans. The toolkit is accessible to all and is adaptable to both school-based student learning opportunities and districtwide professional development focused on strengthening and supporting at-risk students. www.pbslearningmedia.org/resource/4beb6862-c4f0-4604-8a32-c0e73a5ae27d/the-bad-kids-educator-toolkit.

Videos

- On YouTube, search for the video by Asha Gill titled "Eckhart Tolle: How to Respond and Not React" at www.youtube.com/watch?v=UpLwPUxJkGM. In this video, Gill reveals a technique that allows you to respond appropriately in a situation where your buttons are being pushed, so you can feel emotionally calm and in control.

Additional Readings

- Benson, J. (2014). *Hanging in: Strategies for teaching the students who challenge us most.* Alexandria, VA: ASCD. Benson suggests that mistakes should not result in punishment for students, particularly those we find difficult to teach, as this will turn off students' desire to learn.

- Bondy, E., & Ross, D. D. (2008). The teacher as warm demander. *Educational Leadership, 66*(1), 54–58. This short article explains what a warm demander is, how warm demanders support student learning, and how to become a warm demander.
- Stronge, J. H. (2007). *Qualities of effective teachers* (2nd ed.). Alexandria, VA: ASCD. In this extremely practical book, Stronge identifies specific teacher behaviors that contribute to student achievement. The book focuses specifically on what teachers can control: their own preparation, personality, and practices.
- Matias, C., & Zembylas, M. (2014). "When saying you care is not really caring": Emotions of disgust, whiteness ideology, and teacher education. *Critical Studies in Education, 55*(3), 319–337. This article stresses the importance of interrogating the ways that benign emotions (e.g., pity and caring) are sometimes hidden expressions of disgust for "the Other." This phenomenon is particularly relevant because care, sympathy, and love are emotions that are routinely performed by teachers.

Endnotes

1. National Education Association (NEA). (2017). *Code of ethics.* Retrieved from www.nea.org/home/30442.htm
2. Association of American Educators (AAE). (2017). *Code of ethics for educators.* Retrieved from www.aaeteachers.org/index.php/about-us/aae-code-of-ethics
3. *Primary Sources: America's Teachers on Teaching in an Era of Change* (2013). (3rd ed.). Retrieved from www.scholastic.com/primarysources/PrimarySources3rdEditionWithAppendix.pdf (p. 11)
4. Marsh, S. (2015, January 27). Five top reasons people become teachers—and why they quit. *The Guardian.* Retrieved from www.theguardian.com/teacher-network/2015/jan/27/five-top-reasons-teachers-join-and-quit
5. Darling-Hammond, L. (1990). Teacher professionalism: Why and how. In A. Lieberman (Ed.), *Schools as collaborative cultures: Creating the future now* (pp. 25–50). New York: Falmer. Retrieved from http://files.eric.ed.gov/fulltext/ED333064.pdf
6. Phelps, P. H. (2003). Teacher professionalism. *Kappa Delta Pi Record, 40*(1), 10–11. (p. 10)
7. Haberman, 2004, p. 22.
8. Haberman, M. (1995). Selecting 'Star' Teachers for children and youth in urban poverty. *Phi Delta Kappan, 76*(10), 777–781. (p. 780)
9. Haberman (1995, p. 780).
10. Haberman (1995, p. 780).

11. Kugel, P. (1993). How professors develop as teachers. *Studies in Higher Education, 18*(3), 315–328. Retrieved from www.mach.kit.edu/download/HowProfessorsDevelop.pdf

12. Lumpkin, A. (2008). Teachers as role models: Teaching character and moral virtues. *JOPERD, 79*(2), 45–50. (p. 45)

13. Teachers as role models. (n.d.). Retrieved from https://teach.com/what/teachers-change-lives/teachers-are-role-models/

14. Haberman, M. (2004). Can Star Teachers create learning communities? *Educational Leadership, 61*(8), 52–56. (p. 52)

15. Burden, P. R. (2016). *Classroom management: Creating a successful K–12 learning community.* Hoboken, NJ: Wiley.

16. Angelou, M. Retrieved from www.goodreads.com/quotes/663523-at-the-end-of-the-day-people-won-t-remember-what

17. Weissbourd, R. (2003). Moral teachers, moral students. *Educational Leadership, 60*(6), 6–11.

18. Noddings, N. (2003). *Caring: A feminine approach to ethics and moral education* (2nd ed.). Berkeley: University of California Press. (p. 176)

19. Haberman, M. (2011, December 8). The beliefs and behaviors of Star Teachers. *Education Views.* Retrieved from www.educationviews.org/the-beliefs-and-behaviors-of-star-teachers/ (para. 16)

20. James, M. (2016, September 1). React vs. respond. What's the difference? *Psychology Today.* Retrieved from www.psychologytoday.com/blog/focus-forgiveness/201609/react-vs-respond

21. Mertz, J. (2013, March 7). A mindful difference: Respond vs. react. Retrieved from www.thindifference.com/2013/03/a-mindful-difference-respond-vs-react/

22. Babauta, L. (n.d.). Learn to respond, not react. Retrieved from https://zenhabits.net/respond/ (para. 3)

23. Teacher Thought. (n.d.). A teacher makes 1500 educational decisions a day. Retrieved from www.teachthought.com/pedagogy/teacher-makes-1500-decisions-a-day/

24. Mertz (2013, para. 3).

25. Haberman, M. (2010). *Star Teachers: The ideology and best practices of effective teachers of diverse children and youth in poverty.* Houston, TX: Haberman Educational Foundation. (p. 191)

26. Haberman, M., & Hill-Jackson, V. (2017). Gentle teaching in a violent society: A postscript for the 21st century. In V. Hill-Jackson & D. Stafford (Eds.), *Better teachers, better schools: What Star Teachers know, believe, and do* (pp. 13–29). Charlotte, NC: Information Age Publishing. (pp. 19–20)

27. Based on Martin Haberman's (2004, pp. 54–57) 11 indicators of good teaching.

28. Pimperton, H., & Nation, K. (2014). Poor comprehenders in the classroom: Teacher ratings of behavior in children with poor reading comprehension and its relationship with individual differences in working memory. *Journal of Learning Disabilities, 47*(3), 199–207.

29. Ayllon, T., & Roberts, M. D. (1974). Eliminating discipline problems by strengthening academic performance. *Journal of Applied Behavior Analysis, 7*(1), 71–76; Burden, P. R. (1995). *Classroom management and discipline: Methods to facilitate cooperation and instruction.* White Plains, NY: Longman; Wolfgang, C. H., & Glickman, C. D. (1986). *Solving discipline problems: Strategies for classroom teachers.* Newton, MA: Allyn & Bacon.

30. Brophy, J. E. (1997). *Motivating students to learn* (3rd ed.). New York: Routledge. (p. 25)

31. Stronge, J. H. (2007). *Qualities of effective teachers.* Alexandria, VA: ASCD. (p. 54)

32. Stronge (2007, p. 16).

33. *Primary sources: America's teachers on teaching in an era of change* (3rd ed.). (2013). Retrieved from www.scholastic.com/primarysources/PrimarySources3rdEditionWithAppendix.pdf (p. 20)

34. *Primary sources* (2013, p. 79).

35. Bianco, A. (2002). *One-minute discipline: Classroom management strategies that work.* New York: Center for Applied Research in Education.

36. Bryan, N. (2017). White teachers' role in sustaining the school-to-prison pipeline: Recommendations for teacher education. *The Urban Review, 49*(2), 326–345.

37. Anti-Defamation League (ADL). (2015). What is the school-to-prison pipeline? Retrieved from www.adl.org/sites/default/files/documents/assets/pdf/education-outreach/what-is-the-school-to-prison-pipeline.pdf (p. 9)

38. ADL (2015, p. 9).

39. U.S. Department of Education. (2016, July 11). School climate and discipline: Know the data. Retrieved from https://www2.ed.gov/policy/gen/guid/school-discipline/data.html

40. Kupchik, A. (2009). Things are tough all over: Race, ethnicity, class and school discipline. *Punishment & Society, 11*(3), 291–317. Retrieved from http://citeseerx.ist.psu.edu/viewdoc/download?doi=10.1.1.838.1681&rep=rep1&type=pdf

41. National Women's Law Center. (2014). *Let her learn: A toolkit to stop school push out for girls of color.* Retrieved from https://nwlc.org/wp-content/uploads/2016/11/final_nwlc_NOVO2016Toolkit.pdf

42. Kids Count. (2012, November). *Zero tolerance and exclusionary school discipline policies harm students and contribute to cradle to prison pipeline.* Columbus, OH: Children's Defense Fund—Ohio. Retrieved from www.cdfohio.org/research-library/2012/issue-brief-zero-tolerance.pdf

43. National Women's Law Center (2014, p. 1).

44. Ayers, W., Dohrn, B., & Ayers, R. (Eds.). (2001). *Zero tolerance: Resisting the drive for punishment in our schools.* New York: New York Press.

45. Haberman, M., & Hill-Jackson, V. (2017). Gentle teaching in a violent society: A postscript for the 21st century. In V. Hill-Jackson & D. Stafford (Eds.), *Better teachers, better schools: What Star Teachers know, believe, and do* (pp. 13–29). Charlotte, NC: Information Age Publishing. (p. 23)

46. Hogan, K. (2008). The Curie 12: A case for teacher activism. In W. Ayers, G. Ladson-Billings, G. Michie, & P. A. Noguera (Eds.), *City kids: More reports from the front row* (pp. 97–102). New York: New Press.

47. Hartlep, N. D. (2012). Teachers' pet projects versus real social justice teaching. In A. Honigsfeld & A. Cohan (Eds.), *Breaking the mold of education for culturally and linguistically diverse students: Innovative and successful practices for the 21st century* (pp. 13–22). Lanham, MD: Rowman & Littlefield. (p. 18)

48. Advancement Project. (2010). *Test, punish, and push out: How "zero tolerance" and high-stakes testing funnel youth into the school-to-prison pipeline*. Retrieved from www.educationjustice.org/assets/files/pdf/Resources/Policy/School%20Discipline %20and%20School-to-Prison%20Pipeline/Test%20punish%20and%20push%20out.pdf

49. Nelsen, J., Lott, L., & Glenn, H. S. (2000). *Positive discipline in the classroom: Developing mutual respect, cooperation, and responsibility*. New York: Three Rivers Press.

50. Kleinfeld, J. (1975). Effective teachers of Eskimo and Indian students. *School Review, 83*, 301–344.

51. Irvine, J. J. (1998). Warm demanders. *Education Week, 17*(35), 56.

52. Ware, F. (2006). Warm demander pedagogy: Culturally responsive teaching that supports a culture of achievement for African American students. *Urban Education, 41*(4), 427–456. Retrieved from www.arisehighschool.org/wp-content/uploads/2013/06/Ware.Franita_Warm-demander.pdf (p. 452)

53. Bondy, E., Ross, D. D., Hambacher, E., & Acosta, M. (2012). Becoming warm demanders: Perspectives and practices of first year teachers. *Urban Education, 48*(3), 420–450. Retrieved from www.researchgate.net/profile/Elyse_Hambacher/publication/258198644_Becoming_Warm_Demanders_Perspectives_and_Practices_of_First_Year_Teachers/links/54e5062a0cf276cec172f34c.pdf (p. 436)

6

Surviving in a Bureaucracy

This chapter deals with a teacher's ability to work within a school environment that is depersonalized, bureaucratic, and impersonal. Teachers who have the ability to survive in a bureaucracy are also more effective in the classroom and more likely to remain on the job.

Learning Outcomes

Upon completion of this chapter, you will be able to
- Develop the mindset required to survive the bureaucracy in your school.
- Identify the characteristics required to survive in a bureaucracy.
- Transfer the practices and behaviors of Star Teachers who know how to survive in a bureaucracy to your own school.

Interstate New Teacher Assessment and Support Consortium (InTASC) Standards

Standard #3: Learning Environments
The teacher works with others to create environments that support individual and collaborative learning and that encourage positive social interaction, active engagement in learning, and self-motivation.

★ ★ ★ ★ ★ ★ ★ ★ ★ ★ ★

Defining *Bureaucracy*

Meetings, paperwork, more meetings, more paperwork: such is the mundane work of K–12 teachers in U.S. schools. As Haberman writes, the "paperwork, the conflicting rules and policies, the number of meetings, the interruptions, the inadequate materials, the lack of time, large classes, and an obsessive concern with test scores are just some of the demands that drive" teachers out of the profession and define the activities of bureaucratic schools.[1] Haberman notes that Star Teachers function effectively even in school bureaucracies where the educators are often disconnected from stakeholders.[2] Here's how Nicholas D. Hartlep and Sara A. McCubbins define such teachers:

> Teachers who are successful at surviving in a bureaucracy tend to recognize and accept the demands of the school bureaucracy, and they do not let organizational stress such as meetings, school notices, etc., take away too much time and energy that could be spent teaching children. These teachers tend to be experts at using the informal structure of the school to accomplish their goals (i.e., knowing which secretary, janitor, aide, or other teacher will help them with what they want or need in a way that provides the least amount of hassle) and often set up networks of likeminded colleagues who serve as a support group, not all of whom are teachers at the same school or even teachers at all.[3]

Hartlep and McCubbins speak to how and why working in bureaucracies can be dispiriting, especially when administrators seem to be ephemeral. As Donald Sanders and Marian Schwab pointed out more than 30 years ago, "Teachers are placed at the bottom of a bureaucratic structure permeated with the presumption that those higher up know better how to define and carry on the work of teaching."[4] Effective teachers know who in the school has the power to get things done and who has vital information—and it is not always the principal or department head.

Unreflective teachers may unintentionally prioritize the time they spend filling out paperwork and following policies over planning engaging lessons for their students. Haberman makes the direct claim that schools are designed to feed the bureaucratic machine. "Particularly in districts where the poorest children live," he writes, "school bureaucracies can wear down teachers. It's not the work; it's the time-consuming bureaucratic processes and interruptions that cause Stars to become exhausted."[5]

Ralph Kimbrough and Eugene Todd define a **bureaucracy** as "a pattern of ordering and specifying relationships among personnel in an organization."[6] They write that bureaucracies have the following six dimensions:

1. A division of labor based on functional specialization.
2. A well-defined hierarchy of authority.
3. A system of rules covering the rights and duties of employees.
4. Systematic procedures for dealing with work situations.
5. Impersonal approach to interpersonal relations and the promotion of rational behavior according to organizational goals.
6. Promotion and selection based on technical competence.[7]

David Tyack writes that "during the mid-19th century most American urban school systems became bureaucracies."[8] According to Michael Katz, this was largely because a factory model was the most practical for assimilating immigrants.[9] Frederick Winslow Taylor (1856–1915), considered to be father of scientific management, created an approach to schooling that quickly became paradigmatic, structuring educators' expectations for the increasingly diverse student population of the 20th century.[10] "Taylorism" was a bureaucratic response to formal education. In his 1909 publication *The Principles of Scientific Management,* Taylor outlines the principles of scientific management, which focuses on training and efficiency.[11] E. Wayne Ross points to examples of how modern forms of Taylorism continue to be practiced in U.S. public schools:

• Schools are often large and bureaucratized.
• Students change teachers each year.
• Teachers plan and teach alone.
• Elementary teachers often do not share students.
• Secondary students see many teachers in large groups (the "platoon" system).
• Curriculum is fragmented.
• Students are tracked by ability level.

- Deskilling occurs as teaching is aligned with mandated curriculum and standardized tests.
- There is an emphasis on monitoring or surveillance and other bureaucratic activity.
- Teachers are less and less free to engage students in conversation, inquiry, and open-ended activities.[12]

Like Ross, Richard Rothstein also finds plenty of examples of bureaucratic sensibilities in schools today: "Schools' bureaucratic rules (such as centralized textbook selection, detailed curriculum requirements including the number of minutes spent on specified subjects, demands for attendance accounting and ethnic surveys, and restricted telephone or copying machine use) inhibit teacher creativity and should be reformed,"[13] he writes. Creativity is undervalued and discipline encouraged. School bureaucracies, like manufacturing factories, are most concerned with efficient compliance, depersonalized relationships, and standardized productivity. Thinking differently is not encouraged.

Changing Schools from Bureaucracies to Learning Organizations

Large school districts are arranged to benefit everyone who works in them except their teachers and students. For example, Kevin Smith and Christopher Larimer found that while bureaucratic schooling improves things like rates of student attendance and graduation, it is unable to increase test score achievement.[14]

Because the narrow perspective of running a school like a business fails to address how the interests of students are to be served, Mike Lavell suggests that schools ought to be run according to a **community model of schooling** instead.[15] Unfortunately, as Thomas Sergiovanni writes, schools are increasingly seen as organizations to be run rather than communities where learning takes place.[16] To Haberman, schools are inherently "communal" spaces where ideas are shared, power is egalitarian, learning is modeled, and collaboration is prized.[17] Relationships form the basis of schools as learning organizations. Star Teachers don't preach or lecture, and they tend to be nonjudgmental. According to Haberman, you know a school is a learning organization when "members share a common vision that learning is the primary purpose."[18]

Teacher Stress and Burnout

Michael Fimian defines **teacher stress** as "a hypothetical construct that represents an equilibrium state that exists between the individual responding to environmental demands and the actual environment."[19] Haberman explains that stress leads to **burnout**, which is "a syndrome resulting from teachers' inability to protect themselves against threats to their self-esteem and well-being. . . . When those coping mechanisms fail to stem the demands, then stress increases and threatens the teachers' mental and physical well-being, ultimately leading to teachers quitting or burning out."[20]

In one study, Barry Farber found that "excessive paperwork, unsuccessful administrative meetings, and the lack of advancement opportunities in teaching" were primary sources of teacher stress.[21] The stress and frustration of bureaucratic teaching policies, practices, and culture can stifle teachers' creativity and spoil their desire to continue putting effort into instruction. Consider what happens when teachers who are burnt out continue to show up in the classroom every day: according to Haberman, such teachers "use significantly less task-oriented behavior and provide less positive reinforcement for their students" than do their colleagues.[22]

Depersonalization

Less discussed but equally as problematic as absenteeism is "**presenteeism**," or the practice of staying in school and teaching despite feeling sick or mentally unfit to do so, which has been found to lead to further depersonalization.[23]

Depersonalization is a common response for stressed teachers, since it preserves mental health by allowing them to "go through the motions" while temporarily hiding their emotional exhaustion.[24] Abhishek Totawar and Ranjeet Nambudiri note that the negative consequences of teachers distancing themselves psychologically include job dissatisfaction, absenteeism, and attrition or lack of commitment.[25]

Job Dissatisfaction. It increasingly seems that rules, procedures, and paperwork are becoming the focus of teachers instead of actual teaching. This can lead to teachers becoming dissatisfied with their work. Teacher dissatisfaction leads to a **vicious cycle** in bureaucratic schools. School bureaucracy leads to teacher dissatisfaction, and teacher dissatisfaction results in more bureaucracy because teachers become alienated from their work. National surveys have found that a majority of K–12 teachers are stressed and dissatisfied with their jobs. For example, according to the 2012 MetLife Survey of the American Teacher, "Teacher satisfaction has declined 23 percentage points since 2008, from 62% to 39% very satisfied, including five percentage points since last year, to the lowest level in 25 years."[26] The survey also points out a finding that will surprise few teachers: "Stress among teachers has increased since 1985."[27]

Why are teachers stressed and dissatisfied? Why has stress and dissatisfaction increased over the past three decades? It is because teaching has become less and less about teaching and learning and more and more about achievement on high-stakes tests, mandates from the central office, and working with fewer resources. There is a silver lining, though. Research has found that teachers who regularly use stress-reducing strategies can increase their ability to cope with the profession's demands, better positioning them to focus their energies on doing a stellar job educating students.[28]

Absenteeism. The headline of Alejandra Matos's *Washington Post* story reads "1 in 4 U.S. teachers are chronically absent, missing more than 10 days of school."[29] Matos reports on a teacher who was absent from her classroom for 19 days. It is unfortunate that as schools become more bureaucratic and more impersonal, the important issue of **absenteeism** is likely to go unresolved. Miller, Murnane, and Willett note that "teachers who are required to report absences directly to their principal by telephone are absent less often than teachers who report their absences indirectly, to either a centralized reporting center or a school-based message machine."[30] A majority of teacher absences fall into three categories: (1) professional development, (2) sick days, or (3) personal days.[31]

There is evidence that schools with a high percentage of black or Latinx students disproportionately experience teacher absence,[32] which creates stress among other school staff. Consider, for example, substitute teachers, who do not know the school policies and procedures well and must teach from absent teachers' lesson plans. Their lack of awareness tends to disrupt student learning. Moreover, substitute teachers may not be well qualified to teach a given class in the first place. Some states don't require substitute teachers to hold a teacher license or have training in the subject and grade level they will be teaching. The minimum education required to be a substitute teacher across the United States ranges from high school completion to two years of college. And, of course, if no substitute is found to fill in for an absent teacher, the effects on learning are even worse.

Allison Ross writes about the difficulty of finding substitute teachers in Kentucky's Jefferson County Public Schools (JCPS): "Unable to find subs to fill in, school administrators or other certified school personnel are being forced to step away from their normal duties to take over classrooms. In some cases, students whose teachers are out sick are being split up and dispersed to other teachers' classrooms for the day because a substitute can't be found."[33] She continues: "Schools that were more likely to have sub requests go unfilled were those who had higher percentages of children who qualified for free or reduced-price lunches—a common indicator of poverty. Schools that have been deemed priority schools by the state also tended to have more sub requests go unfilled."[34]

In his report "Teacher Absence as a Leading Indicator of Student Achievement," Raegen Miller writes that

> On any given school day, up to 40 percent of teachers in New Jersey's Camden City Public Schools are absent from their classrooms. Such a high figure probably would not stand out in parts of the developing world, but it contrasts sharply with the 3 percent national rate of absence for full-time wage and salaried American workers, and the 5.3 percent rate of absence for American teachers overall.[35]

Between 2012 and 2013, the National Council on Teacher Quality (NCTQ) collected data from 40 large school districts across the nation and "found that, on average, teachers missed nearly 11 days out of a 186-day school year. This is considered frequently absent. Still, 16 percent of those teachers missed 18 or more days—equivalent to about 10 percent of the school year—and were considered chronically absent" (see Figure 6.1).[36] Research has found that teacher absences negatively affect 4th-grade student achievement in mathematics.[37]

Many scholars have offered policy recommendations to reduce teacher absenteeism. For example, Geoffrey Smith writes that schools and districts should establish innovative policies to encourage attendance.[38] The first step in addressing teacher absences is to track them and determine whether they are school-related. For Smith, a comprehensive attendance improvement plan includes some of the following action items:

Figure 6.1 **Teacher Attendance Rates Across 40 School Districts**

Teachers were in the classroom, on average, 94 percent of the school year.			
Number of Districts	Number of Teachers	Attendance Rate	Average Days Absent
40	234,031	94%	11
Excellent Attendance (3 or fewer days absent)	Moderate Attendance (4–10 days absent)	Frequent Absence (11–17 days absent)	Chronic Absence (18 or more days absent)
16%	40%	28%	16%

Source: From *Roll Call: The Importance of Teacher Attendance* (p. 3), by the National Council on Teacher Quality, 2014, Washington, DC: Author. Copyright 2014 by the National Council on Teacher Quality. Adapted with permission.

- Review board policy. Establish innovative policies to encourage attendance, not just reducing absenteeism. Research suggests that there is a correlation between policies and absenteeism.
- Appoint an attendance manager and systemwide policies that encourage teacher attendance.
- Track attendance via an automated system.
- Create rules and standards regarding attendance standards.
- Collect attendance data and review it for improvement. This may require surveying teachers about their absences.
- Write a plan that sets short- and long-term goals for improving overall attendance. This work should involve teachers.
- Train school leaders to emphasize the importance of attendance.
- Offer teachers the ability to sell back their unused sick leave.
- Improve work conditions for school employees.
- Remind employees that employee assistance programs exist. Encourage personnel who have excessive absences to access this resource.
- Offer compensation for unused sick leave upon separation from the school system.
- Provide an incentive for master teachers who volunteer for assignments in failing schools.
- Remind employees that sick leave is a benefit reserved for illness, not an entitlement.

- Hold administrators accountable for administering policies and site administrators for any abuse of the attendance policies.[39]

Smith goes on to share practices to reduce school related absences: "(a) review policies to ensure that limits are placed on when, where, why, and who pays for absences; (b) schedule staff development outside of school hours; (c) ensure that sponsorship of student activities does not increase teacher absenteeism; (d) reduce the number of teachers used as chaperones on school sponsored trips; (e) promote school-wide inservice when students are on campus; and (f) regularly review printouts/data on school related absence."[40]

Attrition or Lack of Commitment. In 1990, Haberman and William Rickards lamented that "[n]ationally, approximately one-half of beginning teachers leave teaching in the first six years."[41] Nearly three decades later, teacher **attrition** still remains high.[42] As Leslie Baldacci writes, "one-third of new teachers quit after three years and nearly half bail out after five years."[43] Research that has been conducted on why K–12 teachers leave the profession has been important to the field.[44] Mary Brownell, Stephen Smith, Janet McNellis, and David Miller found that special education teachers left the profession because they "felt unsupported, unprepared, overwhelmed by student needs or job responsibilities, disempowered, or all of these."[45]

In *A Possible Dream: Retaining California Teachers So All Students Learn,* Ken Futernick notes that "the factor cited most frequently as a reason for leaving was bureaucratic impediments."[46] The weight of bureaucratic conditions forces teachers out of the profession. There are six main reasons teachers leave the profession: (1) climate and culture, (2) students and inability to support learners,[47] (3) lack of autonomy, (4) lack of a career ladder, (5) lack of resources, and (6) low pay.[48]

Leib Sutcher, Linda Darling-Hammond, and Desiree Carver-Thomas liken the teaching workforce to a leaky bucket.[49] They write that hundreds of thousands of teachers leave the profession each year, most before retirement age. Retaining teachers is important not only for student achievement, but to save money; The Alliance for Excellent Education, citing the research of Richard Ingersoll, estimates that states spend between $1 billion and $2.2 billion a year on costs related to teacher turnover.[50]

Teacher absenteeism and attrition have been associated negatively with student achievement. For example, Matthew Ronfeldt, Susanna Loeb, and Jim

Wyckoff concluded, in their study of teacher turnover on over 1.1 million New York City 4th and 5th grade student observations over 10 years, that "students in grade levels with higher turnover score lower in both ELA and math."[51]

Bureaucratic Climate and Culture

According to Sherry Joiner and Jennifer Edwards, whereas "climate refers to the morale or attitude of the organization, the culture refers to the expectations or unwritten rules that the organization establishes as their norm behaviors."[52] (See Figure 6.2 for differences between climate and culture.)

Figure 6.2 **Contrasting School Climate with Culture**

Climate	Culture
Monday versus Friday	Gives Mondays permission to be miserable
Attitude or mood of the group	Personality of the group
Provides a state of mind	Provides a (limited) way of thinking
Flexible, easy to change	Takes many years to evolve
Based on perceptions	Based on values and beliefs
Feel it when you come in the door	Members cannot feel it
Is all around us	Is part of us
The way we feel around here	The way we do things around here
First step to improvement	Determines if improvement is possible
It's in your head	It's in your head

Source: From *School Culture Rewired: How to Define, Assess, and Transform It* by Steve Gruenert and Todd Whitaker, p. 10, Copyright 2015 ASCD. Adapted with permission.

School climate refers to the school's effects on students, including teaching practices; diversity; and the relationships among administrators, teachers, parents, and students.[53] **School culture** refers to how teachers and other staff members work together and the set of beliefs, values, and assumptions they share.[54] A positive school climate and culture promotes students' ability to learn. If the climate or culture are not supportive of teachers, then attrition is more likely.

Jonathan Cohen, Libby McCabe, Nicholas Michelli, and Terry Pickeral's review of the literature found that a positive school climate is associated with and predictive of teacher **retention**.[55]

Lack of Teacher Autonomy

The concept of **teacher autonomy** refers to the professional independence of teachers in K–12 schools, especially the degree to which they can make autonomous decisions about what they teach to students and how they teach it. Unfortunately, evidence suggests that teacher autonomy has declined over the last decade.[56] Schools are full of **teacher-proof** and packaged curricula, which offensively imply that teachers are unable to think for themselves and are designed to reduce their autonomy. Having to teach using scripted curriculum and not being allowed to have input in the development of curriculum are both correlated with teacher attrition.[57]

In an international study of bureaucratic school structures and teacher self-efficacy in elementary schools, Ali Çağatay Kılınç, Serkan Koşar, Emre Er, and Zeki Öğdem found that teachers in schools structured to allow for more teacher autonomy had higher levels of self-efficacy than their peers.[58] National studies of teacher autonomy find that there are ways that schools can provide autonomy to their teachers, while other studies have found that teachers can also claim autonomy and **self-efficacy** for themselves.

Lack of a Career Ladder

A year following the publication of *A Nation at Risk,* Susan Rosenholtz and Mark Smylie cautioned that "for teachers to remain in teaching, the rewards must outweigh the frustrations. If they do not, the likelihood of defection from teaching increases substantially."[59] Career ladders are such reward systems, and Rosenholtz and Smylie pointed out that their absence "is a major reason that teachers leave the profession."[60] Research by Katrien Struyven and Gert Vanthournout found the same to be true in 2014—that lack of future prospects is the main reason for leaving the profession early.[61]

Lack of Resources

Public school teachers work within a system that requires—each year—teachers to do more with less. As funding for schools declines, teachers frequently must purchase classroom items with their own money.

A lack of resources extends beyond spending one's own money for supplies to such issues as lack of subject-matter training, deteriorating building conditions, and an absence of coaching and mentoring,[62] all of which make for a disempowering and isolating experience. As Carla Claycomb notes when discussing retention of high-quality teachers in urban schools,[63] induction programs "integrate teachers into the social life of their school by providing them with a network of new and experienced teachers with which to share concerns and discuss issues."[64]

Low Pay

Low pay for teachers has its origins in the "feminization" of the teaching field in the late 1800s. As demand for schools grew, more teachers were needed, and school organizers realized they could pay young women a smaller salary than their male counterparts. In their book *Women's Work? American Schoolteachers, 1650–1920,* Joel Perlmann and Robert A. Margo note that "by taking advantage of the fact that women were available to staff the schools at lower average wages than men, school boards could realize significant savings; this was so in rural as well as in urban areas."[65] According to Joan Jacobs Brumberg, "At the beginning of the 19th century, one in ten teachers was a woman. By 1920, 86% of American teachers were female, most of whom were employed at the elementary level."[66]

The norm of low teacher salaries has remained consistent in the United States for nearly 180 years—an indicator of the enduring lack of professional esteem and public value of teaching.[67] Susan Rosenholtz and Mark Smylie note that "low starting salaries and low professional status are major impediments to attracting the most academically talented" teachers.[68] According to Sylvia Allegretto and Lawrence Mishel, "The opportunity cost of becoming a teacher and remaining in the profession becomes more and more important as relative teacher pay falls further behind that of other professions."[69] Andy Jacob, Elizabeth Vidyarthi, and Kathleen Carroll find that compensation matters greatly to "irreplaceables"—teachers who are so successful they are nearly impossible to replace, but who too often vanish from schools due to unsatisfactory conditions. Their research identifies lack of compensation as one of the top three reasons that would cause such teachers to leave the classroom.[70]

The Mindset of Star Teachers Who Are
Able to Survive in a Bureaucracy

Star Teachers are plugged in and attentive of the school environment. They understand that you may not always be able to change your situation, but you can change the way you respond to it. They are aware that they teach in a bureaucracy but don't allow it to incapacitate them or kill their energy.

The characteristics of dysfunctional school bureaucracies include the following: (1) Superintendents come and go; (2) systems are highly centralized (human resource personnel boast about their increased inefficiency for managing large numbers of teacher applicants); (3) the chain of command moves downward; (4) the downward flow of directives generates an upward flow of misinformation; (5) there is a lack of transparency for how federal, state, and local funds are used; (6) academic units begin to operate as silos; (7) administrators often compete to protect themselves and bigger budgets that do not affect teachers or students; (8) there is a motivation by every bureaucrat to protect the system and not teachers and students; (9) bureaucratic functionaries are clever at selectively following and circumventing the rules for their own gains; (10) decisions are made by committees so no one person is held accountable; and (11) lower-level staff resort to surviving the present administration.[71]

Teachers are able to survive in a bureaucracy as a result of (1) **situational awareness,** or awareness that they work in a mindless bureaucracy and understanding of environmental and institutional elements and events and (2) **intrapersonal awareness,** or awareness of the personal or physical toil that bureaucracies extract from teachers and a willingness to develop mechanisms and structures of support.

Situational Awareness

Star Teachers realize how their students are mistreated and ignored by the school system but are able to avoid burnout and return year after year—partly because they spend little time trying to change the system. Susan Beltman, Caroline Mansfield, and Anne Price emphasize the importance of teachers using coping techniques outside the school environment to improve resilience.[72] Coping techniques may include seeking help from other colleagues or moving on whether the situation resolved as planned. Star Teachers are aware of the dysfunction of their school environments, but their devotion to children's learning motivates them to adjust, cope, and remain in these bureaucracies. Star Teachers are not oblivious to these bureaucratic conditions and are not afraid to replace unproductive administrative work with "more proactive decision-making strategies."[73]

Intrapersonal Awareness

When teachers are aware that they work within bureaucracies, they are better able to cope with and manage the organizational stress that is endemic to schools. Minimizing stress and working with other teachers who are also aware of their common working conditions can prevent physical fatigue and emotional frustration. Teachers have a limited amount of time and energy, and they should redirect as much as they can from dealing with stress to better serving students. Intrapersonal awareness or awareness of the personal or physical toil (e.g., knowing what e-mails to answer, knowing what professional development to engage in, knowing what meetings matter, placing students and parent needs first) can help teachers retain their energy and mental health.

According to Richard Schwab, Susan Jackson, and Randall Schuler, "Emotionally exhausted teachers may do what many individuals in their situation have done; they cope by depersonalizing their co-workers and students and by putting distance between themselves and others."[74] Star Teachers cope more effectively than their less successful peers by not depersonalizing their colleagues. Instead, they survive and thrive in bureaucracies by setting up networks of like-minded colleagues who serve as a support group and using informal structures to help them accomplish their teaching tasks.

The Behaviors of Star Teachers Who Are Able to Survive in a Bureaucracy

Star Teachers know how to move into "protective" action when the bureaucracy becomes a drain on their time, energy, or commitment to learners. The ability to survive in a bureaucracy requires that Star Teachers conduct themselves in ways that shield both their instructional space and their personhood. As Haberman writes,

> Star Teachers in large urban school systems are well aware they work in mindless bureaucracies. They recognize that even good teachers will

eventually burn out if they are subjected to constant stress, so they learn how to protect themselves from an interfering bureaucracy. As they gain experience, they learn the minimum things they must do to function in these systems without having the system punish them. Ultimately, they learn how to gain the widest discretion for themselves and their students without incurring the wrath of the system. Finally, they set up networks of a few like-minded teachers, or they teach in teams, or they simply find kindred spirits. They use these support systems as sources of emotional sustenance.[75]

Two of the most important skills Star Teachers leverage to survive in a bureaucracy are (1) organizational prowess and (2) personal prowess or teacher resilience.

Organizational Prowess

Star Teachers have **organizational prowess**,[76] or the ability to selectively navigate the demands of the bureaucracy. Bypassing certain procedures, policies, and people in the school is extremely beneficial because it saves precious time and energy. Star Teachers know what's really "going on" in the school and who the important individuals are who can assist them when necessary. They are prepared in advance when timelines, deadlines, or other bureaucratic changes are made and able to respond quickly and efficiently (e.g., a Star Teacher might fill out report cards well before deadline because she remembers the time everyone procrastinated and caused the school's computer system to crash). Star Teachers are also adept at prioritizing tasks (e.g., by responding only to the most pressing e-mails from the school bureaucracy).

Star Teachers have learned certain techniques that help them block out the bureaucratic noise so they can be fully present for their students. For instance, Star Teachers may avoid eating lunch in the staff lounge, using that time to get work done instead and avoiding the toxicity of colleagues' gossip. Choosing to eat lunch alone is a "protective" behavior that insulates teachers from the negativity and harsh criticism of others. Star Teachers choose to avoid sitting near coworkers who have nothing positive to share. Conversely, Star Teachers know when to speak up and when to be quiet during these meetings. They also know how to avoid committees that do not accomplish results—Stars do not want to work hard to accomplish little.

Star Teachers pick their battles intentionally and selectively. Consider the story of Ms. Caroleen Bennings, a third-year high school English teacher who teaches in the Chicago Public Schools (CPS), and her level of organizational prowess. Ms. Bennings wanted her students to have a homecoming dance, so she requested to be the coordinator of the homecoming committee. She understood that in this role she would be the chief organizer for the festivities.

Ms. Bennings quickly learned that the weekends were the best days of the week for the handful of students who were interested in co-planning the event, so she was wise to have befriended the janitor, who kindly opened the building up for her and her students. The school's principal did not like teachers entering the school on weekends for a variety of reasons, but Ms. Bennings didn't ask for permission, preferring to plead ignorance of school policy and to ask for forgiveness if she got caught. As previously discussed, Star Teachers are subversive practitioners.[77] After being reprimanded, Ms. Bennings informed her students that the homecoming planning committee would now be doing its work during class time by aligning it to classroom goals: students created informative and persuasive materials using writing strategies Ms. Bennings was teaching them, for example, and wrote and delivered short speeches to be read over the PA system before and after school.

Ms. Bennings was ultimately able to use the informal and impersonal school environment to help her students, such as befriending the school janitor. She is now in her 12th year at the same high school and still teaching freshman English. The success she has had with her students is especially notable given that "within five years, the typical CPS school loses over half of its teachers" and "many schools turn over half of their teaching staff every three years."[78]

Personal Prowess or Teacher Resilience

To Haberman, the "physical and emotional stamina" of Star Teachers is the embodiment of **resilience**.[79] The concept of "**teacher resiliency**" is difficult to define,[80] but fundamentally it is a kind of **personal prowess** that allows teachers to recover quickly from difficulties, frequently achieved through networking with peers, mentors, and loved ones. Teacher resilience is highly correlated with effectiveness:[81] Resilient teachers don't give up on their students, even if teaching them is challenging or they are physically tired. Indeed, although resilience is surely a form of toughness, it is a form of physical self-care (exercise, sufficient sleep, a well-balanced diet) and mental self-care (maintaining strong relationships with family and colleagues, obtaining counseling when needed, managing stress).

Resilience is the capacity to recover quickly from difficulties, or toughness. As shown in Figure 6.3, there are four dimensions of resilience:

1. **Physical:** Teachers must be fit, have stamina, be energetic, and know how to rest and recover so they can be effective throughout the long school year.
2. **Mental:** Teachers must believe in themselves and have a positive outlook.
3. **Emotional:** Teachers must resist acting on impulse and maintain a healthy (that is, realistic) amount of optimism.
4. **Spiritual:** Teachers must be empathetic and have some form of spirituality that helps them maintain their values and beliefs.

Research has found that teacher resilience contributes to their staying in the profession.[82] This is not surprising given Geoffrey Borman and N. Maritza Dowling's findings that teacher attrition is high in "schools with a lack of collaboration, teacher networking, and administrative support."[83]

The American Psychological Association (APA) shares the following 10 ways to build resilience:

1. **Make connections.** Good relationships with close family members, friends or others are important. Accepting help and support from those who care about you and will listen to you strengthens resilience. Some people find that being active in civic groups, faith-based organizations, or other local groups provides social support and can help with reclaiming hope. Assisting others in their time of need also can benefit the helper.
2. **Avoid seeing crises as insurmountable problems.** You can't change the fact that highly stressful events happen, but you can change how you interpret and respond to these events. Try looking beyond the present to how future circumstances may be a little better. Note any subtle ways in which you might already feel somewhat better as you deal with difficult situations.

Figure 6.3 **Four Dimensions of Resilience**

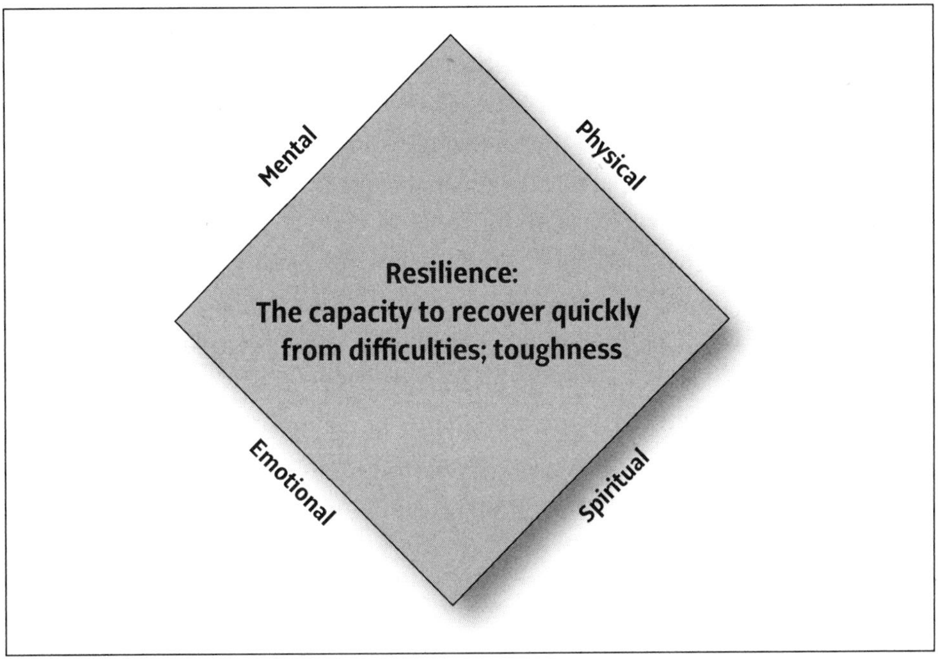

Mental

Physical

**Resilience:
The capacity to recover quickly
from difficulties; toughness**

Emotional

Spiritual

Source: Content copyright 2018 John Martin. Adapted with permission.

3. **Accept that change is a part of living.** Certain goals may no longer be attainable as a result of adverse situations. Accepting circumstances that cannot be changed can help you focus on circumstances that you can alter.

4. **Move toward your goals.** Develop some realistic goals. Do something regularly—even if it seems like a small accomplishment—that enables you to move toward your goals. Instead of focusing on tasks that seem unachievable, ask yourself, "What's one thing I know I can accomplish today that helps me move in the direction I want to go?"

5. **Take decisive actions.** Act on adverse situations as much as you can. Take decisive actions, rather than detaching completely from problems and stresses and wishing they would just go away.

6. **Look for opportunities for self-discovery.** People often learn something about themselves and may find that they have grown in some respect as

a result of their struggle with loss. Many people who have experienced tragedies and hardship have reported better relationships, greater sense of strength even while feeling vulnerable, increased sense of self-worth, a more developed spirituality and heightened appreciation for life.

7. **Nurture a positive view of yourself.** Developing confidence in your ability to solve problems and trusting your instincts help build resilience.

8. **Keep things in perspective.** Even when facing very painful events, try to consider the stressful situation in a broader context and keep a long-term perspective. Avoid blowing the event out of proportion.

9. **Maintain a hopeful outlook.** An optimistic outlook enables you to expect that good things will happen in your life. Try visualizing what you want, rather than worrying about what you fear.

10. **Take care of yourself.** Pay attention to your own needs and feelings. Engage in activities that you enjoy and find relaxing. Exercise regularly. Taking care of yourself helps to keep your mind and body primed to deal with situations that require resilience.[84]

Finally, consider the example of Terry, an elementary school teacher with eight years' experience. Terry has been an effective 1st and 2nd grade teacher and has been applying to be a district literacy coach, so far with no success. Despite having a master's degree and strong performance reviews, she has been turned down twice for the position. Though she is denied an opportunity to climb the career ladder, she continues to maintain her positive attitude and remain focused on her students. Terry is a Star Teacher.

Summary

Teachers' ability to survive in a bureaucracy helps them to be there mentally and physically for learners. Unfortunately, the inhumane routines of school systems often lead to burnout in the form of job dissatisfaction, absenteeism, or lack of commitment and teacher attrition. Star Teachers maintain a mindset that includes both situational awareness and intrapersonal awareness, both of which help them to avoid burnout. These teachers also display organizational prowess and personal prowess or teacher resilience, attributes which protect them from the school bureaucracy. Star Teachers also devise support structures to prevent themselves from becoming overburdened by the system. By not allowing the routine of the school to affect them and by taking care of themselves, Star Teachers are better able to take care of their students.

Key Words

absenteeism	attrition	bureaucracy
burnout	community model of schooling	depersonalization
"hard-to-staff-schools"	intrapersonal awareness	job satisfaction
organizational prowess	personal prowess	presenteeism
resilience	retention	school climate
school culture	self-efficacy	situational awareness
teacher autonomy	teacher-proof curriculum	teacher resiliency
teacher stress	vicious cycle	

Extension Exercises

1. Read "75 Examples of How Bureaucracy Stands in the Way of America's Students & Teachers" written by the BroadCenter, available at www .coreeducationllc.com/blog2/75-examples-of-how-bureaucracy-stands-in-the-way-of-students-and-teachers/.
   - Identify three to four main concepts from the essay that you think are worth remembering.
   - Identify two quotes that resonated with you and explain why.
   - Identify one question from the essay that prompted you to reflect.
   - Did anything in the essay contradict what you already knew or believed? If so, what?
   - Is there something you wish the author explained more?

2. Review Chandra Shaw's "Shut Up! And Let Me Teach: Ending the Assault on Teacher Autonomy" video, available at www.youtube.com/watch?v=f4l9fjdO2SI.
   - Do you agree or disagree with Ms. Shaw's points?

- What are two quotes from the video that resonated with you and why?
- Think of one question you have after viewing the video and reflect on it with colleagues.

3. Obtain a copy of your district's organizational flow chart and answer these questions:
   - Is the structure highly, moderately, or slightly bureaucratic? Identify four ways that this structure is positive or needs improvement.
   - Does the structure allow various stakeholders (e.g., students, families/parents, teachers) to participate equitably? Identify four ways to improve communication across stakeholder groups.
   - Name four bureaucratic practices in your grade level or subject area in your school. Next, share one or two strategies for each that may end or overhaul the practice for the benefit of teachers and learners.

Going Further

Web Resources

- The website *MindTools: Essential Skills for an Excellent Career* allows interested teachers to take the "Burnout Self-Test" here: www.mindtools.com/pages/article/newTCS_08.htm.
- The *Everyday Health* website contains many helpful resources for everyday physical, mental, and emotional health. Interested people can sign up for their newsletter, too: www.everydayhealth.com.
- Check out the website *Teacher Self-Care* for strategies to help you stay afloat in the bureaucracy: http://teacherselfcare.org/.

Additional Readings

- Kipps-Vaughan, D. (2013). Supporting teachers through stress management. *Principal Leadership, 13*(5), 12–16. In this short read, Kipps-Vaughan, who was a school psychologist for 25 years, shares how school psychologists can help promote healthier schools by providing stress reduction programming for teachers to reduce teacher absenteeism, turnover, and burnout.

- Mazzone, M. N., & Miglionico, B. J. (2014). *Stress-Busting Strategies for Teachers: How Do I Manage the Pressures of Teaching?* Alexandria, VA: ASCD. This book is a wellspring of hope and possibility. Veteran educators Nora Mazzone and Barbara Miglionico offer simple, proven tactics to help teachers manage the stresses of their work. Reading the book you will learn how to (1) employ healthy practices that positively affect your mindset; (2) react, generalize, and maintain to create a positive environment; (3) identify and use your ideal professional pace; (4) exploit your intrinsic preferences for how to get the work done; and (5) make food and exercise choices that will better fuel your mind and body.
- Mendler, A. N. (2014). *The Resilient Teacher: How Do I Stay Positive and Effective When Dealing with Difficult People and Policies?* Alexandria, VA: ASCD. This is an essential book for teachers who wish to survive in a bureaucracy. Mendler shares strategies that will help you to (1) communicate tactfully but forthrightly with administrators, colleagues, and students whose actions interfere with your ability to do your job properly; (2) confidently and convincingly express your thoughts and expectations to all stakeholders; and (3) increase your influence with coworkers, students, and parents.

Endnotes

1. Haberman, M. (2017). Selecting "Star" Teachers for children and youth in urban poverty. In V. Hill-Jackson & D. Stafford (Eds.), *Better teachers, better schools: What Star Teachers know, believe, and do* (pp. 1–11). Charlotte, NC: Information Age Publishing. (p. 8)

2. Haberman, M. (1995). Selecting 'Star' Teachers for children and youth in urban poverty. *Phi Delta Kappan, 76*(10), 777–781.

3. Hartlep, N. D., & McCubbins, S. A. (n.d.). *What makes a Star Teacher? Examining teacher dispositions, professionalization, and teacher effectiveness using the Haberman Star Teacher Pre-Screener.* Retrieved from www.habermanfoundation.org/Articles/PDF/WhatMakesAStarTeacher.pdf

4. Sanders, D. P., & Schwab, M. (1980). A school context for teacher development. *Theory into Practice, 19*(4), 271–277. (p. 273)

5. Haberman, M. (n.d.). Empowering children through effective education. Retrieved from www.habermanfoundation.org/Articles/Default.aspx?id=81

6. Kimbrough, R. B., & Todd, E. A. (1967). Bureaucratic organization and educational change. *Educational Leadership, 25*(3), 220–224. Retrieved from https://pdfs.semanticscholar.org/92f6/f2027bfcb10cbe79407ce6185c3a237b4130.pdf (p. 220)

7. Kimbrough & Todd (1967, pp. 220–221).

8. Tyack, D. (1967). Bureaucracy and the Common School: The example of Portland, Oregon, 1851–1913. *American Quarterly, 19*(3), 475–498. (p. 476).

9. Katz, M. (1971). *Class, bureaucracy, and schools: The illusion of educational change in America.* New York: Praeger.

10. Gray, F. (1993). Why we will lose: Taylorism in America's high schools. *Phi Delta Kappan, 74*(5), 370–374.

11. Taylor, F. W. (1909). *The principles of scientific management.* New York: Harper. Retrieved from www.saasoft.com/download/Taylor_FW_Principles_of_Scientific_Management_1911.pdf

12. Ross, E. W. (2010). Exploring Taylorism and its continued influence on work and schooling. In E. Heilman (Ed.), *Social studies and diversity teacher education: What we do and why we do it* (pp. 33–37). New York: Routledge. (p. 36)

13. Rothstein, R. (1993, Spring). The myth of public school failure. *The American Prospect.* Retrieved from http://prospect.org/article/myth-public-school-failure (para. 61)

14. Smith, K. B., & Larimer, C. W. (2004). A mixed relationship: Bureaucracy and school performance. *Public Administration Review, 64*(6), 728–736. Retrieved from http://mavdisk.mnsu.edu/parsnk/Linked%20Readings/Pol%20680/POL%20680%20readings/ksmith.pdf

15. Lavell, M. (1982). Secondary school organization: Bureaucracy or community? *School Organisation, 2*(1), 21–29.

16. Sergiovanni, T. J. (1994). *Building community in schools.* San Francisco: Jossey-Bass.

17. Haberman, M. (2004). Can Star Teachers create learning communities? *Educational Leadership, 61*(8), 52–56.

18. Haberman (2004, p. 52).

19. Fimian, M. J. (1982). What is teacher stress? *The Clearing House, 56*(3), 101–105. (p. 101)

20. Haberman, M. (2017). Teacher burnout in black and white. In Hill-Jackson & Stafford (2017, pp. 31–32).

21. Farber, B. A. (1984). Stress and burnout in suburban teachers. *Journal of Educational Research, 77*(6), 325–331. (p. 327)

22. Haberman (2017, p. 33).

23. Totawar, A. K., & Nambudiri, R. (2012). An overview of depersonalization in the organizational context. *IMJ, 4*(2), 64–72. (p. 67)

24. Zabel, M. K., Dettmer, P. A., & Zabel, R. H. (1984). Factors of emotional exhaustion, depersonalization, and sense of accomplishment among teachers of the gifted. *Gifted Child Quarterly, 28*(2), 65–69.

25. Totawar & Nambudiri (2012).

26. MetLife Survey of the American Teacher. (2013, February). Retrieved from www.metlife.com/assets/cao/foundation/MetLife-Teacher-Survey-2012.pdf (p. 6)

27. MetLife Survey (2013, p. 45).

28. Jennings, P. A., Frank, J. L., Snowberg, K. E., Coccia, M. A., & Greenberg, M. T. (2013). *Improving classroom learning environments by cultivating awareness and resilience in education (CARE): Results of a randomized controlled trial. School Psychology Quarterly, 28*(4), 374–390. Retrieved from http://www2.apa.org/pubs/journals/features/spq-0000035.pdf .

29. Matos, A. (2016, October 26). 1 in 4 U.S. teachers are chronically absent, missing more than 10 days of school. *Washington Post.* Retrieved from www.washingtonpost.com/local/education/1-in-4-us-teachers-are-chronically-absent-missing-more-than-10-days-of-school/2016/10/26/2869925e-9186-11e6-a6a3-d50061aa9fae_story.html?utm_term=.597cfe7155e6

30. Miller, R. T., Murnane, R. J., & Willett, J. B. (2007, August). *Do teacher absences impact student achievement? Longitudinal evidence from one urban school district.* Cambridge, MA: National Bureau of Economic Research. Retrieved from www.nber.org/papers/w13356.pdf

31. Wert, A. (2014, June 9). *Teacher absences are under attack (again).* Retrieved from www.frontlineeducation.com/Blog/June_2014/Teacher_Absences_Are_Under_Attack_(Again)

32. Miller, R. (2012). *Teacher absence as a leading indicator of student achievement: New national data offer opportunity to examine cost of teacher absence relative to learning loss.* Washington, DC: Center for American Progress. Retrieved from www.americanprogress.og/wp-content/uploads/2012/11/TeacherAbsence-6.pdf

33. Ross, A. (2017, February 24). Substitute teachers are in short supply at JCPS. *Courier Journal.* Retrieved from www.courier-journal.com/story/news/education/2017/02/24/wanted-substitute-teachers-jcps/97521582/ (para. 12)

34. Ross (2017).

35. Miller, R. (2012, November). Teacher absence as a leading indicator of student achievement. Retrieved from https://cdn.americanprogress.org/wp-content/uploads/2012/11/TeacherAbsence-6-INTRO.pdf (p. 1)

36. National Council on Teacher Quality. (2014). *Roll call: The importance of teacher attendance.* Washington, DC: Author. Retrieved from www.nctq.org/dmsView/RollCall_TeacherAttendance (p. 3)

37. Miller et al. (2008).

38. Smith, G. G. (2001). Increasing teacher attendance. *SubJournal, 2*(1), 8–17. Retrieved from http://88pqz2md3zt3enasj4b54xk180s.wpengine.netdna-cdn.com/wp-content/uploads/2014/08/IncreasingTeacherAttendance.pdf

39. Smith (2001, pp. 10–11).

40. Smith (2001, p. 13).

41. Haberman & Rickards (1990).

42. Sutcher, L., Darling-Hammond, L., & Carver-Thomas, D. (2016, September). *A coming crisis in teaching? Teacher supply, demand, shortages in the U.S.* Learning Policy Institute. Retrieved from https://learningpolicyinstitute.org/sites/default/files/product-files/A_Coming_Crisis_in_Teaching_BRIEF.pdf

43. Baldacci, L. (2006). Why teachers leave. . . and why new teachers stay. *American Educator.* Retrieved from www.aft.org/sites/default/files/periodicals/Teacher.pdf

44. Buchanan, J. (2010). May I be excused? Why teachers leave the profession. *Asia Pacific Journal of Education, 30*(2), 199–211.; Haberman, M., & Rickards, W. H. (1990). Urban teachers who quit: Why they leave and what they do. *Urban Education, 25*(3), 297–303.

45. Brownell, M. T., Smith, S. W., McNellis, J. R., & Miller, M. D. (1997). Attrition in special education: Why teachers leave the classroom and where they go. *Exceptionality, 7*(3), 143–155. (p. 148)

46. Futernick, K. (2007). *A possible dream: Retaining California's teachers so all students learn.* Sacramento: California State University. Retrieved from www.wested.org/wp-content/uploads/2016/11/139941242532061.TeacherRetention_Futernick07-3.pdf (p. viii)

47. Simos, E. (2013). Why do new teachers leave? How could they stay? *The English Journal, 102*(3), 100–105. Retrieved from https://wiuenglishlangartsmethods.files.wordpress.com/2013/01/ej1023why.pdf

48. Futernick (2007, p. 12).

49. Sutcher, L., Darling-Hammond, L., & Carver-Thomas, D. (2016, September 15). A coming crisis in teaching? Teacher supply, demand, and shortages in the U.S. Retrieved from https://learningpolicyinstitute.org/product/coming-crisis-teaching

50. Alliance for Excellent Education. (2014, July). *On the path to equity: Improving the effectiveness of beginning teachers.* Washington, DC: Alliance for Excellent Education. Retrieved from http://all4ed.org/wp-content/uploads/2014/07/PathToEquity.pdf

51. Ronfeldt, M., Loeb, S., & Wyckoff, J. (2012, January). *How teacher turnover harms student achievement.* Washington, DC: National Center for Analysis of Longitudinal Data in Education Research. Retrieved from www.caldercenter.org/sites/default/files/Ronfeldt-et-al.pdf

52. Joiner, S., & Edwards, J. (2008). Novice teachers: Where are they going and why don't they stay? *Journal of Cross-Disciplinary Perspectives in Education, 1*(1), 36–43. (p. 47) Retrieved from http://people.wm.edu/~mxtsch/Teaching/JCPE/Volume1/JCPE_2008-01-07.pdf

53. ASCD. (2017). Retrieved from www.ascd.org/research-a-topic/school-culture-and-climate-resources.aspx (para. 1).

54. ASCD (2017, para. 2).

55. Cohen, J., McCabe, L., Michelli, N. M., & Pickeral, T. (2009). School climate: Research, policy, practice, and teacher education. *Teachers College Record, 111*(1), 180–213.

56. Sparks, D., & Malkus, N. (2015, December). *Public school teacher autonomy in the classroom across school years 2003–04, 2007–08, and 2011–12.* Retrieved from https://nces.ed.gov/pubs2015/2015089.pdf

57. Westervelt, E. (2016, September 15). Frustration. Burnout. Attrition. It's time to address the national teacher shortage. NPR. Retrieved from www.npr.org/sections/ed/2016/09/15/493808213/frustration-burnout-attrition-its-time-to-address-the-national-teacher-shortage

58. Kilinç, A. Ç., Kosar, S., Er, E., & Öğdem, Z. (2016). The relationship between bureaucratic school structures and teacher self-efficacy. *McGill Journal of Education, 51*(1), 615–634. Retrieved from http://mje.mcgill.ca/article/view/9139/7094

59. Rosenholtz, S. J., & Smylie, M. A. (1984). Teacher compensation and career ladders. *The Elementary School Journal, 85*(2), 149–166. (p. 152)

60. Rosenholtz & Smylie (1984, p. 162).

61. Struyven, K., & Vanthournout, G. (2014). Teachers' exit decisions: An investigation into the reasons why newly qualified teachers fail to enter the teaching profession or why those who do enter do not continue teaching. *Teaching and Teacher Education, 43*, 37–45.

62. Kozol, J. (1991). *Savage inequalities: Children in America's schools.* New York: Crown.

63. Claycomb, C. (2000). High-quality urban school teachers: What they need to enter and to remain in hard-to-staff schools. *The State Education Standard, 1*(1), 17–20.

64. Claycomb (2000, p. 20).

65. Perlmann, J., & Margo, R. A. (2001). *Women's work? American schoolteachers, 1650–1920.* Chicago: University of Chicago Press. (p. 118)

66. Brumberg, J. J. (1983). The feminization of teaching: "Romantic sexism" and American Protestant denominationalism. *History of Education Quarterly, 23*(3), 379–384. (p. 379)

67. Darling-Hammond, L. (2010). *The flat world and education: How America's commitment to equity will determine our future.* New York: Teachers College Press.

68. Rosenholtz & Smylie (1984, p. 160).

69. Allegretto, S. A., & Mishel, L. (2016, August 9). *The teacher pay gap is wider than ever: Teachers' pay continues to fall further behind pay of comparable workers.* Washington, DC: Economic Policy Institute. Retrieved from www.epi.org/files/pdf/110964.pdf (p. 19)

70. Jacob, A., Vidyarthi, E., & Carroll, K. (2012). *The irreplaceable: Understanding the real retention crisis in America's urban schools.* Retrieved from https://tntp.org/assets/documents/TNTP_Irreplaceables_2012.pdf

71. Haberman (2004, pp. 180–182).

72. Beltman, S., Mansfield, C., & Price, A. (2011). Thriving not just surviving: A review of research on teacher resilience. *Educational Research Review, 6*(3), 185–207.

73. Niece (2010, p. 8).

74. Schwab, R. L., Jackson, S. E., & Schuler, R. S. (1986). Educator burnout: Sources and consequences. *Educational Research Quarterly, 10*(3), 14–30. Retrieved from http://smlr.rutgers.edu/sites/smlr.rutgers.edu/files/documents/faculty_staff_docs/EducatorBurnout.pdf (p. 15)

75. Haberman (1995, p. 780).

76. Hartlep, N. D., & Associates. (2014). *What makes a Star Teacher? Examining the dispositions of PK–12 urban teachers in Chicago.* Normal, IL: Educational Administration and Foundation. Retrieved from www.educationviews.org/wp-content/uploads/2015/01/Hartlep-and-Colleagues-2014.pdf

77. Hatch, J. A. (2007). Learning as subversive activity. *Phi Delta Kappan, 89*(4), 310–311.

78. Allensworth, E., Ponisciak, S., Mazzeo, C. (2009, June). *The schools teachers leave: Teacher mobility in Chicago Public Schools.* Chicago: Consortium on Chicago School Research. Retrieved from http://consortium.uchicago.edu/sites/default/files/publications/CCSR_Teacher_Mobility.pdf (p. 1)

79. Haberman (2004, p. 53).

80. Beltman, S., Mansfield, C., & Price, A. (2011). Thriving not just surviving: A review of research on teacher resilience. *Educational Research Review, 6*(3), 185–207.

81. Gu, Q., & Day, C. (2007). Teachers resilience: A necessary condition for effectiveness. *Teaching and Teacher Education, 23*, 1302–1316. Retrieved from https://moo27pilot.eduhk.hk/pluginfile.php/379346/mod_resource/content/2/Gu%20%20Day%20(2007).pdf

82. Arnup, J., & Bowles, T. (2016). Should I stay or should I go? Resilience as a protective factor for teachers' intention to leave the teaching profession. *Australian Journal of Education, 60*(3), 229–244.

83. Borman, G. D., & Dowling, N. M. (2008). Teacher attrition and retention: A meta-analytic and narrative review of the research. *Review of Educational Research, 78*(3), 367–409. (p. 396)

84. www.apa.org/helpcenter/road-resilience.aspx

7

Accepting and Admitting Fallibility

Haberman's dimension of fallibility refers to teachers' willingness to admit mistakes and correct them. Doing this establishes the classroom climate and models for students how they should respond to their own mistakes.

Learning Outcomes

Upon completion of this chapter, you will be able to

- Identify the mindsets of Star Teachers who admit making mistakes in the classroom.
- Self-reflect on your own mindset and how it affects your teaching.
- Identify the practices and behaviors of Star Teachers who admit to being fallible and apply them to your own instruction.

Interstate New Teacher Assessment and Support Consortium (InTASC) Standards

Standard #2: Learning Differences
The teacher works with others to create environments that support individual and collaborative learning, and that encourage positive social interaction, active engagement in learning, and self-motivation.

Standard #9: Professional Learning and Ethical Practice

The teacher engages in ongoing professional learning and uses evidence to continually evaluate his/her practice, particularly the effects of his/her choices and actions on others (learners, families, other professionals, and the community), and adapts practice to meet the needs of each learner.

★ ★ ★ ★ ★ ★ ★ ★ ★ ★ ★

Defining *Fallibility*

All K–12 teachers are fallible—that is, they are prone to make mistakes in the classroom. Indeed, we all are: "to err is human." But how normal is it to admit our mistakes? Doing so is an essential characteristic of Star Teachers. The **"fallibility"** of teachers—their ability to be "real" and "authentic" with their students and admit when they made a mistake—are highly consequential for students of all grade levels. As Haberman points out, "Individuals who cannot recognize, admit, or abide mistakes in themselves are not likely to be tolerant of others' mistakes."[1] The striking difference between the fallibility of Star Teachers and the fallibility of pre-Star Teachers lies in the nature of their respective admissions.

The Nature of Fallibility for Star Teachers

Although most teachers admit their errors and chalk them up to being human, Star Teachers admit to mistakes that break trust with students, whereas ineffective teachers admit only to inconsequential mistakes like misspelling something on the whiteboard. "The difference between Star Teachers and pre-Star Teachers is in the nature of the mistakes that they recognize and own up to. Stars acknowledge serious problems and ones having to do with human relations; [pre-Stars] confess to spelling and arithmetic errors," Haberman writes.[2] Pre-Stars never disclose larger mistakes and would never expose these errors to others. Star Teachers, by contrast, acknowledge huge missteps such as "breaking trust: e.g., misjudging a child in some important way, blaming or publicly embarrassing a student for something. Although they know their children quite well, they confess errors of occasionally rushing to judgment too quickly without getting all the facts about a particular incident. Although their errors of judgment are rare, Stars are willing to confess to serious lapses, which may result in breaking trust with a child."[3]

As previously discussed, Star Teachers understand the importance of maintaining and growing teacher-student relationships. When a teacher breaks trust with a student, repairing the relationship in an authentic way becomes the only common-sensical thing to do. Embarrassing a student, ridiculing a student, being sarcastic with a student, or mistakenly blaming a student are some ways that teachers break trust. Pre-Star Teachers are oblivious to how breaking trust can occur in the classroom because their perception of student-teacher relationship is based on roles and love: students love their teacher, and teachers love their students (who love their teachers). Star Teachers don't fall into this trap; they understand the importance of professional instead of personal relationships with their students.

Fallibility as a Strength

Popular culture in the United States treats making mistakes as something that should be avoided at all cost. When we do make mistakes, being willing and able to admit them can prove challenging.[4] But why is admitting mistakes so difficult for some? And why is admitting our mistakes perceived as bad? The reason for both is that these admissions are perceived by many to show weakness. Who likes to be seen as weak? Mistakes are hidden instead of used productively because individuals wish to be viewed as strong.

Do teachers want mistakes to be hidden or made open to the classroom community? Mistakes, whether made by teachers or students, should not be associated with being weak or ineffective. According to Michael Rogers, admitting to errors "provides permission," "builds trust," and helps everyone involved to learn.[5] Students, in particular, learn that it is OK to talk about their mistakes in that they can do so without feeling judged or threatened.

Teachers who believe they are never wrong are **narcissist educators.** They are stubborn, irresponsible, and unprofessional, and they are less effective in the classroom than teachers who admit their fallibility. For example, a teacher who is narcissistic may attend a district-required professional development session and learn about an evidence-based practice, only to respond, "That won't work with my students!"

As discussed in Chapter 5, Star Teachers hold a professional orientation toward learners, not a personal one. As Carol Lakey Hess writes,

A narcissistic teacher expects that his or her students will mirror his or her needs, especially needs for admiration and loyalty. Because of the power dynamic inherent in educational relationships, students can easily become "narcissistic supplies" at the teacher's "disposal." . . . Students in narcissistic learning environments, in order to survive, learn to "accommodate" to and gratify the teacher's needs. Usually, this also requires suppressing their own intellectual needs and ideas.[6]

The net effect of being a narcissistic educator is that students will suppress curiosity, will fear making mistakes and doing or saying anything that will upset their teacher, and will not learn as much as they would with a teacher who encourages making mistakes when they lead to deeper understanding. Pre-Stars who are narcissistic, overly sensitive, or **perfectionist** avoid making mistakes as best as they can, and if they do make a mistake, frequently it is an instructional one.

"I'm Only Human": The Mindset of Star Teachers Who Admit Their Mistakes

When teachers are asked, "Do you ever make mistakes?" they answer, "Of course, I'm only human!" or "Everyone makes mistakes."[7] But what types of mistakes do teachers make and which do they confess making? According to Haberman, a "reluctance to admit to serious errors, especially in the presence of children, is typical of teachers who have a problem owning mistakes. They appear to be fearful of admitting mistakes because they believe they will lose stature in the eyes of the children. Actually, the exact reverse is true."[8] It is difficult for students to learn where mistakes are not allowed. The Haberman Star Teacher Pre-Screener Instrument can predict, with remarkable accuracy,[9] whether teachers will model fallibility in the classroom.

Research by Benjamin Apelojg has found that many teachers have a "fear of making mistakes [that] can lead to teacher-centered lessons, and thereby [limit] pupils' possibilities to learn autonomously."[10] Teachers who admit to making mistakes lead by example to show that the classroom is a safe space, one where judgment is suspended and trial-and-error is allowed. This kind of leadership builds a community of trust in the classroom, which ultimately leads to deeper and more personal learning. According to Haberman, "The child so fearful of being wrong doesn't try and once trying stops, learning stops. The surest way to teach children and youth to accept their own fallibility is to have teachers who can accept theirs.". . . The importance of fallibility cannot be overstated.[11] If the classroom climate is one where mistakes are not supposed to happen, then mistakes will be treated as "a sign of weakness or stupidity."[12]

Star Teachers are "failure-tolerant"[13] insofar as they help students see the educational value of mistakes. Because Star Teachers are concerned that students will learn to be afraid of making mistakes, they model learning from errors in their teaching. Teachers know that many of the world's most innovative and successful individuals were not handcuffed by the possibility they would make mistakes. A Star Teacher might say to students, "Practice doesn't make perfect. Nothing is perfect. Practice makes permanent. We need to try things that are hard; otherwise we are not learning as much as we could." Star Teachers express fallibility in a way that centers learning, not error, and that helps to cultivate strong student-teacher relationships.[14]

Star Teachers believe that students should "fall forward" by learning from mistakes. Research by Peter Bieling, Anne Israeli, Jennifer Smith, and Martin Antony found that "individuals high in perfectionism set a higher standard for the exam, were more likely to fall short of their goals, and experienced more negative affect about the exam, whether they had met their goal or not."[15] As this study shows, focusing on getting things "correct" or "perfect" can lead to maladaptive behavior and cause distress for students. Instead, students should focus on learning, which by its essence involves making errors.

Behaviors of Star Teachers Who Demonstrate Fallibility

Star Teachers understand that intelligence and learning are effort-based and that making mistakes is a function of taking risks in the classroom. They demonstrate fallibility in two distinct ways: (1) by admitting to big mistakes to engender trust among learners, and (2) by cultivating curiosity, creativity, and experimentation using fallibility as a learning tool.

Admitting to Big Mistakes to Engender Trust Among Learners

Star Teachers who admit their mistakes are being vulnerable and authentic with their students.[16] Being vulnerable and authentic comes more naturally in learning environments that are student- rather teacher-centered. Haberman points out that strong-handed teachers are not effective and will not lead to positive learning outcomes: "Schools begin teaching students a dysfunctional way of relating to authority in kindergarten. Young children are readily controlled by authoritarian, directive teaching and simple rewards. As children mature, however, they come to realize that school authorities lack any real power to make them comply."[17]

When students don't hear their teacher admit to making mistakes, they receive the message that mistakes are to be avoided. But as Haberman points out, "Children and young people cannot learn in classrooms where mistakes are not allowed."[18] Hunter Maats and Katie O'Brien write that the goal for teachers should be to teach students to embrace mistakes, not avoid making them.[19]

When students feel safe and respected, they are better able to learn, so mistakes should be addressed openly before distrust enters the classroom environment and depersonalization ensues. When this happens, the learning environment deteriorates into an unhealthy, unengaging, lifeless classroom. As Stephen Brookfield writes in his book *The Skillful Teacher: On Technique, Trust, and Responsiveness in the Classroom,* to cultivate trust and respect, "you have to make students feel safe."[20]

Bobbi Morehead writes that Star Teachers "know they are human beings with flaws, so instead of trying to cover up the flaws, they use that knowledge to uncover learning opportunities for their students which in turn makes the classroom truly a life lab of authentic learning experiences."[21] Patricia Phelps writes, "Fallibility and persistence are important in any human endeavor, but especially in teaching . . . we should help prospective teachers admit, embrace, and value their errors."[22]

Breaking **trust** or negatively affecting the teacher-student relationship are foremost concerns in student-centered classrooms. Trust refers to confidence and understanding. According to Combs, Harris, and Edmonson, "In [a classroom] with high trust, when the [teacher] says the wrong thing or says it in the wrong way, students still understand what was intended and give the [teacher] latitude to make mistakes. In contrast, when a [teacher] makes a mistake in a low-trust [classroom], distrust of his or her intentions leads to problems and creates a barrier to meaningful [learning]."[23]

Admitting mistakes has at least five positive outcomes:

1. It earns respect.
2. It strengthens the classroom.
3. It's a form of leading by example.
4. It builds a culture of trust in the classroom.[24]
5. It leads to deeper and more personal learning.[25]

Students **respect** teachers who are open and honest with them because they can trust them. **Vulnerability** strengthens the classroom because it humanizes everyone and breaks down barriers, differences, and hierarchies. As Beaudoin writes, "Respect is important because it contributes to a context of safety, openness, and reflection; this context is crucial for the brain to effectively process and encode academic material, as opposed to being preoccupied with emotional concerns."[26]

Consider the 4th grade classroom of Mr. Johnson, a Star Teacher, on a late Tuesday afternoon after recess. Mark, a boisterous 10-year-old, bounces into class and exclaims that Terrance hit him. This accusation doesn't surprise Mr. Johnson because Terrance is always one short fuse away from lashing out. Mr. Johnson asks, "Terrance, why did you hit Mark?" A look of confusion comes over Terrance's face, but Mr. Johnson recognizes this as a tactic to thwart responsibility. "But I didn't—" The Star Teacher impatiently interrupts. "Terrance, I need you to apologize right now, young man. That behavior is not acceptable in our classroom." Begrudgingly, Terrance squeaks out "sorry" to Mark, who slyly slides into his chair with his tongue wagging at Terrance. Star Teachers sometimes make mistakes by not following the recommendations in this book, but when they realize a mistake has been made, they address it.

The rest of the afternoon and the following morning, Terrance is uncharacteristically withdrawn. Keisha, who is known for being a peacemaker, slides a note to Mr. Johnson and shares that it was Mark who hit Terrance on the playground the prior day; afraid of getting into trouble, he plotted to make it seem the other way around. Mr. Johnson feels deeply remorseful. He realizes that his relationship with Terrance has been bruised and needs to be healed right away, so he takes immediate action by calling Terrance to the front of the class and apologizing for accusing him of hitting Mark. After his apology, Terrance's facial expression shows that while trust had been broken, Mr. Johnson, the Star Teacher, is on the road to repairing it because a child's natural reflex is forgiveness.[27] Soon after, Terrance forgives Mr. Johnson and their relationship is repaired.

When teachers admit mistakes, students notice and integrate the practice into their daily lives. As Bill Schorr writes, "Children can be taught to feel shame when they make a mistake, or they can be taught to be excited about mistakes as opportunities to learn."[28] It is "caught, not taught." Star Teachers rarely break trust with students, but when it is broken, they immediately seek to repair it. Robert J. Walker shares three solutions that teachers can use when they break trust by making mistakes in the classroom:

1. When a student is mistakenly accused, the teacher is willing to apologize to the student.
2. The teacher is willing to make adjustments when students inform the teacher there was material on the test they were not told to study or when errors are made in grading.
3. The teacher is willing to give students an opportunity to redo a project if she did not explain an important step in the assignment.[29]

Stephen Brookfield writes, "Trust is not given to teachers as a right, and teachers cannot assume that it exists a priori. It must be earned."[30] He points out that "public declarations of fallibility from teachers who have clearly earned credibility are prized by students."[31]

Cultivating Curiosity, Creativity, and Experimentation Using Fallibility as a Learning Tool

Because school is fast-paced, teachers tend to call on students who are quick to grasp a lesson due to existing background knowledge. Indeed, the school culture, as a whole, measures, records, and ranks school achievement, competency, and learning: words correct per minute (WCPM) on running records for reading, the number of correct answers on spelling tests, the number of rote-memorized arcane historical facts recited correctly on a social studies test. These are just a few concrete examples of traditional instruction valuing error-free responses.

Students who do not make mistakes are seen to be intelligent and capable, while students who do are viewed as less intelligent rather than slow to grasp a specific concept. Exacerbating these falsehoods, popular television and print media socialize people into believing that mistakes and failure are not helpful to the learning process. Prodigies and autodidacts are believed to be born, not made, through countless hours of repetitive practice and trial-and-error. It is not uncommon to hear parents tell their children, "It's OK—math didn't come easy to me either." The subtle insinuations are that you should avoid things that don't come easy to you and that moving outside your comfort zone is not necessary.

Learning Requires Us to Make Mistakes

The following scenario is classic. A teacher returns essays to her 6th grade students. When Jillian receives her essay back, she sees the red pen marks and is devastated. When students like Jillian see red pen marks, they interpret them to indicate their level of worth as writers.[32] This can have a soul-crushing effect on these students' attitudes and willingness to write future essays. "Why should I try again?" they may ask themselves. "The same thing will happen. I'm just not good at writing."

By contrast, other students interpret the red marks as pointing out opportunities for enhancing their writing ability. "Oh, I see what I did incorrectly here," they say to themselves. "I agree. I *did* write that sentence in the passive voice. Mrs. Smith's feedback was just what I needed. I will revise my essay and it will be better." These students understand that they are not perfect—no one is. They see their mistakes as part of the greater learning process (especially when it comes to writing).

Alina Tugend describes how a culture that praises exemplary performance can cause children to become "**victims of excellence**," reluctant to take intellectual or learning risks for fear of not excelling or not getting the "right" answer right away.[33] Victim-of-excellence students conduct a cost-benefit analysis in their minds: "Do I take a risk and possibly be wrong, or not take a risk and definitely be right?" This reality is sad, unfortunate, and unnecessary.

The fear of making mistakes can be seen in Figure 7.1.

Figure 7.1 **Learning from Our Mistakes**

As Meriwynn Mansori writes, "If we want to create [perseverant], capable, problem-solving students, we need to allow them to make mistakes that encourage them to learn and grow. Students learn best when their affective filter is low. When mistake-making is perceived as bad, it is detrimental to learning."[34] Teachers should teach and model persistence in the classroom,[35] perhaps by hanging up a poster that reads something like, "The worst thing about making a mistake is being afraid of making one."

Stars also understand the all-important practice of allowing enough wait time for students to respond to questions without feeling pressured to get the answer right. They encourage students to take their time and think about it, adding that all responses, even incorrect ones, are valid. The body language of Star Teachers during wait time conveys their interest in learners' ideas, pushing not for a correct answer, but a thoughtful choice. Star Teachers encourage stick-with-it-ness in students through their verbal and nonverbal responses.

Thomas Edison did not fail 2,000 times making the incandescent lightbulb; he found 2,000 ways *not to* make an incandescent light bulb. Mistakes are stepping stones for success. As the expression has it, "The key to increasing your success is to increase your rate of failure." Because gradual improvement through practice so often occurs behind closed doors, many students are clueless about how much effort goes into performing at a high level. The more and harder you practice, the likelier you are to experience failures—so sometimes if you're failing a lot, it paradoxically means you're succeeding. Too often, when students see other students succeeding, they just chalk it up to them being born that way instead of to practice.

Richard Curwin shares the following nine ways to teach with mistakes.[36]

1. Stop marking errors on tests and papers without explaining why they're wrong. Give enough explanation to help your student understand what went wrong and how to fix it. A big red **X** is insufficient.

2. Give students a chance to correct their mistakes and redo their work. This allows mistakes to become learning opportunities.

3. Improvement must become a significant factor in the evaluation process. The more a student improves, the higher his or her grade. Nothing shows learning from mistakes more than improvement.

4. When a student makes a mistake in a class discussion, don't say things like, "No, wrong, can anyone help him?" Don't just call on someone else without further comment. Instead, ask the student, "Why do you think so? Can you give an example? If you could ask yourself a question about your answer, what would it be?"

5. If a teacher asks, "Who was the first president of the United States?" and a student answers, "Barack Obama," instead of saying, "You're wrong," try saying, "Barack Obama is a president, you're right about that. However, he wasn't the first. Let's go further back in history." Even silly answers can be responded to in this way.

6. If a student needs help with an answer, let him or her choose a classmate to help. Call the helper something like a "personal consultant."

7. Instead of (or at least in addition to) walls filled with students' achievements, have a wall where students can brag about their biggest mistakes and what they learned from them.

8. Have bi-weekly class meetings where students share a mistake they made, what happened after, and what they learned.

9. Be sure to tell the class about your own mistakes, especially if they are funny, and what you learned from them.[37]

Coaching Perseverance

Deep learning requires making mistakes.[38] Haberman notes that "as children move through grades, they become less willing to try for fear of making mistakes and being embarrassed in front of their peers. They also become less willing to seek help from teachers—particularly if this help is given publicly in front of peers."[39] Teachers who encourage students to persevere in the face of mistakes are helping them to develop growth mindsets. Perseverant students "value hard work, learning, and challenges and see failure as a message that they need to change tasks in order to succeed next time."[40]

Teachers further foster a growth mindset in students by adding the word *yet* to the end of complaints (e.g., I can't do long division *yet*; I don't have the skills to answer this question *yet*; I don't understand dependent and independent clauses *yet*), implying that ability is something that grows over time.[41] Star Teachers also ask questions that help students own their learning and think through solutions, such as "What did you learn from today's lesson?" and "What other strategies could you have tried to achieve different results?" But most important, Star Teachers establish a **culture of effort** and risk taking. Star Teachers do not hide the fact that learning a new concept will be tough and are sensitive to the fact that some learners are fearful of public failure. Haberman explains:

> One Star Teacher I observed told the class directly: "Look, if you're learning to parachute out of airplanes, you've got to get it right the first time; otherwise there won't be a second time. But that's not the way we learn in this classroom, or the way we learn most things in life. We learn by trying, correcting, getting better, trying again. I make dozens of mistakes every day, and I'll show them to you. And if you

see one that I miss, I would appreciate your help. Let me know about it." This teacher, from day one, systematically created a classroom atmosphere effort and deemphasized children's notions of native ability that somehow should lead them to knowing content without engaging in the hard work of studying, thinking, trying, correcting, and redoing.[42]

The Star Teacher Haberman describes is modeling a fearless acceptance of fallibility. Such a gesture sends a powerful message that effort, persistence, success, and failure are all welcome components of learning. Star Teachers understand that for most students, academic achievement is often a result of continuous, persistent effort and not some magical talent. "Star Teachers demonstrate their commitment to eliciting, fostering, and rewarding effort in their daily teaching, in their marking and grading, and in the way they discuss their students' work with parents and the students themselves," writes Haberman. "Their ideology considers no alternative."[43]

Summary

What do you call a teacher who is both willing to admit her mistakes and is highly tolerant of students' mistakes? A Star Teacher. This chapter has focused on fallibility, or a teacher's willingness to admit mistakes and correct them. Classrooms with Star Teachers who are unafraid of making public mistakes are spaces where deep learning can take place because learning requires making multiple mistakes and persisting in the face of them. Star Teachers want students to respond to their mistakes in the process of learning, and classrooms where students feel safe and engaged without worrying about mistakes reflecting poorly on them.

Key Words

culture of effort	fallibility	narcissist educators
perfectionist	respect	trust
victim of excellence	vulnerability	

Extension Exercises

1. Review *Rethinking Schools'* Q&A, "What Do I Do When I Realize I've Made a Mistake with a Child?" available at www.rethinkingschools.org/static/ publication/newteacher/NTQA2.pdf. Make a list of any mistakes you have made and how you responded. If you responded in a way that was not public, write down how you will respond in the future to similar mistakes.

2. Consider the message in "Three Ways to Celebrate Mistakes in Class." View the video at www.youtube.com/watch?v=hGafkyjaQWk. Three strategies are shared: (1) Start classes with the norm that you love and want mistakes; (2) don't just praise mistakes—say why they are important; and (3) give work that encourages mistakes.

   • Do you agree or disagree with the suggestions in the video?
   • Do you already do these things in your classroom?
   • How can you utilize these suggestions in your own practice?

3. Go online at www.mindsetkit.org/topics/celebrate-mistakes and test one of the activities with your students. After delivering the lesson to your students, talk with a colleague about how it went and what you gained from the experience. While you're online, have your students take the Mindset Test. Do they agree or disagree with their results? Why or why not?

4. Check out the book *The Girl Who Never Made Mistakes* (2011) by Gary Rubinstein and Mark Pett, published by Sourcebooks. Read it to your 5th–8th grade students. Use the lesson plan found at www.thenedshow .com/assets/a4-the-girl-who-never-made-mistakes-primary-lesson-plans-the-ned-show.pdf and use it with your students.

Going Further

Web Resources

   • The Haberman Educational Foundation (HEF) website contains valuable resources for teachers. Those interested can take the Star Teacher Pre-Screener, which tests for fallibility, for $20 here: www.habermanfoundation .org/Evaluation-Tools/.

- The American Psychological Association (APA) website has many resources that address student-teacher relationships here: www.apa.org/education/K12/relationships.aspx.
- The *Talks with Teachers* podcast archives episodes that teachers will find both personally and professionally interesting here: https://talkswith-teachers.podbean.com. Especially relevant to this chapter is Episode 60, featuring 2014 National Teacher of the Year Sean McComb: http://talk-swithteachers.com/60-2014-national-teacher-year-sean-mccomb/.
- Teachers can use the "Grit Lesson Plan: The Perseverance Walk" to help students develop grit and perseverance: www.edutopia.org/pdfs/rmr/edutopia-rsrchmaderelevant-grit-perseverance-walklesson.pdf. A video is also available here showing Amy Lyon's 5th grade lesson on perseverance.

Videos

- The video "Michael Margolis: How Vulnerability Creates Trusting Relation-ships" can be found on YouTube at www.youtube.com/watch?v=_i2yIaFmHzk. In the video, educator and entrepreneur Michael Margolis discusses how truth gets attention, empathy establishes connection, and vulnerability reminds people of shared values and similar interests. Teachers who are interested in cultivating deep relationships with their students will benefit from viewing this video.

Additional Readings

- Costa, A. L., & Kallick, B. (Eds.). (2008). *Learning and leading with Habits of Mind: 16 essential characteristics for success.* Alexandria, VA: ASCD. This book is rife with examples of how teachers must use mistakes in the class-room to support learning. Authors Arthur Costa and Bena Kallick identify fallibility as a habit of mind.
- Haberman, M. (2004). *Star Teachers: The ideology and best practices of effec-tive teachers of diverse children and youth in poverty.* Houston, TX: Haberman Educational Foundation. Chapter 13 of this book addresses fallibility. Teachers will benefit from reading this section to better understand what fallibility means and its consequences in the classroom.

- Phelps, P. H. (2000). Mistakes as vehicles for educating teachers. *Action in Teacher Education, 21*(4), 41–49.
- Young, E. (2009). What makes a great teacher? *Phi Delta Kappan, 90*(6), 438–439. This short article discusses the dispositions great teachers possess and how they affect practice. Teachers who are strapped for time will find this reading accessible and enlightening. According to author Erin Young, great teachers do more than simply advance student learning.

Endnotes

1. Haberman, M. (2004). *Star Teachers: The ideology and best practices of effective teachers of children and youth in poverty.* Houston, TX: Haberman Educational Foundation. (p. 189)

2. Haberman, M. (1994). Selecting "Star" Teachers for children and youth in urban poverty. *Phi Delta Kappan, 76*(10), 777–781. (p. 780)

3. Haberman (2004, p. 187).

4. Why it's hard to admit to being wrong. (2007, July 20). *NPR.* Retrieved from www.npr.org/templates/transcript/transcript.php?storyId=12125926

5. Rogers, M. G. (n.d.). Leaders—Should you admit a mistake? 3 reasons I would. Retrieved from www.teamworkandleadership.com/2015/02/leaders-should-you-admit-a-mistake-3-reasons-i-would-video.html

6. Hess, C. L. (n.d.). When Narcissus teaches: Teaching, mentoring and the danger of narcissism. Retrieved from http://old.religiouseducation.net/member/02_papers/hess.pdf (p. 7)

7. Haberman (1994, p. 780).

8. Haberman (2004, p. 188)

9. Hartlep, N. D., & Associates. (2014). What makes a Star Teacher? Examining the dispositions of PK–12 urban teachers in Chicago. Retrieved from http://educationnews.educationviewsor.netdna-cdn.com/wp-content/uploads/2015/01/Hartlep-and-Colleagues-2014.pdf

10. Apelojg, B. (n.d.). Teachers do not make mistakes? Two explorative case studies: Relationships between biographical aspects, thinking and behavioral patterns and experiences in classes. First results of a qualitative study on the aspect of dealing with mistakes. Retrieved from www.depositonce.tu-berlin.de/bitstream/11303/5491/3/08_Apelojg.pdf

11. Haberman (2004, p. 190).

12. Haberman (2004).

13. Farson, R., & Keyes, R. (2002). The failure-tolerant leader. *Harvard Business Review, 80*(8), 64–71.

14. Brookfield, S. D. (1990). *The skillful teacher.* San Francisco: Jossey-Bass. Retrieved from http://cte.virginia.edu/wp-content/uploads/2014/03/Building-Trust-With-Students.pdf

15. Bieling, P. J., Israeli, A., Smith, J., & Antony, M. M. (2003). Making the grade: The behavioural consequences of perfectionism in the classroom. *Personality and Individual Differences, 35*(1), 163–178.

16. Haberman (2004).

17. Haberman (2004, p. 65).

18. Haberman, M. (2017). Selecting "Star" Teachers for children and youth in poverty. In V. Hill-Jackson & D. Stafford (Eds.), *Better teachers, better schools: What Star Teachers know, believe, and do* (pp. 1–11). Charlotte, NC: Information Age Publishing. (p. 9)

19. Maats, H., & O'Brien, K. (2014, March 20). Teaching students to embrace mistakes. *Edutopia.* Retrieved from www.edutopia.org/blog/teaching-students-to-embrace-mistakes-hunter-maats-katie-obrien

20. Brookfield, S. D. (2015). *The skillful teacher: On technique, trust, and responsiveness in the classroom* (3rd ed.). San Francisco: Wiley. (p. 230)

21. Morehead, B. (2007). *Exposing Star Teachers of children in poverty.* Unpublished doctoral dissertation, Western Michigan University. Retrieved from http://scholarworks.wmich.edu/cgi/viewcontent.cgi?article=1900&context=dissertations (p. 33)

22. Phelps, P. H. (2000). Mistakes as vehicles for educating teachers. *Action in Teacher Education, 21*(4), 41–48. (p. 47)

23. Combs, J. P., Harris, S., & Edmonson, S. (2015). Four essential practices for building trust. *Educational Leadership, 72*(7), 18–22. (p. 18)

24. Llopis, G. (2015, July 23). 4 reasons great leaders admit their mistakes. *Forbes.* Retrieved from www.forbes.com/sites/glennllopis/2015/07/23/4-reasons-great-leaders-admit-their-mistakes/2/#7e8368f76038

25. Newland, A. (2012, February 4). Good teachers learn from their mistakes. *The Guardian.* Retrieved from www.theguardian.com/teacher-network/2012/feb/04/teachers-mistakes-classroom-control

26. Beaudoin, M. N. (2011). Respect—Where do we start? *Educational Leadership, 69*(1), 40–44. (p. 40)

27. Van Manen, M. (20156). *The tone of pedagogy* (2nd ed.). New York: Routledge. (p. 88)

28. Schorr, B. (n.d.). Mistakes as opportunities for learning. Retrieved from www.positivediscipline.com/sites/default/files/mistakes-teacher-tools-sample.pdf

29. Walker, R. J. (2013). *12 characteristics of an effective teacher: Inspirational stories of teachers who inspired others to become teachers.* Morrisville, NC: Lulu Publishing.

30. Brookfield (1990, p. 164).

31. Brookfield (1990, pp. 168–169).

32. Semke, H. D. (1984). Effects of the red pen. *Foreign Language Annals, 17*(3), 195–202. Retrieved from www.learner.org/workshops/tfl/resources/s3_redpen.pdf

33. Tugend, A. (2011, September 6). The role of mistakes in the classroom. *Edutopia.* Retrieved from www.edutopia.org/blog/benefits-mistakes-classroom-alina-tugend

34. Mansori, M. (n.d.). Modeling mistakes and creating trust in the classroom. Retrieved from https://medium.com/synapse/modeling-mistakes-and-creating-trust-in-the-classroom-ea5b94335917

35. Rice, L. H. (2013). Teaching and modeling persistence: Setting goals. Retrieved from http://theeducatorsroom.com/2013/10/teaching-modeling-persistence-setting-goals/

36. TeachThought. (n.d.). 9 ways to help students learn through their mistakes. Retrieved from www.teachthought.com/pedagogy/9-ways-help-students-learn-mistakes/

37. Curwin, R. (2014, October 28). It's a mistake not to use mistakes as part of the learning process. *Edutopia.* Retrieved from www.edutopia.org/blog/use-mistakes-in-learning-process-richard-curwin

38. Schroder, H. S., Fisher, M. E., Lin, Y., Lo, S. L., Danovitch, J. H., & Moser, J. S. (2017). Neural evidence for enhanced attention to mistakes among school-aged children with a growth mindset. *Developmental Cognitive Neuroscience, 24,* 42–50.; Doyle, T., & Zakrajsek, T. (2013). *The new science of learning: How to learn in harmony with your brain.* Sterling, VA: Stylus. (p. 96)

39. Haberman, M. (1995). *Star Teachers of children in poverty.* Indianapolis, IN: Kappa Delta Pi. (p. 76)

40. Guido, M. (2016, December 22). 10 ways teachers can instill a growth mindset in students. Retrieved from www.prodigygame.com/blog/growth-mindset-in-students/

41. Guido (2016).

42. Haberman (1995, p. 76).

43. Haberman (1995).

8

Am I a Star Teacher?
Developing Dispositions
That Support Student Learning

It is certainly possible for both novice and veteran teachers to develop into Star
Teachers, but doing so requires a great deal of work and introspection. "[Star]
Teachers are not born," writes Haberman. "They develop the appropriate ideology and relationship skills by reflecting upon, learning from, and benefitting
from their life experiences."[1] Teachers committed to embracing a growth mindset
can mature and progress as effective educators.

With the Every Student Succeeds Act (ESSA),[2] teachers have an opportunity
to reinvent their professional development goals in accordance with their individualized needs. Effective teaching is not one-size-fits-all, and effective professional development shouldn't be either. The development needs of a first-year
teacher are not the same as those of a teacher with 15 years under his or her belt.
Currently teachers are held accountable by value-added measurements (VAMs)—
high-stakes, summative evaluations based on student improvement. Rather than
improve instruction, VAMs undermine it:[3] Research shows that they are burdensome,[4] demoralizing,[5] and unreliable for determining effective practice.[6]

In their book *Making Teachers Better, Not Bitter: Balancing Evaluation, Supervision, and Reflection for Professional Growth,* Tony Frontier and Paul Mielke envision
new teacher evaluation frameworks that replace the ranking model with a developmental one, noting that teacher evaluation systems were founded on ideas
related to performance and not growth.[7]

Haberman's seven dispositions (persistence, protecting learners and learning, ability to put theory into practice, approach to at-risk learners, professional versus a personal orientation to learners, ability to survive in a bureaucracy, and fallibility) are not items on a checklist or means of high-stakes evaluation, but are goals that teachers use to take ownership of their professional progress by adjusting their dispositional skills to better match those of hypothetical Star Teachers. They are meant to help teachers move away from district-directed evaluations and choose their own low-stakes, formative goals toward becoming Star Teachers.

The five stages of development on the way to becoming a Star Teacher are as follows for each disposition:

1. **Pre-Star:** The teacher has a common knowledge or an understanding of basic techniques and concepts and *rarely* performs the actions associated with the disposition. This stage of development denotes an open but naive understanding of dispositional behavior and its significance.

2. **Developing:** The teacher has gained classroom experience with the disposition and *sometimes* asks for help understanding and performing dispositional behaviors.

3. **Proficient:** The teacher is *regularly* successful at completing tasks associated with one of Haberman's seven dispositions. Help from an expert may be required from time to time, but the teacher can usually perform dispositional behaviors independently.

4. **Accomplished:** The teacher *consistently* performs the actions associated with the disposition without assistance. He or she is recognized by peers as a go-to person for questions about the disposition.

5. **Star:** The teacher is known as a distinguished expert in the disposition by his or her peers. Star Teachers almost *always* provide support for and guidance in the disposition to others with humility (see Appendix).

Haberman believed in the potential of every K–12 educator to become a distinguished Star Teacher, writing, "There is every reason to believe that even greater numbers of potential teachers . . . can be selected and coached to do as well as these [S]tar [T]eachers."[8] Using Haberman's seven dispositions as a guide, teachers can learn to avoid the burdens of restrictive school or district systems, more deeply contemplate their effectiveness as teachers, and ultimately become empowered to create a professional development plan that is personalized and growth-oriented.

Why Use the Ideas in this Book for Your Practice?

What Makes a Star Teacher synthesizes Haberman's research-based recommendations about relational dispositions into a framework that can improve instruction. The purpose of the book is to serve not as a rigid to-do list but rather as a guide to support your professional growth through identification of goals, strategies, resources, and intended results. By reading the book and using its ideas and the online study guide, you will learn how to

- Develop a clear vision of the dispositions of Star Teachers.
- Self-assess by tracking and reflecting on evidence for dispositional activities.
- Set goals for further learning.

The overall aim of this chapter is to improve instruction through formative assessment of teacher dispositions. *What Makes a Star Teacher* is designed to be used as a standalone manual—you do not need to purchase other books by Dr. Haberman or on the topic of teacher dispositions to fully understand it. To get the most out of the book, we recommend discussing key points in the text with peers, sharing the strategies you try in the classroom and your observations of how they are working, completing one or more Star Tracker activities, as well as the extension exercises in each chapter, to help you understand the differences between pre-Star and Star Teachers. Whether you have elected to work alone or alongside colleagues, we encourage you to read and respond individually to the ideas presented in each chapter.

The Star Teacher Development Protocol

Our Star Teacher Developmental Protocol (STDP) is an experiential, hands-on approach for teachers who are interested in the personal development of Haberman's seven dispositions. The protocol is underpinned by best practices and research maintaining that teachers learn best when they work alongside peers on hands-on strategies that they can immediately try out in the classroom and when they have time to reflect on their practice. The STDP is an open-ended formative assessment that involves the following steps (see Figure 8.1):

1. The teacher reflects on his or her relational dispositions, professional standards, and student learning objectives and identifies professional growth goals.
2. The teacher engages in a pre-conference.
3. The teacher completes a peer observation.
4. The teacher traces progress toward goals over the course of the year.
5. The teacher completes a post-conference to review goal attainment and discuss how professional development enhanced his or her effectiveness.

In the STDP process, peers engage in a combination of independent study and ongoing collaboration with an instructional partner, including peer observation. Although being observed in the classroom can be unsettling for some teachers, observations support professional growth for both the observer and the observed. The observed teacher is able to have a trusted colleague share valuable feedback on his or her dispositional behaviors in the classroom, and the observer is able to watch dispositional behaviors in action, articulate their strengths and weaknesses, and compare them to his or her own. The process enables teachers to

- Connect with their colleagues in collaborative relationships,
- Reflect on and gain insight into their instructional skills, and
- Engage in public discourse about best teaching practices.[9]

Peer observation often occurs as a low-stakes, friendly, summative exercise in which teachers "buddy up to observe each other teach and discuss what happened during a single teaching encounter."[10] In "Rethinking Classroom Observation," Emily Grimm, Trent Kaufman, and Dave Doty note that teacher-driven peer observation helps teachers to focus on their own development, immediately apply what they've learned to their classrooms, and refine their skills because they are provided "with a classroom-embedded process to refine their instruction. Through teacher-driven observation, teachers engage peers in gathering and analyzing classroom data—data that speak to the unique context of their own classrooms. This approach has demonstrated potential to meaningfully improve instruction and student achievement."[11]

Peer observation is an effective form of professional development because it

- Is embedded into teachers' workdays;
- Is flexible in design, content, and time;
- Is continuous;
- Supports initiating and maintaining change; and
- Leverages expertise within schools.[12]

Figure 8.1 **The Star Teacher Developmental Protocol**

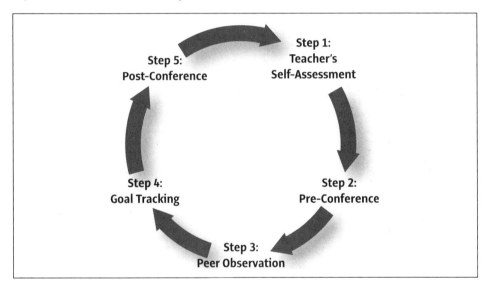

Source: Adapted from: Ball, D. L. & Cohen, D. K. (1999). Developing practice, developing practitioners: Toward a practice-based theory of professional education. In G. Sykes & L. Darling-Hammond (Eds.), *Teaching as the learning profession: Handbook of policy and practice* (pp. 3–32). San Francisco: Jossey-Bass.

Peer observation provides teachers a shared vision on which to base professional and instructional conversations.[13] Successful peer observations are guided by seven principles: they are purposeful, autonomous, constructive, ethical, flexible, collaborative, and inclusive (see Figure 8.2).

Step 1: Teacher Self-Assessment

The STDP, which is modeled after other peer-observation protocols (e.g., Gibbs's Reflective Teaching Cycle), starts with the teacher reflecting on his or her relational dispositions, professional standards, and student-learning objectives.

The teacher conducts a self-assessment by reviewing data and reflecting on professional practices to determine teacher and student needs, then conducts an in-depth analysis of Haberman's seven dispositions. The teacher's goals should include collecting evidence of practices that positively affect student outcomes.

The teacher begins his or her self-assessment by reviewing the five stages of teacher development (see p. 193) and Haberman's seven dispositions. After determining a specific disposition that he or she would like to develop further, then they would complete a self-assessment (see Figure 8.3).

Figure 8.2 **Principles of Peer Review**

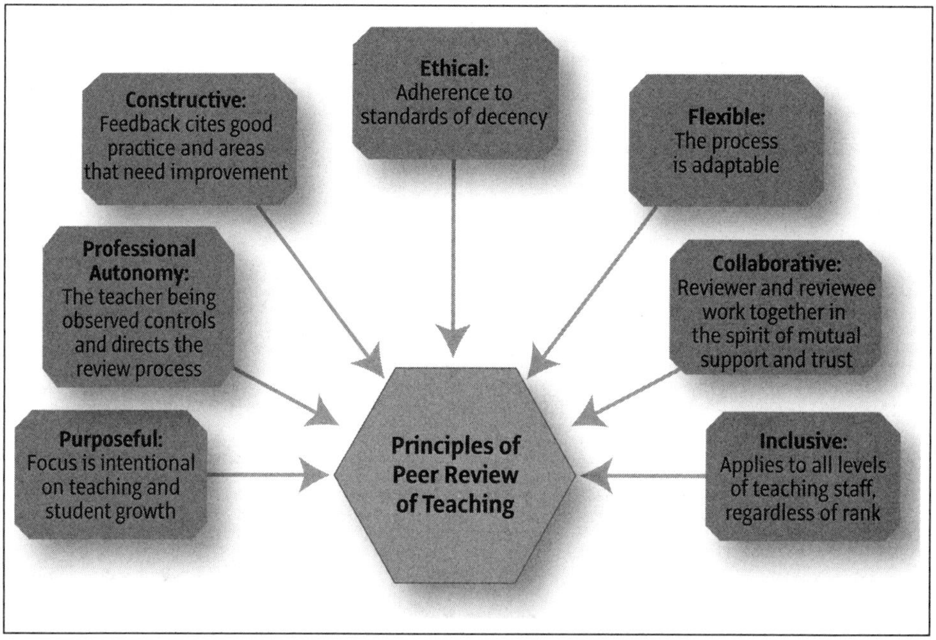

Step 2: Pre-conference

The teacher meets with a trusted peer who will perform the classroom observation to ensure that they are both clear about goals and actions. During the pre-conference, the teacher shares with his or her peer the goals identified in the self-assessment. This is also an opportunity for the teacher to outline the support systems needed to achieve the goals, as well as the means for tracking evidence of progress or goal attainment. If trust and confidentiality are present, peer

Figure 8.3 **Self-Assessment of Dispositions**

Disposition / Professional Goal: _____

_____

_____

Related professional standards (consider national, state, district, and subject matter): _____

_____

_____

_____

Related student standard(s) to professional goal: _____

_____

_____

_____

Behaviors or actions needed to accomplish the goal: _____

_____

_____

_____

Timeline for completion:

  Milestone 1: _____ Date: _____

  Milestone 2: _____ Date: _____

Completion Date: _____

Evidence of Goal Attainment: _____

_____

_____

_____

observation can stimulate confidence in a teacher as well as promote reflective thinking.[14] During this step, the two teachers set the parameters of the observation and select a date. They can also choose which chapters of this book to focus on, although open dialogue should be a key element of this and any future meetings.[15]

Step 3: Peer Observation

The peer observation determines how proficiently the observed teacher is implementing the disposition he or she selected (see Appendix). The most valuable part of the process is in the dialogue and reflections that the two teachers share. The observer is less like a supervisor and more like a critical friend, sharing feedback that is honest, collegial, and constructive in a nonjudgmental environment. However, these conversations are only productive if the teachers are willing to develop relationships, take risks, and engage in collaborative reflection.[16]

Step 4: Tracking the Evidence

The teacher tracks evidence of goal attainment and dispositional behaviors using such tools as portfolios, electronic profiles, students' classroom or state reporting data, recordings of lessons and interactions with students, and personal reflections. During this step, which may last for several lessons or over the entire academic year, teachers should also consider additional professional development activities such as attending workshops, reading books and articles, and watching videos.

Step 5: Post-Conference

In the last stage of the STDP, the teacher and peer observer reflect on goals attained and how much the dispositional behaviors enhanced instructional practice. They discuss further goals and create a professional development plan if needed. This is also an opportunity to celebrate successes, identify areas for continued learning, and record lessons learned. Using the Appendix as the guide, the teacher assigns himself or herself a score between 1 and 5 based on his or her stage of development: (1) Pre-Star, (2) Developing, (3) Proficient, (4) Accomplished, or (5) Star. This score is not meant for public dissemination, but to empower the teacher with the knowledge of his or her dispositional growth. During the conference, the two teachers may plan to further the development of the disposition, abandon training, or move forward with a different one of Haberman's seven dispositions and newly identified goals.

Teachers involved in the STDP process should always find ways to celebrate the important milestone of having experienced it. Because the STDP is designed to be ongoing, teachers may decide to repeat the above cycle of steps for every one of Haberman's dispositions. Upon the successful assessment of all seven dispositions, the teacher may then elect to record his or her results on a dispositions summary form (see Figure 8.4). Authors' note: Because the STDP is an integrated process in which each stage supports the next, all five stages must be completed from beginning to end for each disposition that is being assessed.

Summary

Star Teachers persistently seek what works for learners, unapologetically protect learners, link theory and practice, see students as at promise and not at risk, value respect above love from their students, effectively navigate the bureaucracy of schools, own their faults, and are willing to grow. Although Star Teachers make the job look easy, as any educator knows, the art of teaching requires plenty of time, practice, and development.

Beginning in 1959, Haberman conducted more than 5,000 classroom observations upon which the Star Teacher framework was founded. This first-generation research focused on teachers' mindsets and behaviors. He wrote more than 200 major papers, 150 refereed articles, 20 research projects, 50 chapters and monographs, and 8 books.

The second generation of Haberman's research emerged in the early 1990s, when he formulated a Star Teacher Pre-Screener to help school districts identify and hire Star Teachers. The pre-screener consists of 50 questions and evaluates teachers' dispositions, knowledge, and skills. Nearly 400 school districts around the country have used Haberman's selection and interview protocols to identify and hire teachers with Star potential. (For more information, visit www.habermanfoundation.org.)

For the third generation of Haberman's research, we have translated the theories from his landmark book *Star Teachers of Children in Poverty,*[17] and the follow-up companion book *Star Teachers: The Ideology and Best Practice of Effective Teachers of Diverse Children and youth in Poverty*[18] into observable behaviors, strategies, and assessment tools in this book.

Figure 8.4 **Dispositions Summary**

In the chart below, specify how often you perform each disposition: routinely, consistently, regularly, sometimes, or rarely. If you are not certain, leave the box blank.					
Disposition	Star	Accomplished	Proficient	Developing	Pre-Star
1. Persistence					
2. Protecting Learners and Learning					
3. Putting Theory into Practice					
4. Approaching Learners Who Are at Risk					
5. Orienting to Learners: Professional Versus Personal					
6. Surviving in a Bureaucracy					
7. Accepting and Admitting Fallibility					

Endnotes

1. Haberman, M. (2010). *Star Teachers: The ideology and best practice of effective teachers of diverse children and youth in poverty* (1st ed., third printing). Houston, TX: Haberman Educational Foundation. (p. 216)

2. Every Student Succeeds Act (ESSA) of 2015, Pub. L. No. 114–95 (2015).

3. Frontier, T. & Mielke, P. (2016). *Making teachers better, not bitter: Balancing evaluation, supervision, and reflection for professional growth.* Alexandria, VA: ASCD; Hartlep, N. D., Hansen, C. M., & Horn, B. R. (2015). Measuring the dispositions that make teachers effective. Cambridge, MA: Scholars Strategy Network. Retrieved from https://scholars.org/brief/measuring-dispositions-make-teachers-effective.

4. Hinchey, P. H. (2010). *Getting teacher assessment right: what policymakers can learn from research.* National Education Policy Center, School of Education, University of Colorado at Boulder, Boulder, CO.

5. Darling-Hammond, L., Amrein-Beardsley, A., Haertel, E. H., & Rothstein, J. (2011, September). *Getting teacher evaluation right: A background paper for policy makers.* (American Education Research Association, National Academy of Education). Retrieved from https://edpolicy.stanford.edu/sites/default/files/publications/getting-teacher-evaluationright-challenge-policy-makers.pdf

6. Glazerman, S., Loeb, S., Goldhaber, D., Staiger, D., Raudenbush, S., & Whitehurst, G. (2010, November 17). *Evaluating teachers: The important role of value-added.* Washington, DC: The Brookings Institution. Retrieved from www.brookings.edu/wp-content/uploads/2016/06/1117_evaluating_teachers.pdf

7. Frontier & Mielke (2016).

8. Haberman, M. (1995). *Star Teachers of children in poverty.* Indianapolis, IN: Kappa Delta Pi. (p. 3)

9. Newman, L., Roberts, D., & Schwartzstein, R. (2012). Peer observation of teaching handbook *MedEdPORTAL Publications.* Retrieved from https://hms.harvard.edu/sites/default/files/assets/Sites/Academy/files/MedEdPortalPeer%20observation%20handbook.pdf (p.1)

10. Newman et al. (2012, p. 1).

11. Grimm, E. D., Kaufman, T., & Doty, D. (2014). Rethinking classroom observation. *Professional Learning: Reimagined, 71*(8), 24–29. (p. 25)

12. Blank, R. K. (2013). What research tells us: Common characteristics of professional learning that leads to student achievement. *Journal of Staff Development, 34*(1), 50–53.

13. Pressick-Kilborn, K., & Riele, K. (2008). Learning from reciprocal peer observation: A collaborative self-study. *Studying Teacher Education: A journal of self-study of teacher education practices, 4*(1), 61–75. doi:10.1080/17425960801976354

14. Gosling, D., Mason, O., & Connor, K. (Eds.). (2009). *Beyond the peer observation of teaching* [SEDA Paper 124]. London: Staff and Educational Development Association.

15. Harris, K. L., Farrell, K., Bell, M., Devlin, M., & James, R. (2008). *Peer review of teaching in Australian higher education* [Report]. Sydney: Australian Learning and Teaching Council; Weller, S. (2009). What does "peer" mean in teaching observation for the professional development of higher education lecturers? *International Journal of Teaching and Learning in Higher Education, 21*(1), 25–35.

16. Schuck, S., Aubusson, P., & Buchanan, J. (2008). Enhancing teacher education practice through professional conversations. *European Journal of Teacher Education, 31*(2), 215–227.; Tremlett, R. (1992) Peer support for improved teaching, *New Academic,* Summer, 16–17.; Weller (2009).

17. Haberman, M. (1995). *Star Teachers of children in poverty.* Indianapolis, IN: Kappa Delta Pi.

18. Haberman (2010).

Appendix:
Star Teacher Rubrics

Haberman's Seven Dispositions for Effective Teaching

Disposition 1: Teacher Persistence

Teacher persistence is reflected in an endless search for what works best with each student. Indeed, Star Teachers define their jobs as asking themselves constantly, "How might this activity have been better—for the class or for a particular individual?"

Star	Accomplished	Proficient	Developing	Pre-Star
• Persists with the lesson until there is evidence that all students demonstrate mastery of the objective. • Establishes a classroom environment that is safe, inviting, and sparks imagination. • Consistently tiers content as well as formative and summative assessments in order for learners to determine level of proficiency. • Consistently provides opportunities for students to utilize their individual learning patterns, habits, and needs to achieve high levels of academic and social-emotional success. • Utilization of multiple forms of data to problem solve and enhance student learning by adapting instructional practices.	• Persists with the lesson until there is evidence that most students demonstrate mastery of the objective. • Establishes a classroom environment that is safe, inviting, and sparks imagination. • Consistently tiers content as well as formative and summative assessments in order for learners to determine level of proficiency. • Consistently provides opportunities for students to utilize their individual learning patterns, habits, and needs to achieve high levels of academic and social-emotional success. • Utilization of multiple forms of data to problem solve and enhance student learning by adapting instructional practices.	• Persists with the lesson until there is evidence that most students demonstrate mastery of the objective. • Establishes a classroom environment that is safe, inviting, and sparks imagination. • Regularly tiers content as well as formative and summative assessments in order for learners to determine level of proficiency. • Regularly provides opportunities for students to utilize their individual learning patterns, habits, and needs to achieve high levels of academic and social-emotional success.	• Persists with the lesson until there is evidence that most students demonstrate mastery of the objective. • Establishes a classroom environment that is safe and inviting. • Sometimes tiers content as well as formative and summative assessments in order for learners to determine level of proficiency.	• Persists with the lesson until there is evidence that some students demonstrate mastery of the objective. • Establishes a classroom environment that is safe and inviting.
Sources of evidence	Lesson plan with differentiated instructional techniques; classroom layout; classroom artifacts; assessment tools; analysis of student data; Teacher Grit score; Teacher Efficacy score; etc.			

Disposition 2: Protecting Learners and Learning

Protecting Learners and Learning refers to making children's active involvement in productive work more important than curriculum rigidities and uneven school rules. Effective teachers not only recognize all the ways in which large school organizations impinge on students but find ways to make and keep learning the highest priority.

Star	Accomplished	Proficient	Developing	Pre-Star
• Protects learners from classroom distractions or school bureaucracies. • Displays enthusiasm for learning by sharing his/her interests in the course content. • Transcends the explicit curriculum with relevant content outside of the traditional curriculum.	• Protects learners from classroom distractions. • Consistently displays enthusiasm for learning by sharing his/her interests in the course content. • Transcends the explicit curriculum with relevant content outside of the traditional curriculum.	• Regularly displays enthusiasm for learning by sharing his/her interests in the course content. • Regularly protects learners from classroom distractions. • Transcends the explicit curriculum with relevant content outside of the traditional curriculum.	• Sometimes displays enthusiasm for learning by sharing his/her interests in the course content. • Sometimes protects learners from classroom distractions.	• Rarely displays enthusiasm for learning by sharing his/her interests in the course content.
Sources of evidence	Curriculum materials; teacher enthusiasm; classroom management tactics (e.g., attendance procedures); passion results; etc.			

Disposition 3: Putting Theory into Practice

Theory into Practice explains the teacher's ability to put theory or research into practice. Conversely, it also refers to the teacher's ability to understand how specific teaching behaviors support concepts and ideas about effective teaching. In addition, this dimension predicts the teacher's ability to benefit from professional development activities and grow as a professional practitioner.

Star	Accomplished	Proficient	Developing	Pre-Star
• Crosswalks from theory to practice, and from practice to theory • Leads colleagues collaboratively in and beyond the school to identify professional development needs through detailed data analysis and self-reflection. • Seeks resources and collaboratively fosters faculty knowledge and skills. • Develops and fulfills the school and district improvement plans through professional learning communities, grade- or subject-level team leadership, committee leadership, or other opportunities beyond the campus. • Engages in all scheduled activities, professional learning communities, committee, grade-or subject-level team meetings as directed.	• Leads colleagues collaboratively in and beyond the school to identify professional development needs through detailed data analysis and self-reflection. • Seeks resources and collaboratively fosters faculty knowledge and skills. • Develops and fulfills the school and district improvement plans through professional learning communities, grade- or subject-level team leadership, committee leadership, or other opportunities beyond the campus. • Engages in all scheduled activities, professional learning communities, committee, grade-or subject-level team meetings as directed.	• Seeks resources and collaboratively fosters faculty knowledge and skills. • Develops and fulfills the school and district improvement plans through professional learning communities, grade- or subject-level team leadership, committee leadership, or other opportunities beyond the campus. • Regularly engages in all scheduled activities, professional learning communities, committee, grade-or subject-level team meetings as directed.	• Seeks resources and collaboratively fosters faculty knowledge and skills. • Develops and fulfills the school and district improvement plans through professional learning communities, grade- or subject-level team leadership, committee leadership, or other opportunities beyond the campus. • Sometimes engages in all scheduled activities, professional learning communities, committee, grade-or subject-level team meetings as directed.	• Seeks resources and collaboratively fosters faculty knowledge and skills. • Develops and fulfills the school and district improvement plans through professional learning communities, grade- or subject-level team leadership, committee leadership, or other opportunities beyond the campus. • Rarely engages in most scheduled activities, professional learning communities, committee, grade-or subject-level team meetings as directed.
Sources of evidence	Professional development portfolio; implementation of PD strategies; PD leadership roles, e.g., PLCs; Teacher's Mindset Score results; Curiosity Quiz; Survey of Reflective Practice score; etc.			

Disposition 4: Approaching Learners Who Are At Risk

Stars' **approach to at-risk children** is one in which they assume personal accountability for their students' learning, in spite of the fact that they cannot control all in-school and out-of-school influences on learners, and form productive relationships with students to seed educational breakthroughs.

Star	Accomplished	Proficient	Developing	Pre-Star
• Maintains high expectations for all learners. • Maintains positive teacher-student relationships with all learners. • All lessons connect to students' prior knowledge, experiences, interests, and future learning expectations across content areas. • Guidance for students to apply their strengths, background knowledge, life experiences, and skills to enhance each other's learning. • Sustains feedback to students, families, and other school personnel while maintaining confidentiality.	• Maintains high expectations for most learners. • Maintains positive teacher-student relationships with most learners. • All lessons connect to students' prior knowledge, experiences, interests, and future learning expectations across content areas. • Guidance for students to apply their strengths, background knowledge, life experiences, and skills to enhance each other's learning. • Consistent feedback to students, families, and other school personnel while maintaining confidentiality.	• Maintains high expectations for most learners. • Maintains positive teacher-student relationships with most learners. • Most lessons connect to students' prior knowledge, experiences, interests, and future learning expectations across content areas. • Guidance for students to apply their strengths, background knowledge, life experiences, and skills to enhance each other's learning. • Regular feedback to students, families, and other school personnel while maintaining confidentiality.	• Maintains high expectations for most learners. • Maintains positive teacher-student relationships with most learners. • Most lessons connect to students' prior knowledge, experiences, interests, and future learning expectations across content areas.	• Maintains high expectations for some learners. • Maintains positive teacher-student relationships with some learners. • Some lessons connect to students' prior knowledge, experiences, interests, and future learning expectations across content areas.
Sources of evidence	Empathy scores; teaching philosophy; teacher-student interactions; student examples; lesson plan assessments; empathy quiz results; etc.			

Disposition 5: Orienting to Learners: Professional Versus Personal

Star Teachers maintain a **professional orientation to learners** by displaying respect and care about children, even when learners do things they regard as despicable.

Star	Accomplished	Proficient	Developing	Pre-Star
• Respects students and places learners before the curriculum. • Monitors behavior subtly, reinforces positive behaviors appropriately, and intercepts misbehavior fluidly. • Encourages and monitors student behavior subtly and responds to misbehavior swiftly. • Students and the teacher create, adopt, and maintain classroom behavior standards. • All students know, understand, and respect classroom behavior standards.	• Consistently monitors behavior subtly, reinforces positive behaviors appropriately, and intercepts misbehavior fluidly. • Consistently encourages and monitors student behavior subtly and responds to misbehavior swiftly. • Students and the teacher create, adopt, and maintain classroom behavior standards. • Most students know, understand, and respect classroom behavior standards.	• Regularly monitors behavior subtly, reinforces positive behaviors appropriately, and intercepts misbehavior fluidly. • Regularly encourages and monitors student behavior subtly and responds to misbehavior swiftly. • Students and the teacher create, adopt, and maintain classroom behavior standards. • Most students know, understand, and respect classroom behavior standards.	• Sometimes monitors behavior subtly, reinforces positive behaviors appropriately, and intercepts misbehavior fluidly. • Sometimes encourages and monitors student behavior subtly and responds to misbehavior swiftly. • The teacher creates, adopts, and maintains classroom behavior standards. • Most students know, understand, and respect classroom behavior standards.	• Rarely monitors behavior subtly, reinforces positive behaviors appropriately, and intercepts misbehavior fluidly. • Rarely encourages and monitors student behavior subtly and responds to misbehavior swiftly. • The teacher creates, adopts, and maintains classroom behavior standards. • Some students know, understand, and respect classroom behavior standards.
Sources of evidence	Student interviews; classroom climate; discipline records and referrals; class celebrations; display of rules; teacher philosophy; peer-to-peer interactions; teacher-to-student interactions; personality type results; etc.			

Disposition 6: Surviving in a Bureaucracy

Ability to **survive in a bureaucracy** deals with a teacher's ability to work within a school environment that is depersonalized, bureaucratic, and impersonal. Teachers who can survive in a bureaucracy are better able to remain on the job, and ultimately are more effective in the classroom.

Star	Accomplished	Proficient	Developing	Pre-Star
• Maintains a healthy perspective about working conditions. • Utilizes resources and peers to effectively navigate the demands and duties within a learning organization. • Utilizes self-care to preserve emotional, physical, spiritual, and mental health.	• Consistently maintains a healthy perspective about working conditions. • Consistently utilizes resources and peers to effectively navigate the demands and duties within a learning organization. • Consistently utilizes self-care to preserve emotional, physical, spiritual, and mental health.	• Regularly maintains a healthy perspective about working conditions. • Regularly utilizes resources and peers to effectively navigate the demands and duties within a learning organization. • Regularly utilizes self-care to preserve emotional, physical, spiritual, and mental health.	• Sometimes maintains a healthy perspective about working conditions. • Sometimes utilizes resources and peers to effectively navigate the demands and duties within a learning organization. • Sometimes utilizes self-care to preserve emotional, physical, spiritual, and mental health.	• Rarely maintains a healthy perspective about working conditions. • Rarely utilizes resources and peers to effectively navigate the demands and duties within a learning organization.

Sources of evidence
Resilience and emotional quotient scores; professional learning communities or critical friends; work-out and diet plans; work-life balance schedules; review of personal diary; review of email schedules; Teacher Burnout Scale; teacher's attendance record; School Culture Assessment score; Resiliency Quiz score results; Emotional Quotient Quiz results; Surviving Bureaucracy Inventory; Organizational Flow Chart; etc.

Disposition 7: Accepting and Admitting Fallibility

Fallibility refers to the teacher's willingness to admit mistakes and correct them. This dimension of teacher behavior establishes the classroom climate for how students respond to their mistakes in the process of learning.

Star	Accomplished	Proficient	Developing	Pre-Star
• Utilizes teacher and student mistakes as 'teachable moments.' • Acknowledges small and large mistakes. • Provides a classroom climate where innovation and creativity are nurtured. • Provides opportunities for students to establish high academic and social-emotional expectations for themselves. • Addresses student mistakes and follows through to ensure student mastery. • Provides opportunities for students to self-monitor and self-correct mistakes.	• Consistently utilizes teacher and student mistakes as 'teachable moments.' • Consistently acknowledges small and large mistakes. • Consistently provides a classroom climate where innovation and creativity are nurtured. • Consistently provides opportunities for students to establish high academic and social-emotional expectations for themselves. • Consistently addresses student mistakes and follows through to ensure student mastery. • Consistently provides opportunities for students to self-monitor and self-correct mistakes.	• Regularly utilizes teacher and student mistakes as 'teachable moments.' • Regularly acknowledges small and large mistakes. • Regularly provides a classroom climate where innovation and creativity are nurtured. • Regularly provides opportunities for students to establish high academic and social-emotional expectations for themselves. • Regularly addresses student mistakes and follows through to ensure student mastery. • Regularly provides opportunities for students to self-monitor and self-correct mistakes.	• Sometimes utilizes teacher and student mistakes as 'teachable moments.' • Sometimes provides opportunities for students to establish high academic and social-emotional expectations for themselves. • Sometimes addresses student mistakes and follows through to ensure student mastery. • Sometimes provides opportunities for students to self-monitor and self-correct mistakes.	• Rarely provides opportunities for students to establish high academic and social-emotional expectations for themselves. • Rarely addresses student mistakes and follows through to ensure student mastery. • Rarely provides opportunities for students to self-monitor and self-correct mistakes.
Sources of evidence	Teacher-to-student interactions; instructional behavior (questioning); climate; Narcissist Quiz; Students' Mindset Quiz results; etc.			

Index

The letter *f* following a page number denotes a figure.

time
    barrier to reflective practice, 86–87
    in classroom management, 52–54, 132
    lost learning, 51–52
    make every minute count, 51
    noninstructional use of, 52–54
    on task, 52
time on task, 52
trust, 176–178

victim, blaming the, 105
victims of excellence, 179–180

"Victory at Buffalo Creek: What Makes a School
    Serving Low-Income Hispanic Children Suc-
    cessful" (Haberman), 12–13

warm demanders, 136
"What Teachers Say About Reflection" (Canning),
    88
Women's Work? American Schoolteachers, 1650–
    1920 (Perlmann & Margo), 155
writing, reflective, 89

zero-tolerance policies, 133, 135

About the Authors

 **Valerie Hill-Jackson** began her teaching career with the Camden Board of Education in Camden, New Jersey—one of the nation's poorest urban school districts. She received her Interdisciplinary Doctorate in Educational Leadership degree from St. Joseph's University in Philadelphia and is currently the director of Educator Preparation and School Partnerships in the College of Education and Human Development and a clinical professor of teacher education in the Department of Teaching, Learning, and Culture at Texas A&M University.

Hill-Jackson received the prestigious American Educational Research Association/Spencer Fellowship and the Lead Star Award for her research in childhood lead poisoning and community education. Additionally, Dr. Hill-Jackson won Maybelline's Women Who Empower Through Education Award, the Upton Sinclair Award, a Fulbright Fellowship to Cardiff University, and a Melbern G. Glasscock Non-Tenure Track Faculty Research Fellowship.

Dr. Hill-Jackson's books include *Transforming Teacher Education: What Went Wrong with Teacher Training and How We Can Fix It* (2010); *Better Principals, Better Schools: What Star Principals Know, Believe, and Do* (2016); *Better Teachers, Better Schools: What Star Teachers Know, Believe, and Do* (2017); and *Teacher Confidential: Personal Stories of Stress, Self-Care, and Resilience* (2018). Visit her website at www.teacher-confidential.com.

Nicholas D. Hartlep began his career as a 1st grade teacher in Rochester, Minnesota, before receiving a PhD in Urban Education at the University of Wisconsin–Milwaukee (UWM). He also has a master's in K–12 education and bachelor's in elementary education, both conferred from Winona State University. Dr. Hartlep is an associate professor of urban education and the chair of the Early Childhood/Elementary Education department in the School of Urban Education at Metropolitan State University in Saint Paul, Minnesota. He also serves as the graduate program coordinator within the School of Urban Education.

Dr. Hartlep has published 19 books, the most recent being *Asian/American Scholars of Education: 21st Century Pedagogies, Perspectives, and Experiences* with coeditors Amardeep K. Kahlon and Daisy Ball (2018) and *The Neoliberal Agenda and the Student Debt Crisis in U.S. Higher Education,* with Lucille L. T. Eckrich and Brandon O. Hensley (2017). In 2015, he received the University Research Initiative Award from Illinois State University and a Distinguished Young Alumni Award from WSU. In 2016, UWM presented him with a Graduate of the Last Decade Award for his prolific writing. In 2017, Metropolitan State University presented him with both the 2017 Community Engaged Scholarship Award and the President's Circle of Engagement Award. In 2018, the Association of State Colleges and Universities (AASCU) granted Dr. Hartlep the John Saltmarsh Award for Emerging Leaders in Civic Engagement Award. Follow his work on Twitter at @nhartlep or at his website, www.nicholashartlep.com.

Delia Stafford is president and CEO of the Haberman Educational Foundation (HEF). She has a bachelor's in education from Harding University in Searcy, Arkansas, and a master's in education administration, elementary education, and teaching from Texas Southern University. In 1994, Stafford chartered the HEF to promote the research of Martin Haberman. Thanks largely to the foundation, Haberman's education models are being used in more than 370 school districts across the United States, especially in schools with large populations of students who are classified as at risk.

For almost a decade, Stafford directed the nation's largest district-based alternative teacher certification program in the Houston Independent School District and has been recognized twice by the White House for her advocacy of students at risk. She has written on such subjects as teacher education in urban school districts, violence prevention, the belief of effective teachers, student resilience, and the practical implementation of research. Stafford is the coauthor to *Better Principals, Better Schools: What Star Principals Know, Believe, and Do* (2016) and *Better Teachers, Better Schools: What Star Teachers Know, Believe, and Do* (2017). Learn more about the HEF at www.habermanfoundation.org.

Related ASCD Resources: Teacher Effectiveness

At the time of publication, the following resources were available (ASCD stock numbers in parentheses). For up-to-date information about ASCD resources, go to www.ascd.org. You can search the complete archives of *Educational Leadership* at www.ascd.org/el.

Print Products

The 12 Touchstones of Good Teaching: A Checklist for Staying Focused Every Day, by Bryan Goodwin and Elizabeth Ross Hubbell (#113009)

Engaging Students with Poverty in Mind: Practical Strategies for Raising Achievement, by Eric Jensen (#113001)

Intentional and Targeted Teaching: A Framework for Teacher Growth and Leadership, by Douglas Fisher, Nancy Frey, and Stefani Arzonetti Hite (#116008)

Keeping It Real and Relevant: Building Authentic Relationships in Your Diverse Classroom, by Ignacio Lopez (#117049)

Learning in the Fast Lane: 8 Ways to Put ALL Students on the Road to Academic Success, by Suzy Pepper Rollins (#114026)

Qualities of Effective Teachers, 3rd edition, by James H. Stronge (#118042)

Teach, Reflect, Learn: Building Your Capacity for Success in the Classroom, by Pete Hall and Alisa Simeral (#115040)

ASCD myTeachSource®

Download resources from a professional learning platform with hundreds of research-based best practices and tools for your classroom at http://myteachsource.ascd.org/.

For more information, send an e-mail to member@ascd.org; call 1-800-933-2723 or 703-578-9600; send a fax to 703-575-5400; or write to Information Services, ASCD, 1703 N. Beauregard St., Alexandria, VA 22311-1714 USA.

WHOLE CHILD
TENETS

1 HEALTHY
Each student enters school healthy and learns about and practices a healthy lifestyle.

2 SAFE
Each student learns in an environment that is physically and emotionally safe for students and adults.

3 ENGAGED
Each student is actively engaged in learning and is connected to the school and broader community.

4 SUPPORTED
Each student has access to personalized learning and is supported by qualified, caring adults.

5 CHALLENGED
Each student is challenged academically and prepared for success in college or further study and for employment and participation in a global environment.

THE WHOLE CHILD

The ASCD Whole Child approach is an effort to transition from a focus on narrowly defined academic achievement to one that promotes the long-term development and success of all children. Through this approach, ASCD supports educators, families, community members, and policymakers as they move from a vision about educating the whole child to sustainable, collaborative actions.

What Makes a Star Teacher relates to the **engaged** and **supported** tenets.

For more about the ASCD Whole Child approach, visit **www.ascd.org/wholechild.**

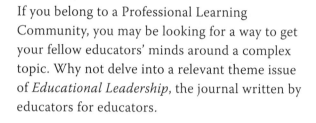